R. R. Inskeep

The Peopling of Southern Africa

David Philip
Cape Town & London

This book is the first in a series The Peoples of Southern Africa.
Series editors: W.D. Hammond-Tooke and M.E. West
Editor for this volume: M.E. West

Grateful acknowledgements are due to the Mauerberger Trust for generous financial assistance in the publication of this volume.

First published in 1978 by David Philip, Publisher (Pty) Ltd, 217 Werdmuller Centre, Claremont, Cape, South Africa
Published in the U.S.A. 1979 by Harper & Row Publishers, Inc., Barnes & Noble Import Division
Distributed in the U.K. by Global Book Resources Ltd, 109 Great Russell Street, London WC1B 3ND

ISBN 0 949968 69 2 (David Philip, Cape Town)
ISBN 0 06 493220 6 (Barnes & Noble, New York)

cover
This magnificent head, modelled in clay, fired and decorated, formed part of the ritual paraphernalia of Early Iron Age farmers at Lydenburg, in the eastern Transvaal. Its height is 38 cm to the crown, not including the animal surmounting it.

Lay-out by Sydney-Anne Wallace

Reproduction by Hirt & Carter, Cape Town

Printed and bound by Printpak (Cape) Ltd, Dacres Avenue, Epping, Cape, South Africa

Contents

To my parents, Adi, and my former students

Preface

This introductory book on Southern African (mostly South African) prehistory is not written for my colleagues nor for advanced students. As the editors requested, it is for the use of university students and for anyone who wants to know something of the peoples of prehistoric Southern Africa. It is not a source-book, and details of sites and their contents are included only where they have particular relevance to an argument. Nor has it seemed relevant to include tedious arguments about the interpretation of radiocarbon dates.

My chief concern has been to convey what I think the evidence means in terms of the origins and development of Southern African populations. In doing so I have tried to give some indication of the nature of the evidence on which the conclusions are based, for much of the interest and challenge of unravelling the past lies in the processes by which conclusions are reached rather than in the often limited and mundane conclusions that are attainable. Often the evidence can have more than one interpretation and those presented here are the interpretations favoured by the author, sometimes his own and sometimes other people's. However, almost all the interpretations will prove to be transient as further research produces better answers and, indeed, better questions.

The foundations of archaeological research in South Africa were laid in the 1920s, '30s, and '40s by such men as John Goodwin, 'Peter' van Riet Lowe, Hewitt, Stapleton, and B.D. Malan. But in more recent years something of a revolution in the pace and character of research has taken place at the hands of a newer generation. Much of what is of value in this book is drawn from their work. It would be tedious to give an exhaustive list of those whose work I have drawn upon, but there are a number of friends and colleagues who have been more than generous in their help and encouragement, and whose research work (much of it unpublished) has been of particular value. I think especially of Hilary and Janette Deacon, who pioneered a new approach to Holocene studies in the south-east Cape, and of John Parkington, Frank Schweitzer and Graham Avery, who are doing the same in the south-west Cape; of Richard Klein, whose faunal studies have done so much to put flesh on the bones of prehistory. The vast regions to the north have seen equally painstaking and imaginative workers, though fewer in

number. Notable among them are Tim Maggs, Tony Humphreys, Garth Sampson and Pat Carter. Little that is known of the prehistory of the Transvaal has not sprung directly or indirectly from the work of Revil Mason and his colleagues, while the greater part of what is known of the australopithecines is drawn from the patient work of Raymond Dart, Phillip Tobias, Bob Brain and John Robinson. In the matter of fossil man and the animals that surrounded him I have drawn heavily on the work of Laurie Wells, Basil Cooke, Brett Hendey and Ronald Singer. In the essential matter of chronology all of us are indebted to John Vogel of the National Physical Laboratory in Pretoria. To these in particular I owe a special debt for their friendship as well as their scholarship. But there are many others and I hope they will recognise, despite the absence of references, the areas that would have been thinner without their efforts.

To Adi, and to Leslie Keeley in particular, I am grateful for many hours of patient typing and for helpful comments.

R.R. Inskeep
Oxford, 1976

Further Reading

At the request of the publisher I have omitted references from the body of the text. The reading lists for each chapter, which can be found at the back of the book, are intended to provide a guide for the reader who wishes to look more closely at the evidence on which this book is based, or to read other prehistorians' views. The lists are not lists of works referred to by the author; these would be far more numerous. Wherever possible books of general interest have been included. But there are few such books of direct relevance to our subject, and for those who would explore further there is often no alternative but to turn to articles in journals. Of journal references only those considered to be of major interest or importance have been included. Many important articles are not included, but may be found listed in the references accompanying the books and articles cited.

1

Looking at the Landscape

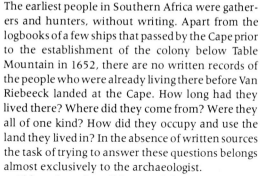

The earliest people in Southern Africa were gatherers and hunters, without writing. Apart from the logbooks of a few ships that passed by the Cape prior to the establishment of the colony below Table Mountain in 1652, there are no written records of the people who were already living there before Van Riebeeck landed at the Cape. How long had they lived there? Where did they come from? Were they all of one kind? How did they occupy and use the land they lived in? In the absence of written sources the task of trying to answer these questions belongs almost exclusively to the archaeologist.

Although oral traditions and the study of contemporary languages sometimes help, we mostly have to reconstruct the past from scraps of evidence dug from the ground. We are restricted to what survives best: stone, bone and shell – and, if we are fortunate, under special conditions we may find wood and vegetable matter. But nowhere can we study the role of individuals in the past, no matter how important they might have been. We can never know the names by which prehistoric peoples knew themselves – or even if they bothered with such names. The nature of archaeological evidence is such that we are best able to discover details of human anatomy (from skeletal remains) and of technology and economy: the tools, weapons, utensils and ornaments that peoples used, and the way they subsisted.

The first step in trying to understand how prehistoric man lived is to learn as much as possible of the natural history of the region under study. This is difficult where modern industry and farming have disturbed the natural order of things, but fortunately in Africa sufficient survives to give us a good clue as to the plant and animal life of most regions a century or two ago, before the disturbance became too great. Establishing this information for the recent past is difficult enough. Projecting it into the remote past must be done with care, as important climatic changes have affected vegetation zones and animal life associated with them.

If we need to know what the landscape had to offer we also need to know what people at different times and places took out of it. The chemical analysis of human bone may be able to identify the presence or absence of certain classes of food in the diet. Primarily, however, our knowledge comes from the food residues which have survived in archaeologi-

cal sites. Since bones survive much more commonly than plant remains the picture heavily overemphasises the role of meat in the diet. None the less animal bones and teeth, eggshell fragments and mollusc shells can tell us a great deal about food preferences, man's skill in securing meat, and indeed what was locally available.

The evidence for reconstructing the past is gleaned from archaeological sites and these vary a great deal in what they have to tell. Caves and rockshelters are valuable for two reasons. They represent permanent, ready-made homes and so have often attracted occupants over many thousands of years. Secondly they provide shelter from sun, wind and rain, so that the deposits accumulated in them are generally well preserved. The fillings of such sites consist of rock fragments from roof and walls, soil blown or washed in by wind and rain, organic remains brought in by animals, including nesting birds, and the rubbish left by man. The rubbish left by one group may be buried by that of another. If the site is unoccupied for long enough a sterile layer of soil and rock debris may accumulate between occupations. The result is a layering of deposits with the oldest at the bottom and the youngest at the top. The approach of the archaeologist is to peel away the layers one by one in the reverse order from that in which they were laid down. Each layer will contain an *association* of artefacts and food-remains plus perhaps the remains of bugs, beetles, bats and birds (including owl pellets) that shared the site with man. This is the raw material for reconstructing the past.

Away from caves, nature (especially in Southern Africa) is less kind. The major part of human living must have been done in the open, and there are plenty of stone tools to bear witness to it. But exposure to dramatic alternations of heat and cold,'heavy rain and long dry seasons, and often acid soil conditions, have generally destroyed all traces of organic remains. In a few areas of lime-rich soil, bones have become fossilised, but such occurrences are rare. All too often even the stone tools have been washed, from where they were left, into accumulations of soil and rock at the foot of a slope, or caught up by a river into the gravels in its bed. They become parts of geological deposits and in such situations can tell us very little.

But occasionally open sites are covered rapidly by blown sand or become submerged beneath the waters of a rising lake where they are gently covered by mud. If found subsequently they may preserve in a striking manner the internal arrangements of the original campsite. In such a situation we may learn more about the group size and its internal social arrangements than in a cave. In the open the group can spread out and settle into its preferred arrangements of family groupings, adults and children, working and sleeping areas, and so on. In a cave or shelter the group must fit into the space available and such distinctions are generally lost.

The Resources of the Landscape

A glance at the map (fig. 1) tells us that there are a number of major vegetation zones in Southern Africa. In the west and south-west these tend to comprise scrubby, succulent plants adapted to the drier conditions of the western part of the sub-continent. In the centre is a huge area of grassland important in the past, as at present, as grazing for wild animals and cattle. Large areas of this grassland in the east and north-east (sourveld) lose much of their nourishment value and palatability in the winter months. The grassveld is an almost treeless area. Enclosing these areas, to the north and east, are vast expanses of bushveld or savannah with variable mixtures of grasses, shrubs and trees. In the drier areas of the north-west, thorn trees often give the veld a characteristic appearance. Elsewhere a greater variety of trees occur in varying densities from forest patches to open parkland. True temperate, evergreen forests are rare, surviving mainly in the Knysna forest in the south, and as patches on the wetter, east-facing slopes south of Lesotho, and in the eastern Transvaal.

Work in progress at Nelson Bay Cave.

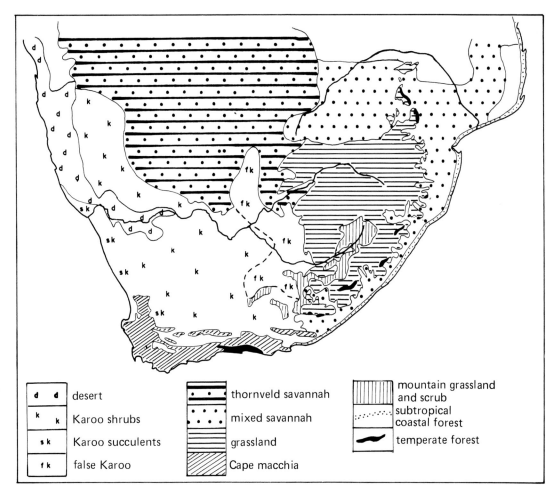

d d	desert	• • • thornveld savannah	▦	mountain grassland and scrub
k k	Karoo shrubs	• • • mixed savannah	⋯	subtropical coastal forest
s k	Karoo succulents	═ grassland	⬛	temperate forest
f k	false Karoo	▨ Cape macchia		

1 The main vegetation zones of Southern Africa. The false Karoo represents a recent spread of Karoo shrubs into grassland and thornveld as a result of bad management in the past century or two.

But a description of the botanical features of the landscape does not in itself say much about how generous that landscape might have been to prehistoric man. For this it is more profitable to turn to the writings of early travellers and to naturalists who have enquired specifically about the usefulness of the veld to man. Early travellers in particular help us to catch a glimpse of how things were before European guns devastated the game, and farms and cities altered the vegetation. An example may suggest a different and more helpful way of looking at things.

Captain Cornwallis Harris journeyed from the south-east Cape to the Transvaal and back on a hunting expedition in 1836. His party followed a route from Grahamstown to Kuruman by way of Graaff-Reinet, and then in a broad arc northward and eastward to the Cashan (Magaliesberg) mountains near Pretoria. From here he hunted north to the valley of the Limpopo and back to Magaliesberg before travelling east and south and finally south-westward across the Vaal and back to Graaff-Reinet through the heart of the present day Orange Free State (fig. 2). He began his journey in mid-winter (July, the height of the dry season) and reached Kuruman towards the end of September. Rains began about mid-October and continued intermittently to the end of his journey at the height of summer in late January. Thus in the first half of his journey (to the Molopo River) the landscape was seen in its most parched condition, at the end of the dry season, whereas the Transvaal and Free State sections were viewed in the rainy season. But despite this, the irregularity of the thunderstorms resulted in occasional water shortages on the return journey across the grasslands, and more than once we are made aware of the difficulties of finding fuel

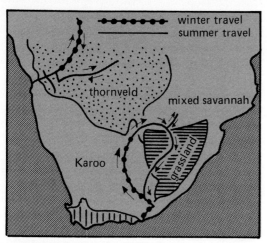

2 *The approximate routes followed by Cornwallis Harris in 1836/7 and Galton in 1850/1. Water was sometimes in short supply for both travellers and Cornwallis Harris sometimes lacked fuel for fires, but neither ran short of meat.*

for fires or branches to enclose the oxen at night.

Between Port Elizabeth and Grahamstown they saw little game, and the first part of the journey to Graaff-Reinet had 'the same barren, uninteresting character . . . but generally more level, less abundantly watered, and more thickly covered with brushwood and succulent dwarf trees, called by the colonists speckboom.' 'Several small herds of springbucks', and guinea fowl in abundance were seen at one of the farms en route. As they advanced, 'the country became more open and practicable, and was covered with large herds of spring-bucks.' On September 6th they saw 'large troops of those eccentric animals the Gnoos', and the following day 'the face of the country was literally white with spring-bucks . . . pouring down like locusts from the endless plains of the interior.' But the route to the Orange was dry, and he speaks somewhat bitterly of the 'drought which had . . . removed every vestige of vegetation', of 'plains of arid land . . . variegated with a few black and sickly shrubs. . . . Over the wide desolation of the stony waste not a tree could be discerned. The days were oppressively hot . . . the nights were piercingly cold.' Here he saw a Korana running down an ostrich on foot, and ostrich eggs were offered by 'Bushmen' women.

North of Kuruman, 'our march was a very hot one across measureless plains (of) . . . red sand, abounding at intervals with long coarse grass . . . troops of unwieldy ostriches . . . grazing (and) extensive areas of waving grass . . . decorated with larger shrubs . . . the day was intolerably hot.' But the scenery was

changing, 'we might now imagine ourselves in an extensive park . . . a soft carpet of luxuriant green grass, spangled with flowers, and shaded by spreading mokaalas' *(Acacia giraffae).* They now saw 'small troops of striped quaggas . . . and of brindled gnoos . . . troops of ostriches and spring-bucks.' 'As we advanced the game became hourly more abundant . . . hartebeests, quaggas, and brindled gnoos were everywhere to be seen.' Then came the 'Choo Desert', followed by 'Immense sandy flats, with a substratum of lime, . . . uniformly covered with *mokaala* trees, low thorn bushes, and long grass.' Here they saw 'a vast herd of zebras . . . more gnoos, with sassaybes and hartebeests, pouring down from every quarter, until the landscape literally presented the appearance of a moving mass of game.'

From this point onwards Harris is repeatedly excited by the beauty of the landscape and the abundance of game and of trees and grass, interrupted here and there by less bountiful stretches.

Fourteen years later, in August 1850, Francis Galton landed at Walvis Bay, and in March 1851 he embarked on a journey that took him via the east side of Etosha Pan to Ondongua in Ovamboland, and back again. Almost the whole of this journey lay within the western part of the thornveld; only the most northerly part (Ovamboland) lay within an area of mixed savannah. The journey was accomplished in the period from late summer (March) well into winter (August). On his return from Ovamboland he immediately set out eastwards in an endeavour to reach Lake Ngami, but was obliged to turn back from Tunobis (Rietfontein), about 250 miles east of his starting point (Windhoek). This journey occupied the period from late winter to midsummer and lay within the heart of the thornveld country (fig. 2).

Galton's description of the desert country west of the thornveld is not very extensive. But he does mention the abundance of whales off the coast, which no doubt provided a bonus in meat whenever a whale was stranded, and the Nara melons that covered numerous sandy hillocks about half a mile inland from Walvis Bay. The melons were said to form the staple diet of the 'Hottentots' during the season that they were available. We catch a suggestion of seasonal movement in his remark that when the Nara are not available the 'Hottentots' move from the Bay area to the Swakop River valley with their cows and oxen 'to give them a good feed.' At Otjimbingwe on the Swakop he speaks of 'large herds of zebra . . . that came down nearly every afternoon (October) to drink' and, on the evidence of a sailor who had spent the past seven years in and about the Swakop, formed the opinion that the valley 'must

Another early traveller was William J. Burchell. This is 'Crossing the Karro' from his Travels in the Interior of Southern Africa, *vol. 1, 1822.*

have swarmed with game when it was first seen by Europeans'. Ostrich eggs were brought to him soon after landing, and he mentions edible gums from the thorn trees farther inland. On his trip to the Erongo he ran into a large herd of zebra, and mentions the numerous leopards having 'nothing to feed on except baboons and steinboks . . .'. At Otjimbingwe he learned how, in the evening as darkness fell, the local inhabitants quite unconcernedly ran with torches to drive off a lion from the giraffe it had been seen to kill. In March, on his way northwards 'we saw our first herd of wild animals; I counted about one hundred hartebeests in one place, and Anderson four hundred gnus in another'.

There is frequent mention of Damaras and 'Bushmen' using digging-sticks to grub up 'pig nuts' on which some groups were said to subsist, and one man they encountered 'had his wallet full of young birds, just taken out of the nest . . . to eat'. The great water he had expected at Omanbonde, to which hippos came in good years, was dry (he had travelled in one of the driest years in memory), but the water-holes held excellent water, and were visited every night by 'hundreds of desert partridges'. Eight years later one of Galton's party revisited the spot and found 'a sheet of water four and a half miles in extent, abounding with water-fowl, and largely resorted to by a great variety of game and wild animals, such as elephants, rhinoceroses, elands, koodoos, gemsbucks, zebras, pallahs, lions etc. . . . it was a real oasis in the desert'. Galton frequently mentions pitfall traps on both his journeys. At about the latitude of Otavi he 'passed a magnificent set of pitfalls, which the Bushmen who live about these hills had made; the whole breadth of the valley was staked and bushed across. At intervals the fence was broken, and where broken deep pitfalls were made. The strength and size of the timber that was used gave me a great idea of Bushmen industry, for every

tree had to be burnt down and carried away from the hills, and yet the scale of the undertaking would have excited astonishment in far more civilised nations. When herds of animals were seen among the hills the Bushmen drove them through this valley up to the fence; this was too high for them to jump, so that they were obliged to make for the gaps, and there tumbled into the pitfalls.'

The journey eastwards was made at the driest possible time of year after an exceptionally dry year. Yet, despite this, game of one sort or another was abundant. They followed the dry bed of the Nosob and soon 'game began to appear in abundance. (They) passed one great herd of springboks that were migrating . . . the tufts of white hair on the backs of the males were as thickly scattered over the country as daisies on a lawn.' Something was shot every day, and a 'buffalo, a gnu, five zebras, two hartebeests and three roebucks were bagged in two nights'. At Olifant Fontein (Gobabis) forty zebra were trapped in pitfalls in one night, and the local 'Hottentot' chief was said to have shot as many rhinoceros in the vicinity on a recent hunting expedition. At Tunobis 'the river-bed was trodden like the ground in a cattle fair by animals of all descriptions. On the return journey the party hunted spring hares at night with sticks. These large, kangaroo-like rodents, weighing up to 6 lbs emerge from their burrows at night to feed.' Galton says, 'We and the Bushmen arranged ourselves in large

A drawing by Cornwallis Harris, from Portraits of Game and Wild Animals of Southern Africa *(1840).*

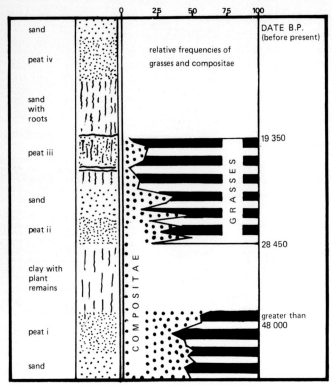

3 Fossil pollens from some sand and peat levels at Florisbad indicate fluctuations between grassland and Karoo vegetation.

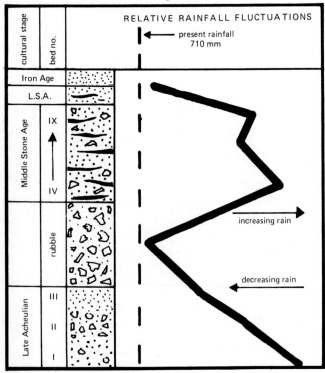

circles, enclosing fresh patches of ground each time, and then beat towards the centre. We generally enclosed two or three . . . and assassinated them with sticks. The sinews of their powerful tails form excellent material for sewing carosses.' Gemsbok calves were also chased on foot and killed. In November the local Bergdamas had poisoned the water-holes in the bed of the Swakop in order to take buffalo that were there at the time, but we are not told the source of the poison.

Accounts such as this create a vivid picture of the composition and abundance of game before European colonisation so drastically changed things, and the picture is the same for almost every part of South Africa. The travellers were mainly concerned with the larger animals, but things do not have to be big to be nourishing, and often small things that go unnoticed are present in great numbers. Tortoises, snakes, frogs, lizards, rats, mice, locusts, flying ants, termites, caterpillars, grubs, birds' eggs and fish are readily available at one time of the year or another, and all help sustain life. The most dramatic accounts of large game belong to the open country of the thornveld, mixed savannah, and grassland, where large herds roamed at will. In the more closed bush areas of the Cape, and in the thickets of mopane country in the north, the great herds may have been missing, or fewer. Hunting techniques may have differed, but game was still abundant.

The Southern African landscape is almost as generous in the matter of plant foods as in meat. Silberbauer records that Central Kalahari hunters pointed out twenty-two species which provided moisture, starch, vitamin C, sugar, fat, protein, riboflavin, salt and iron in various combinations. In the same area the botanist Story was shown no fewer than seventy-nine species used for food and moisture. Each plant was named by Story's guides, and its season and availability were well known. In other parts observers have noted numerous other examples of the use of wild plants.

Where agriculture has replaced hunting and gathering, which it has done throughout most of Southern Africa, information on the uses of wild plants is harder to come by, and less is known than in the regions still occupied by 'Bushmen'. None the less Stevenson-Hamilton lists at least ten species

4 Fluctuations in rainfall as indicated by porosity studies of sand grains at the Cave of Hearths, relative to present rainfall. There are two periods of markedly higher rainfall, and although no absolute values are indicated it seems likely that rainfall never fell below the present-day level.

used for food and moisture in the lowveld some of which are collected in great numbers in times of food shortage, and a survey of the Melville Koppies nature reserve at Johannesburg lists seventeen species of edible fruits, bulbs and roots, ten with edible seed-pods, leaves and young shoots, and four which yield edible gums.

It would be possible to add many more examples and details of the ways in which the natural resources of the landscape were capable of sustaining man, not only in the matter of food but also with the raw materials for clothing and the specialised requirements of a wide variety of tools and weapons. Armed with this knowledge it is perhaps easier to visualise prehistoric man in his landscape, to imagine how he might have lived, and how the artefacts he has left behind might have been employed in the process of living.

The Landscape in the Past

But what of the landscape in the past? The map (fig. 1) summarises the main vegetation types as we see them today, and the outlines are likely to have been much the same throughout the period of man's history in Southern Africa. But there have been changes.

The world-wide temperature changes that produced the 'Ice Ages' of higher latitudes also affected Southern Africa. The timing and degree of these changes are too poorly known to predict their effects in Africa; we only know that they were less dramatic than in temperate latitudes.

The best documentation of temperature change comes from the study of fossil plankton, recovered from the floor of the Mozambique Channel, which shows a rise of about 5°C in the surface waters off the east coast about 10 000 years ago. Fossilised pollen grains from waterlogged deposits at Florisbad (fig. 3), in the southern highveld grasslands, show that several times between 80 000 and 18 000 years ago Karoo vegetation spread at least 200 km eastwards of its original boundary, and the story is repeated for a more recent period at Aliwal North on the Upper Orange. Alternating cycles of deposition and erosion in the Lower Vaal River valley (fig. 6) point to long periods of relatively moist conditions supporting 'lush grassveld' and drier periods with more open vegetation, and evidence for a large and deep lake at Alexandersfontein, near Kimberley, points to a far higher rainfall 16 000 years ago than at the present. Rainfall changes are also documented in the sediments of the Cave of Hearths in

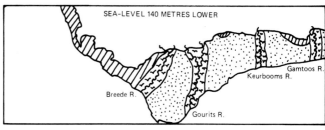

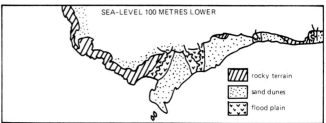

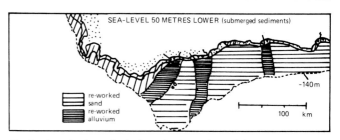

5 *During the last glaciation the lowering of the sea exposed a vast coastal plain off what is now the south coast. The emergence and subsequent drowning of the plain greatly affected the composition of the fauna of the southern region, and seems to have had an important effect on the distribution of man in the Upper Pleistocene.*

the Transvaal (fig. 4).

What might such changes have meant to the prehistoric inhabitants of Southern Africa? Marginally habitable arid areas might have become depopulated during periods of increased aridity while a marked lowering of temperature might have driven populations from the higher mountain regions, but few other areas would be rendered uninhabitable. The savannahs, the grassveld, the macchia, and even the Karoo were, before European disturbance, remarkably well stocked with animal protein and plant foods.

The chief effect of the order of climatic change envisaged would be to shift boundaries between the major ecological zones. It is likely that such shifts induced movement of human populations, but not really easy to see them as prime factors in the emergence of new cultures. Perhaps more dramatic in its effect, at least locally, was the repeated emergence and subsequent drowning of the great plain off the south coast as the sea-levels fell and rose with the waxing and waning of the great continental ice-sheets of the past three million years. The role of changing climates in the story of early man in Africa will emerge only when we have a better understanding of both palaeoclimate and prehistoric human behaviour.

The Landscape and Man

Man as a hunter lives in the landscape like any other animal; he draws his sustenance from it and returns a little to it including, in due course, himself. He cannot be properly understood except in relation to the environment in which he lives. The study of environments now and as they were in the past is an essential concern of the archaeologist. Although man the farmer and herder manipulates and modifies his environment, his scope for doing so is limited by what nature provides.

Many factors have contributed to the making of the landscape. Geological processes have given the continent its form and mass; they have contributed the variety of rocks, and determined their form as mountains, plateaus, plains or valleys. The rocks exercise a strong influence on the nature of the soils that develop on them, or derive from them. Yet ancient though the rocks may be they are not more ancient than the forces of wind and rain and temperature that have acted on them, eroding, shaping and, in the very act of wearing them down, creating from their detritus new rocks to contribute to the land forms of later ages. Climate and geology and living organisms work together to form the soils, rich or poor, deep or thin, that support the mantle of plant life. The plants feed the herbivores and the herbivores feed the carnivores. Exploiting both plants and animals, and paramount among the omnivores, is man.

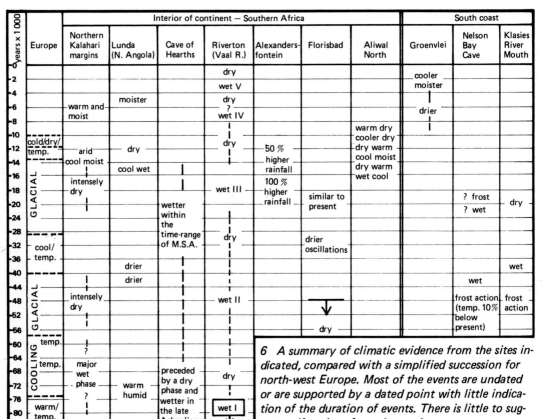

6 A summary of climatic evidence from the sites indicated, compared with a simplified succession for north-west Europe. Most of the events are undated or are supported by a dated point with little indication of the duration of events. There is little to suggest uniformity of trends over large areas.

Climatic Features

The climates of Africa depend primarily on the global character of the high and low pressure belts, the global wind patterns arising from these, and the size and position of the land-mass astride the equator. These global effects are modified in important ways by the cyclic heating and cooling of the continent with the seasonal migration of the sun.

In the southern winter (June, July, August), the south-west corner of the continent is affected by eastward-moving cyclones bringing wild, cold and rainy weather. At this time the interior is cold and dry. With the transition to summer the interior heats up, creating a huge area of low pressure. This, accentuating the inflow of warm, moist air from the Indian Ocean, brings summer rains to most areas excluding the south-west Cape, which now experiences clear, dry weather. Between the winter and summer rainfall areas is a zone likely to experience rain at all seasons.

The relief of the land exercises important influences on rainfall distributions. The Cape Folded Mountains of the south-west Cape receive up to 1 900 mm of rain annually while the 'Swartland' to the west receives between 250 mm and 500 mm and the land to the east of the mountains less than 250 mm. A similar effect is noted on the southern ranges, where the ridges may be very wet but the intervening valleys may be very dry. Such contrasts within short distances exercise important influences on the environment and on man. On the east side of the continent the rainfall tends to be high, but the greatest precipitation occurs over the high peaks

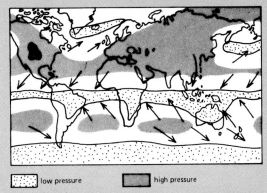

low pressure   high pressure

Ideal distribution of high and low pressure zones and the resultant wind patterns for mid-summer in the southern hemisphere.

of the Natal and Transvaal Drakensberg. Moving west from the Great Escarpment, rainfall declines from 2 500 mm to less than 760 mm, and a broad belt of country along the western edge of the continent receives less than 125 mm.

East of the escarpment and south of the Cape mountains perennial streams are numerous, often flowing during the dry season through otherwise parched and inhospitable country, especially in the east. On the plateau west of the escarpment the only major rivers are the Vaal and the Orange, whose tributaries often flow only weakly, if at all, during the dry season. Many flow only for a few days or hours following a storm. In these seasonally dry, interior regions seasonal lakes (pans) and water-holes assume great importance to man.

Outside of the winter rainfall area most of Southern Africa's rain comes from the Indian Ocean. Rainfall declines steadily from east to west. The interior experiences a great range of temperatures: very hot in summer and cold in winter.

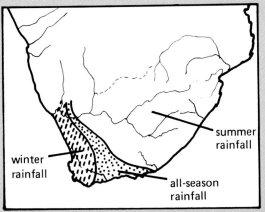

Seasons in which most of the rain falls in the various parts of Southern Africa.

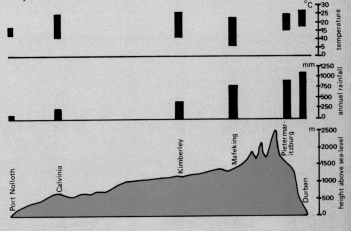

Geological Features

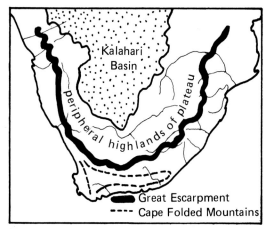

The Cape Folded Mountains were formed some 150 million years ago when marine sediments were squeezed by earth movements against the rigid mass of much older rocks forming the core of the sub-continent. Behind them, and burying much of the southern and eastern part of the more ancient landscape, lie the Karoo rocks, scarcely affected by the folding movements. These near-horizontal rocks give rise to the characteristic 'table-mountain' landscape of much of the interior and the Great Karoo in particular. Following deposition of the Karoo rocks the interior of the continent was gradually uplifted relative to the margins. Erosion of these marginal regions, accompanied by periodic uplift, resulted in the girdle of sloping ground surrounding the plateau interior and separated from it by that dramatic feature the Great Escarpment, which everywhere defines the margins of the plateau.

The uplift was greatest on the eastern side of the continent, giving a gentle tilt to the west, and determining the direction of the drainage of the Vaal and Orange Rivers. The uplift was interrupted in the central region by downwarping, giving rise to the Kalahari Basin, blanketed by sands and devoid of permanent streams, in the area south of the Okavango.

The principal physiographic features of Southern Africa. The Kalahari Basin is almost devoid of drainage. The Peripheral Highlands are drained by two great river systems, the Orange and the Limpopo. The Cape Folded Mountains provide an area of highly variable environments.

(top left) *The Cape Folded Mountains near De Doorns in the south-west Cape.*
(bottom left) *The edge of the Great Escarpment in Natal. To the west lie the great rolling grasslands of the highveld; to the east, foothills with grassy spurs and wooded valleys, and the coast.*
(below) *The Great Karoo near De Aar, with table-top hills in the distance. There is little variation for hundreds of kilometres.*

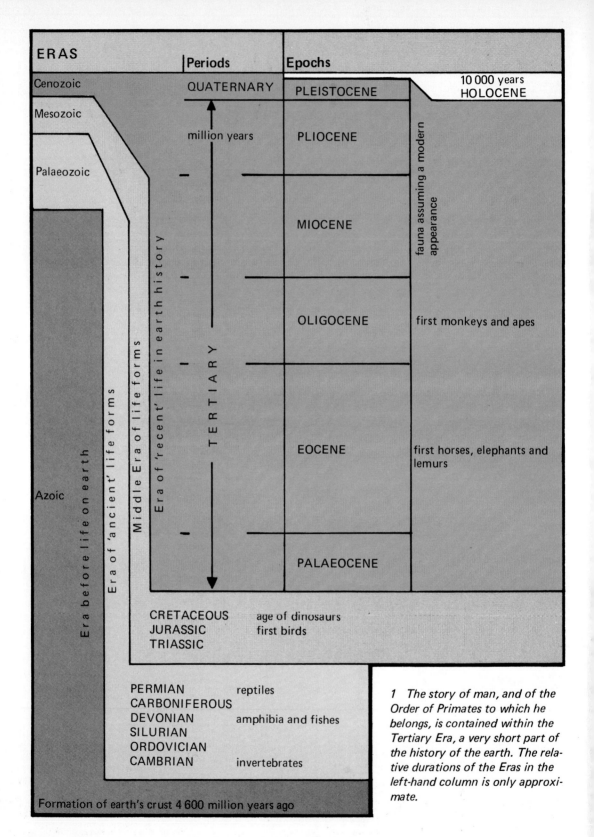

ERAS	Periods	Epochs	
Cenozoic	QUATERNARY	PLEISTOCENE	10 000 years HOLOCENE
Mesozoic	million years	PLIOCENE	
Palaeozoic		MIOCENE	fauna assuming a modern appearance
Azoic	TERTIARY	OLIGOCENE	first monkeys and apes
		EOCENE	first horses, elephants and lemurs
		PALAEOCENE	

Era before life on earth — Era of 'ancient' life forms — Middle Era of life forms — Era of 'recent' life in earth history

CRETACEOUS age of dinosaurs
JURASSIC first birds
TRIASSIC

PERMIAN reptiles
CARBONIFEROUS
DEVONIAN amphibia and fishes
SILURIAN
ORDOVICIAN
CAMBRIAN invertebrates

Formation of earth's crust 4 600 million years ago

1 The story of man, and of the Order of Primates to which he belongs, is contained within the Tertiary Era, a very short part of the history of the earth. The relative durations of the Eras in the left-hand column is only approximate.

2

The Earliest South Africans

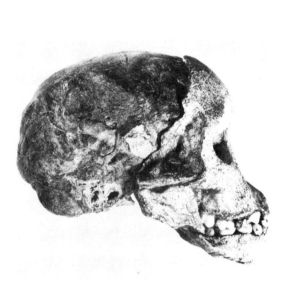

Who were the first inhabitants of Southern Africa? There is no simple answer to the question, and it would be a matter of great interest to know for certain if man evolved from a pre-human ancestor in South Africa, or if he was an immigrant. There is a surprising amount of evidence to consider in any discussion of the question, but it looks as if the first South Africans were immigrants from East Africa, just under 2 million years ago. Their arrival was the consequence of the adoption in East Africa of particularly successful ways of living, involving meat-eating and the regular manufacture of tools and weapons.

If we accept that man evolved from a non-human ancestor, we must decide at what point in his evolution he stopped being pre-human and became 'man'. Now man has a long history, and his evolution as an animal took vastly longer than the time that has elapsed since he first started making tools. Like any other organism he is part of the story of our planet Earth, and it is necessary to fix his origins in the geological time scale.

Geologists divide the history of the earth into four great Eras. The oldest, the Azoic, is without life, unlike the following three, the Palaeozoic, Mesozoic and Cenozoic. The Eras are divided into Periods and the Periods into Epochs (fig. 1). Of these units it is the Tertiary and Quaternary Periods of the Cenozoic that contain the story of man. The Mesozoic was the great age of reptiles, the dinosaurs. As it drew to a close and the dinosaurs diminished in numbers, the tiny mammal-like reptiles that had lurked in the background for millions of years came into their own. From the very beginning of the Tertiary, in the Palaeocene Epoch, tiny insectivorelike creatures appeared. These were members of the Order of Primates, to which man, the apes and all the monkeys belong (fig. 2). With them appeared the first archaic hoofed animals. During the Eocene, from about 58 to 36 million years ago, the ancestors of horses, elephants, pigs, cattle, rhinos and tapirs made their appearance. From the beginning of the Oligocene, some 36 million years ago, the first monkey-like and gibbon-like creatures can be recognised. By 14 million years ago, in the mid-Miocene, a variety of monkeys and apes had evolved. These included Ramapithecus, the earliest representative of the line leading to man (see glossary). By the end of the Pliocene an early form of man was walking the plains of East Africa (fig. 3).

Lest we should think that these important evolutionary changes took place in a placid, unchanging world, we need mention only a few of the major events that occurred during the same interval. At the beginning of the period the continents were still far from their present positions. The great East African Rift valleys had scarcely begun to form, and the Alpine mountain ranges had not yet thrust up their peaks. The early monkeys and gibbons of the Oligocene and their Miocene descendants must often have fled in terror as the earth shook and great volcanoes spewed forth their lava. The movements which thrust up the Alps, the Atlas and the Himalayas had scarcely subsided when the earth was subjected to the first of a series of dramatic climatic changes that covered great areas of the northern hemisphere with ice several times during the past 3 million years. Viewed against such a background man is very much a part of the evolution of our planet and its life-forms.

The biological evolution of man must have proceeded rather slowly by a sequence of small but beneficial changes reflecting adaptations to challenges in his environment. Important among these was the successful attainment of the ability to walk and run in an upright position, not just for short bursts, as some monkeys and apes do, but as a preferred means of getting about. This conferred the advantages of freeing the hands so that they could be used for manipulating and carrying things, and of giving the eyes a higher, and therefore better, viewpoint from which to search for food, or spot the threat of danger soon enough to escape. Then there was the growth of intelligence and the ability to outwit competitors and develop those 'extra-corporeal limbs' that we call 'tools'. Along with these positive developments we must remember that the creature that succeeded in becoming man did so also by avoiding the pitfalls of specialisation. We shall see that at least one of his near relations failed to make the grade, and became extinct, because his teeth specialised to a vegetarian diet and this apparently robbed him of the potential for progress that his more omnivorous relatives retained. Our ancestors never developed the massive arms, long hands and short thumbs of the tree-climbing apes and monkeys. To swing around in the trees you need a long hand with a short thumb, but this is not a good combination for a creature needing a strong, precise grip to fashion and use tools. Whilst these physiological developments were crucial, they were undoubtedly gradual, and did not necessarily all take place at the same time. So it is rather

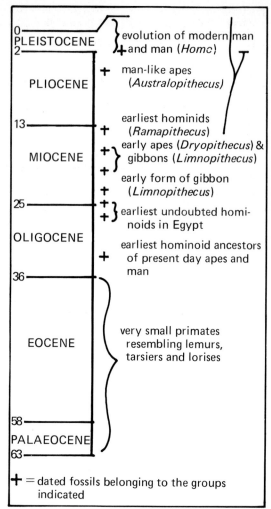

2 The positions within the Tertiary of some fossils relevant to the evolution of man. As yet the direct line to man is not traceable back beyond the late Miocene.

arbitrary to decide at what stage we should call the creature 'man'. The most convenient criterion is the point at which he began to make recognisable tools by regular and repeated techniques.

It is necessary to say 'make' tools because a number of animals use natural objects as tools and it is more than likely that man's pre-human ancestry was marked by a long history of tool-*using*. It is probable that this pre-human stage of tool-using was actually accompanied by a certain amount of tool-making of a simple kind, such as the breaking of sticks and perhaps of bones or stones, which because of the nature of the material or the ultra-simplicity of the object, cannot be recognised as

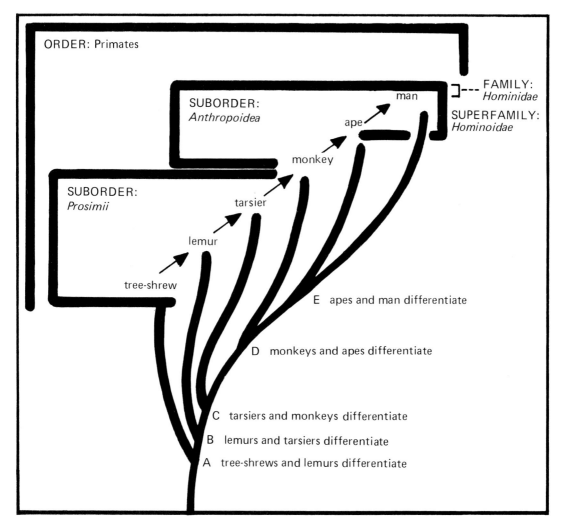

ORDER: Primates

FAMILY:
Hominidae

SUPERFAMILY:
Hominoidae

SUBORDER:
Anthropoidea

man

ape

monkey

SUBORDER:
Prosimii

tarsier

lemur

tree-shrew

E   apes and man differentiate

D   monkeys and apes differentiate

C   tarsiers and monkeys differentiate

B   lemurs and tarsiers differentiate

A   tree-shrews and lemurs differentiate

3   *The apparent evolutionary sequence of the main groups of primates from tree-shrew to man: this is indicated by the oblique arrows across the centre of the diagram. The bold lines indicate in a general way the evolutionary lineage as suggested by the study of fossils and the comparative anatomy of living representatives of the groups. A, B, C, D and E represent the points in the sequence where two lineages begin to differentiate from a common ancestor.*

tools today. For archaeological purposes man becomes recognisable in the geological record when he begins regularly to fracture stone to obtain sharp edges for cutting or chopping or scraping other materials. The oldest such tools found anywhere in the world so far come from just east of Lake Rudolf in Kenya (fig. 4), and from Olduvai Gorge in Tanzania, and are 1,8 million years old.

Geological Considerations

But we must return to man and his possible ancestry in Southern Africa. From the site of Taung in the northern Cape, from Sterkfontein, Swartkrans and Kromdraai near Krugersdorp in the Transvaal, and from Makapansgat further north in the Transvaal, we have a group of fossils which are central to any discussion of human origins south of the Zambezi. But interesting and important as these fossils are they do not represent the earliest stages of the human story. The fossil animal remains from these sites date from very late in the Pliocene or early in the Pleistocene, whereas the ancestry of the human line can be traced back very much further than this, to the late Miocene 14 million years ago and possibly even earlier. Fossils which carry the story well back

4　The principal early-man sites mentioned in this chapter.

into the Miocene are recorded from East Africa, Europe, and India. But if they ever existed in Southern Africa they have not so far been found.

Geological conditions in Southern Africa during the Tertiary were not favourable for the fossilisation of bones, and because of this we have little evidence for periods older than that of the early Pleistocene. It can, however, be argued that it would be unlikely that early representatives of the family to which man and his ancestors belong were living this far south during the major part of the Tertiary. East Africa was an area of considerable geological activity during this period, and particularly so from the mid-Tertiary. The landscape was affected by sagging, which created large inland drainage basins that became filled by lakes. Volcanoes were active, bringing the threat of fire, and incidentally showering down blankets of alkaline ash to bury and preserve the bones of dead animals, including those of our ancestors. At the same time a chain of cracks had begun to appear in the earth's crust causing the foundering of blocks of countryside to form the great Rift Valley. The fossils recovered from Miocene deposits in East Africa indicate, as one geologist has put it, the presence of 'a peneplain [a

Following the pioneer work of the Swedish naturalist Carolus Linnaeus in the middle decades of the eighteenth century, all plants and animals are given two names, a genus name and a species name. The genus name always begins with a capital letter and the species name with a small letter. The species and genus are the basic building materials for biological classification. A *species* may be described as 'a homogeneous group of individuals closely resembling each other and usually capable of interbreeding freely and producing fully fertile offspring'. Examples of interbreeding between different species occur, such as the horse *(Equus caballus)* and the ass *(Equus asinus)*, but the offspring are generally infertile, and the matter stops there. Crossing does not commonly occur in nature, either because the species occupy different areas and do not meet, or because of structural or behavioural differences. A *genus* 'is a group that includes all those closely related species which have arisen from the same immediately ancestral stock'; that is, from the most recent common ancestor. Thus, to say that certain species are members of the same genus is to imply a close relationship between them. Above the level of genus are a number of groupings which increasingly include more and more species and genera and so group together increasingly disparate creatures. Genera may be grouped into Families, Families into Superfamilies, Superfamilies into Suborders, Suborders into Orders, and Orders into Classes. Classes, of which there are six, are the largest subdivisions of the Animal Kingdom.

Members of the Order Primates. The relationship of man to other members of the Order is best seen by reading the table from the bottom upwards. Each step to the left indicates a more remote degree of relationship.

large area levelled by erosion] with ephemeral lakes, active volcanoes of considerable height, a climate generally semi-arid but with a wide range of temperature, and rainfall conditions occurring as a series of altitude zones on the mountains. The vegetation was in accord with this picture, and consisted basically of open savannah on the plains, gallery forests along rivers fed from the mountains, swamps around the lakes, and patches of dense forest on the wetter slopes of the mountains.' This was just the kind of varied and varying environment to provide opportunities and indeed stimulus for experiments in evolution. And there is ample

```
ORDER: Primates

    SUBORDER: Prosimii (the lower primates: tree shrews, lemurs, tarsiers, lorises)

    SUBORDER: Anthropoidea (higher primates: monkeys, apes and men)

        SUPERFAMILY: Ceboidea (New World monkeys)

        SUPERFAMILY: Cercopithecoidea (Old World monkeys)

        SUPERFAMILY: Hominoidea (apes and men)

            FAMILY: Pongidae (apes)
                SUBFAMILY: Hylobatinae (gibbons)
                SUBFAMILY: Dryopithecinae (fossil apes)
                SUBFAMILY: Ponginae (great apes: gorillas, chimps, orang-
                          utans)

            FAMILY: Oreopithecidae (fossil swamp apes)

            FAMILY: Hominidae (men)
                GENUS: Ramapithecus (early man–apes)
                GENUS: Australopithecus (man–apes)
                    SPECIES: A. africanus (gracile man–apes)
                    SPECIES: A. boisei (very robust man–apes)
                GENUS: Homo (men)
                    SPECIES: H. habilis (early Pleistocene men)
                    SPECIES: H. erectus (mid-Pleistocene men)
                    SPECIES: H. sapiens (Late Pleistocene and modern
                             men)
```

evidence that the Order of Primates, the zoological group which includes man and the apes, monkeys and lemurs, and their ancestors, was actively responding in terms of evolutionary experiments.

By contrast Southern Africa remained remarkably stable, geologically, throughout the later part of the Tertiary. Few inland drainage basins were formed, no rifting took place, and there were no volcanoes. Vast areas of the western half of the subcontinent (approximately west of longitude 27[1] east) were blanketed beneath blown sands, under desert conditions. It was not an environment likely to provide a home for evolving primates. At the same time the semi-arid Limpopo trough may have acted as an effective barrier to any movement into the area by higher primates (see page 25) from East Africa. If this assumption is correct these conditions must have changed late in the Tertiary, but before the end of the Pliocene, about 3 to 3½ million years ago. The suggestion that higher primates were absent from Southern Africa in the latter part of the Tertiary may find support in the evidence from Langebaanweg. Here, among the tens of thousands of bones representing at least sixty mammalian species, not a single primate has been found.

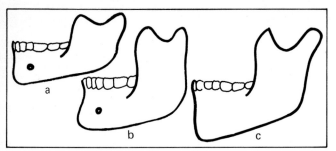

5 Variation in the profile of the mandible in modern man (Homo sapiens): a. Bushman; b. European; c. Negro. Such variation is to be expected within a species.

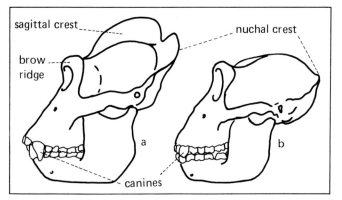

6 Skulls of (a) male gorilla and (b) female gorilla. Note the altogether more massive development of the canines, brow ridge and nuchal crest in the male, and the complete absence of the sagittal crest in the female.

Names and Relationships

When we turn to the man–ape fossils of the early Pleistocene we run into the problem that between East Africa, which we have to take into account, and South Africa there are a large number of fossils with quite an array of names. The names are sometimes a nuisance but it is necessary to learn a few, for not only are they a convenient way of saying what would otherwise take a lot more words, but the names themselves are a kind of code that carries implications about the zoological relationship of the fossils to each other and to the main line of human evolution. An explanation of the naming process may therefore be helpful (see page 25).

The basis for assigning an individual to a particular genus and species is a detailed study of its anatomy. If it is new to science, differing in some significant way from the most similar species that

has been described, it may be given a new species name or, if the differences are sufficiently great, a new genus name, and herein lies a problem for students of fossil man. We have seen that the names indicate a *degree* of relationship; they lead us to think in terms of the ancestry or lineage, or family tree of the individual concerned. We know from the study of living species that the individual members of a species are not identical; they display variation. You have only to think of the range of variation in domestic dogs, all of which belong to the same species, or even in man, another single species. Thus when an anthropologist is faced with a new human fossil which varies from others on record he has to make an assessment as to whether the differences represent variation *within* a species or whether he has a new species or even a new genus. The differences can be very great, as figures 5 and 6 show. The business of giving names to organisms is called taxonomy and working out their evolutionary history is known as phylogeny.

Let us return to the South African man–ape caves and their fossilised remains. The first of this group of fossils, which have become so important in the story of human origins, came to light in 1924. It came with various other fossils from the filling of a cave near Taung in the Harts River valley 130 km north of Kimberley. The skull, that of a child of six years, was almost complete, including the mandible and a full set of teeth (fig. 7). In 1925 Professor Dart stressed the essentially 'humanoid' appearance of the skull and expressed the opinion that it represented a species 'intermediate between living anthropoids (the apes) and man'. He named the creature *Australopithecus africanus*.

In the years following the Taung discovery closely related fossils were found at Sterkfontein (1936), Kromdraai (1938), Makapansgat (1947) and Swartkrans (1948) (fig. 4). These were the dates of the first man–ape fossils to be found. Since then the numbers have grown considerably, with twenty-five to thirty individuals at Sterkfontein represented by a wide range of cranial (skull) and post-cranial parts, at least fourteen individuals at Makapansgat, and eighty-seven at Swartkrans. Although among all these finds the body parts are well represented and tell us a lot that is important, it is the skulls, mandibles and teeth that are most suitable for taxonomic purposes. As might be expected there was a great deal of variation between all these individuals and in an endeavour not to mask differences a variety of new species and genera were created. So by the mid-1950s we had been given *Australopithecus africanus* (Taung), *Australopithecus prometheus*

(Makapansgat), *Plesianthropus transvaalensis* (Sterkfontein), *Paranthropus robustus* (Kromdraai and Swartkrans), *Paranthropus crassidens* (Swartkrans), and *Telanthropus transvaalensis* (Swartkrans). To these, in the twenty-five years since the first Swartkrans discoveries and particularly within the last decade, have been added a number of similar fossils from sites in East Africa. This rapid growth of material for study, combined with a more realistic approach to species variability and a consideration of ecological factors, has led to a welcome reduction in the number of names. Today, all the South African man–apes are accommodated in a single genus *Australopithecus,* containing two species, *africanus* and *robustus.* Let us take a closer look at the physical characteristics of these two species.

7 The beautifully preserved skull of the six-year-old child from Taung. Although this was the first, and therefore the type specimen of the species Australopithecus africanus, *its present taxonomic status is considered uncertain.*

Anatomical matters

The two species seem to have approximately the same stature, about 1,5 m though there is some evidence, particularly from the skull and teeth, that *robustus* was a good deal heavier than *africanus*. The body weights for the two species have been estimated at 36 kg and 28 kg respectively, and *africanus* is often referred to informally as the gracile (slender) australopithecine in contrast to the robust species. So far as the pelvic and limb bones are concerned the general structure is the same in the two species. The manner in which the skull balances on the vertebral column (fig. 8), the form of the lumbar vertebrae, the pelvis and the femur all indicate that both species moved habitually in an upright position. Undoubtedly they walked and ran rather like we do, though the evidence of foot bones from Olduvai in Tanzania shows that the full, springy, striding gait of modern man had not yet evolved. Although the pelves of both species are basically manlike and indicate erect posture, there is a suggestion

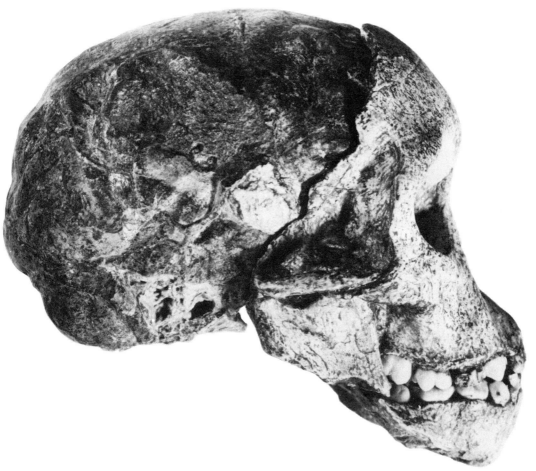

of difference between the two, with *robustus* being slightly less like modern man than *africanus*. A recent suggestion that the limb structure was adapted to allow for marked abilities for climbing is interesting but somewhat difficult to reconcile with the evidence for an open grassland environment unless the adaptation took place elsewhere. That the form of bipedalism might have been different from that of modern man is easier to accept. The evidence for the hand in the South African sites is limited to a wrist-bone, three hand-bones and two finger-bones. The wrist-bone is said to retain important features still found in the wrist structure of chimpanzees. From Olduvai rather better evidence is available and here, again, the hand is said to be 'strangely non-human in many of its characters'. It looks very much as if the development of erect posture and a striding walk had moved ahead more rapidly than the evolution of the hand.

In the matter of brain size, as with the hand, *Australopithecus* had not progressed very far. The mean size for six measurable specimens of *A. africanus* from the South African sites is 442 cubic centimetres. A good specimen of *A. robustus* from Swartkrans measured 530 cc and a robust specimen from Olduvai the same. But too much should not be read into these brain sizes and the differences between them. It has been stressed that 'the weight of the brain is a very poor indicator of its functional value', and it is also true that in the primates the bigger the body size, the bigger the brain. The larger brain of *robustus* compared with *africanus* may reflect no more than greater body size. What is more important is that the brain may be considered as comprising two components: one that is related to body size and another that may vary independently of body size. The latter comprises what have been referred to as 'extra neurons', and it is suggested that it is these that are available to the individual for the development of behavioural responses to the environment. They are the raw material out of which man has progressively developed his culture, and the estimates for the australopithecines place them squarely between the African great apes, and the

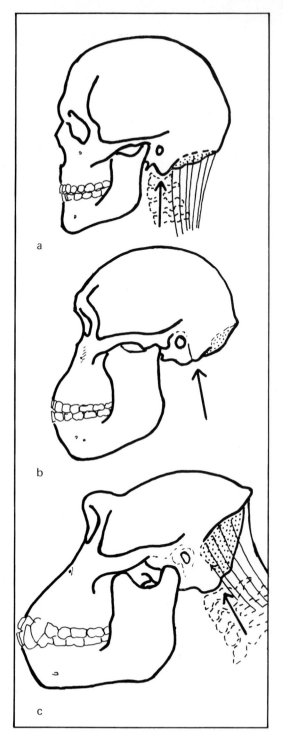

8 Skulls of (a) modern man, (b) Australopithecus africanus, *and (c) a female gorilla. In man and* Australopithecus *the skull is almost balanced on the vertebral column. The neck muscles have less work to do and the area of attachment (nuchal area, stippled) is correspondingly small. These are features associated with an upright (bipedal) habit. In the gorilla, which is primarily quadrupedal, the skull is not supported in the same way,* the neck muscles are altogether more massive and this is reflected in the large area of attachment and the bony ridge (nuchal crest) associated with it.

genus *Homo* (fig. 9).

The remaining anatomical features requiring comment relate to the architecture of the skull, and the character of the teeth. The first thing that strikes one about the australopithecine skull is the ape-like projection of the snout or lower part of the face and jaws, only slightly smaller than modern man, combined with a brain case not much larger than a chimp. But closer inspection reveals a number of important differences (fig. 10). The bony ridges developed for the attachment of muscles are not nearly so pronounced as in the apes, and this applies particularly to the nuchal crest at the back of the skull where the powerful neck muscles attach. Because the skull is more perfectly balanced on the vertebral column there is less work for these muscles to do. Not only is the nuchal crest less developed but it lies much lower, near the base of the skull, much as it does in fossil human skulls. The bony ridges above the eyes are heavy, but they do not match up to the massive shelf of bone found in the apes. In *Australopithecus* the brain case is markedly higher in relation to the face than in the apes. All these features place *Australopithecus* anatomically much closer to *Homo* than to the great apes, but most telling differences are in the teeth and the bony apparatus that contains them.

The incisors in man and the apes fulfil the same functions of nipping and cutting food into manageable-sized pieces, and for this reason are basically similar in shape, though in man and the australopithecines they are reduced in size compared with the apes. The canine teeth are quite a different matter (fig. 11). Although the size of the canines is smaller in the female than in the male, in all of the great apes they are very considerably larger than in man and the australopithecines. Whilst the ape canine may fulfil some function in feeding, such as the stripping of leaves from branches, it serves an even more important function as a fighting weapon and for threat or display in a sexual context within the group. The fossil evidence points to the evolution of the large ape canine from a smaller ancestral form, whereas in man the development has been in the opposite direction so that the canine no longer projects above the general level of the teeth, and often appears chisel-like instead of in its original pointed form. This modification of the canine has important implications for feeding, for with four large canines locking into gaps in the opposing tooth rows the rotary chewing action developed in man cannot occur in apes. In *Australopithecus* the reduction of the canine follows the pattern of human evolution. In the case of the molars and premolars it is difficult to avoid becoming involved in a morass of technicalities, and to steer clear of this it is necessary

9 The estimated 'extra' neurons in the great apes and in man. The figures place the australopithecines squarely between the great apes and the genus Homo, *and suggest a closer affinity with man than with the apes.*

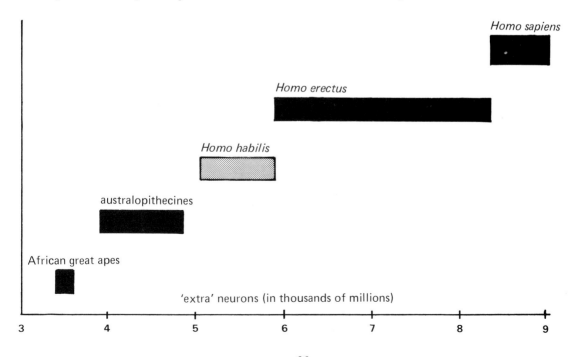

Homo sapiens

Homo erectus

Homo habilis

australopithecines

African great apes

'extra' neurons (in thousands of millions)

3   4   5   6   7   8   9

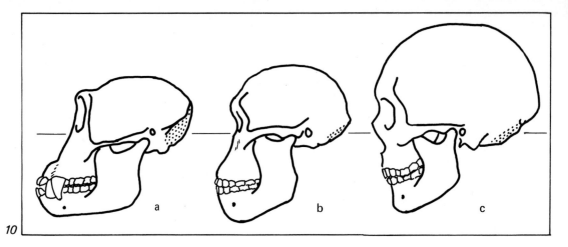

10

10 Skulls of (a) chimpanzee, (b) A. africanus, and (c) modern man, approximately to the same scale. Note the massive canines, brow ridge, and nuchal ridge of the ape, compared with the two hominids. Note also the rounder and higher brain-case of Australopithecus compared with the chimpanzee.

11 Incisor, canine, and premolar teeth of (a) gorilla, (b) chimpanzee, (c) Australopithecus, and (d) modern man, to show the relative sizes of the canine teeth: the roots of the canines are shown black. In the apes the canines serve for fighting and display, as well as for feeding. In man (and Australopithecus) they are reduced to a mere extension of the incisor row, for biting food.

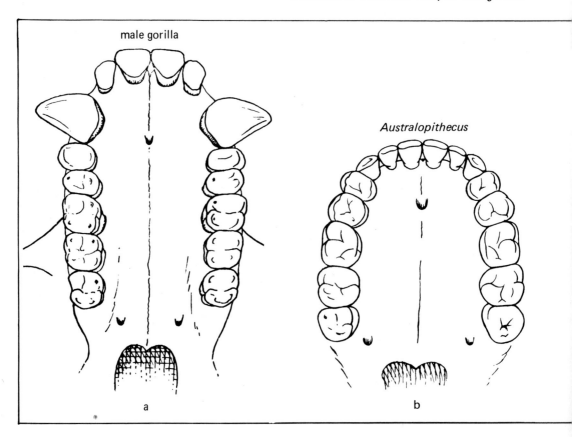

male gorilla

Australopithecus

a

b

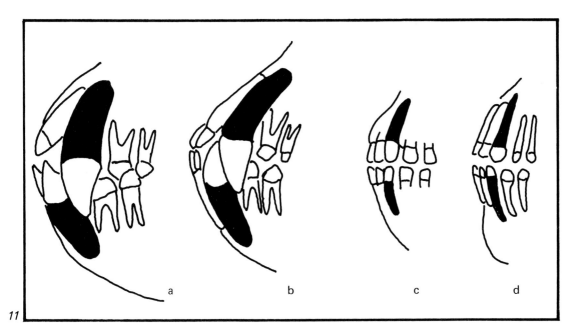

11

to be content with a rather simplified statement. In general the molars and premolars of the apes serve more as a crushing mechanism and tend, even when somewhat worn, to retain an undulating sur-

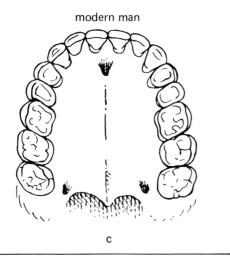

12 *The palate and upper teeth of (a) a male gorilla, (b)* Australopithecus, *and (c) modern man. Note the parallel tooth rows of the gorilla compared with the evenly curved arcades in man and* Australopithecus. *The contrast in the sizes of the canines and incisors is also clearly seen.*

modern man

c

face of cusps and troughs so that the teeth tend to interlock when brought together. In man, and even more so in *Australopithecus*, the premolars rapidly develop a flat grinding surface.

In all these features the australopithecine dentition is clearly human-like rather than ape-like. But the similarity is most clearly revealed in the disposition of the teeth in the palate and jaw (fig. 12).

In the apes the molars and premolars lie in more or less parallel rows, while the incisors tend to form a straight line across the front. To accommodate the highly developed canines there is a marked gap between the incisors and the canines in the upper jaw and between the canines and the premolars in the lower jaw. In man and in the australopithecines the reduction of the canines requires no opposing gap to accommodate them and the teeth lie in a smooth, rounded arch. The lower jaw of apes is strengthened internally by a strong bony plate or buttress low down or midway up the mandible. In man a combination of anatomical changes and changes in feeding habits has resulted in the replacement of this strengthening device by the development of an external growth of bone, the chin.

Although both species of *Australopithecus* can be placed firmly in the Family of men (Hominidae) as distinct from the Family of apes (Pongidae) (see page 25), there are important differences between the two species. The generally greater robustness of the one species has already been mentioned, but the most telling difference is in the teeth. In *A. robustus* the incisors and canines are significantly

31

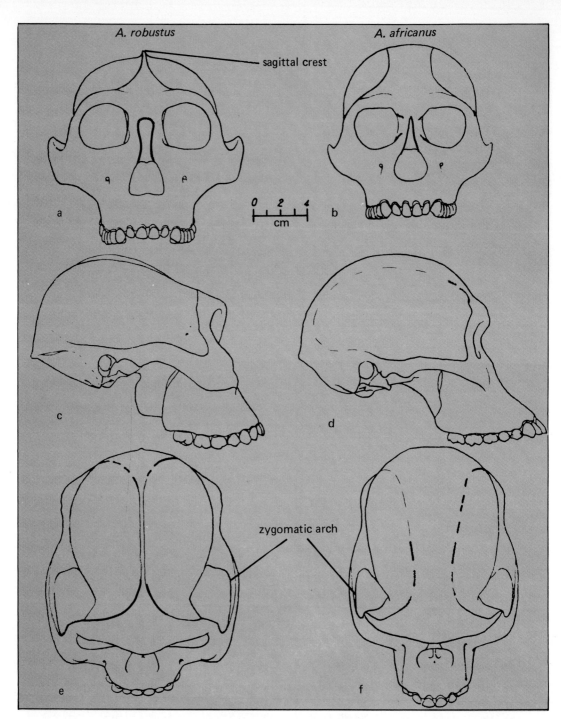

A. robustus

A. africanus

sagittal crest

zygomatic arch

13   The skull of A. robustus *(a, c, e) compared with that of* A. africanus *(b, d, f). Note the (sagital) crest on the top of the* robustus *skull, for the attachment of the great temporalis muscles which help to work the jaw. In* africanus *these muscles are lighter and attach lower on the sides of the skull. The zygomatic arches (best seen in e and f) also reflect the differences in the musculature. Much of the ruggedness of the* robustus *skull is believed to stem from his vegetarian diet: huge, grinding molar teeth and heavy musculature to make them do their work.*

smaller than in *A. africanus,* and the molars and premolars are larger. The contrast between the two is attributed to the fact that *africanus* retained a generally omnivorous diet which may have included a significant amount of meat, while *robustus* appears to have specialised to a vegetarian diet requiring broad grinding surfaces to the teeth, and a very massive musculature to operate them. The evidence for the muscles is very clear and is probably the most striking difference between the two species. The two pairs of muscles responsible for raising the jaw and its teeth against the upper teeth are the masseter muscles and the temporalis muscles. The former are attached to the inner surface of the zygomatic arch (fig. 13) while the latter pass through the arch and spread up over the side of the skull. In man and in *A. africanus* the temporalis muscles reach about three-quarters of the way up the skull where a faint ridge of bone is developed for attachment. In *A. robustus* the huge muscles reach right up to the centre-line of the skull where, because muscle may not attach to muscle, a small bony crest (the sagittal crest) has developed to provide an anchorage. To accommodate both the large temporalis muscle and a comparably large masseter muscle, the zygomatic arch is also very much larger and more rugged than in *A. africanus.* It seems clear that a major distinction between the two species lay in their different dietary and thus behavioural patterns, and these are strongly reflected in the masticatory apparatus. Indeed these differences may have much to do with the overall heaviness of the robust creature compared with his gracile and possibly more active cousin.

The Question of Behaviour

If these creatures qualify anatomically for inclusion in the Family of man, do they also qualify as toolmakers? And if not toolmakers themselves, could they, one or the other, be ancestral to the first toolmaking men in Southern Africa? We must admit at the outset that they do not score too well on either count. What does seem likely is that as creatures not possessed of natural fighting equipment such as large canines or claws, nor built for speed of running, and whose abdomen was vulnerably exposed when standing in their now habitually erect position, they are likely to have made extensive use of weapons for offence or defence. But this is not to say that they fashioned tools. This behaviour may have amounted to no more than a ready predilection for hurling stones or brandishing sticks. The effect

might be enhanced if it were done by several members, or the whole group in concert. It could be a device for discouraging an attacker, or for driving a predator from its kill. This kind of tool-using was proposed in an extreme form at least a quarter of a century ago when Professor Raymond Dart and others claimed to recognise signs of bludgeoning on the skulls of baboons and on skulls and jaws of australopithecines. Of fifty-four fossil baboon skulls from Taung, Sterkfontein and Makapansgat, no less than 80 per cent were said to have been smashed by a severe blow from a club, the weapon being identified as the humerus bone of an antelope. It was not only baboons that were attacked but the australopithecines themselves, and this was taken to indicate not only murder, but cannibalism as well. But these claims have not stood up to closer scrutiny. Some examples are shown clearly to be the result of damage occurring after fossilisation, while the rest cannot be determined one way or the other because there is insufficient information about the enclosing deposits.

Dart went much further than postulating that australopithecines hunted each other and other animals with bone clubs and with stones. He proposed an elaborate culture based on the use of bones, teeth, and horns; the 'osteodontokeratic' culture, as he called it. This elaborate culture was suggested to him mainly by the parts of the fossil animals represented in the breccia (see glossary) from the Makapansgat cave. In the decade between 1945 and 1955 some 7 159 bones were painstakingly extracted from about five tons of breccia. The features that struck Dart were the very high proportion of antelopes, especially small and medium-sized species, and the very uneven representation of the different parts of the skeleton. Skull parts (jaws, teeth, horn-cores) predominated and there were hardly any ribs, vertebrae or tail bones. Front limbs were well represented, but hind limbs were fewer. The extremities of all limbs were very underrepresented. His interpretation of these features was that the parts had been carefully selected by *Australopithecus* and carried back to the cave for use as tools and weapons: saws, knives, scrapers, clubs, daggers, pestles and mortars, spoons, and many other uses. Almost every bone had a use, either in its natural form, or modified. But was this really the correct, or only explanation?

An approach to the answer lies partly in a study of how the caves formed (fig. 14), and partly in considering what other factors may have contributed to the accumulation of bones in the caves. Both of these matters have received very careful attention from Dr. C.K. Brain of the Transvaal Museum. The australopithecine caves today are little more than the heavily eroded remnants of what were formerly large cavern systems in a landscape that has been drastically reduced by erosion. Cavern systems in all stages of development may be seen in the Transvaal, and other limestone areas today. Sometimes these open onto hillsides in the conventional manner of a cave, and sometimes they open as more or less vertical shafts on a flat surface. Such caves may become the lairs of leopard and porcupine, which may carry in bones, while other accumulations can result from the death of sick or wounded animals seeking shelter, as they are known to do in caves. But there are other possibilities.

Brain has shown that the Swartkrans bone breccia accumulated in a near-vertical shaft connecting with a series of chambers below. Although the number of bones or bone fragments recovered now totals more than 14 000, if the shaft was open for several thousand years, as it surely must have been, the rate of accumulation of bones need have been little more than a handful each year. Since nothing approaching a whole skeleton has been found it seems unlikely that natural deaths contributed much. Only about 5 per cent of the bones show signs of porcupine gnawing, and they too must be eliminated as major contributors. Bone accumulations known to be the result of the actions of primitive man are characterised by a high degree of fragmentation, and whilst some splinters and fragments do occur they are not abundant, so that human activity seems not to have played an important part. This leaves a variety of other candidates including lion, leopard, brown hyena, spotted hyena, two extinct hyenas and two extinct sabre-tooth cats. The sabre-tooths can also be disqualified since their dentition is evolved for shearing meat but not for crushing bones, and they would tend to leave whole skeletons. The scavenging hyenas doubtless flourished on the sabre-tooth leftovers, but hyenas crush up and devour all but the largest bones, and it is clear that the Swartkrans bones had not been worked over extensively by hyenas. The most likely candidate singled out by Brain was the leopard, and with this in mind he made a study of a series of leopard kills in the Kruger National Park where hyenas abound, and in a part of Namibia where they do not.

In country where they are not harried by hyenas leopards eat where they kill, taking their fill of meat and doing little damage to the skeleton. In the presence of hyenas they not infrequently lose their kill to the scavengers before getting at it themselves. If they are quick enough they will carry it up into a tree and return to feed on it over a period of several days. At the end, little is left but the head and the lower parts hanging on strips of skin, of which the more fragile bone parts may be chewed up and devoured. The more awkward and the more resistant parts remain and eventually fall to the ground. That there were a variety of scavengers to harry the leopards is clearly attested in the fossil record. Furthermore although trees are sparse in the highveld landscape they are almost invariably present at the mouths of caves and at the head of shafts of the vertical kind found at Swartkrans. In other words the environmental conditions were exactly right for a slow but steady trickle of bones from leopard kills into the Swartkrans breccia. That this was the main source of bones in the deposit is borne out by the pattern of bone occurrence which is entirely consistent with the dining habits of treed leopards. Whereas with antelope remains the post-cranial skeleton is represented by the more resistant parts, in the case of *Australopithecus robustus* the situation is quite different, but it again follows the pattern of destruction observed under experimental conditions with cheetahs eating baboons. In baboons, and in *A. robustus*, the major part of the skeleton is sufficiently delicately constructed for virtually the whole of the post-cranial skeleton to be consumed. From Swartkrans by 1970 a minimum of sixty *A. robustus* were represented by 190 separate pieces, of which only eleven were post-cranial.

This excursion into cave formation and the eating habits of carnivores is vital in relation to the problem of the bone accumulations in the australopithecine caves. Unfortunately we do not at present know if the form of the other caves was similar to Swartkrans, but the mode of their formation and the general similarity of the deposits filling them suggests they were not very different. That they may have been slightly different is suggested by the evidence of Makapansgat, where the incidence of bone splinters appears to be higher than at Swartkrans. This may reflect the human bone-breaking habit, but need mean no more than that conditions at the entrance to Makapansgat were such as to provide a shelter in which *Australopithecus africanus* periodically smashed bones to get at the marrow. The fragments would find their way into the breccia together with contributions from other sources. An explanation similar to that proposed for Swartkrans with a minimal contribution from the cultural behaviour of *A. africanus* would provide a much more plausible interpretation of the Makapansgat bone accumulation than one involving an elaborate bone, tooth and horn culture. A

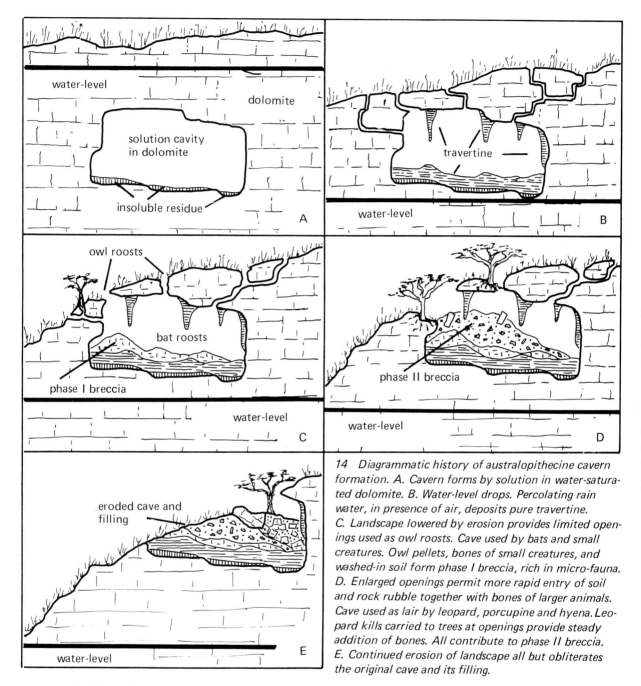

14 *Diagrammatic history of australopithecine cavern formation. A. Cavern forms by solution in water-saturated dolomite. B. Water-level drops. Percolating rain water, in presence of air, deposits pure travertine. C. Landscape lowered by erosion provides limited openings used as owl roosts. Cave used by bats and small creatures. Owl pellets, bones of small creatures, and washed-in soil form phase I breccia, rich in micro-fauna. D. Enlarged openings permit more rapid entry of soil and rock rubble together with bones of larger animals. Cave used as lair by leopard, porcupine and hyena. Leopard kills carried to trees at openings provide steady addition of bones. All contribute to phase II breccia. E. Continued erosion of landscape all but obliterates the original cave and its filling.*

recent study of 2 000 bones from Makapansgat has shown that porcupines played a much more important role in assembling the accumulation than had hitherto been recognised. The preponderance of antelope in both Makapansgat and Swartkrans reflects the kind of kill pattern to be expected in open plains country, rather than the selection of antelope parts by australopithecenes.

AUSTRALOPITHECUS AFRICANUS

Australopithecus africanus *A close relative of the ancestors of man about 2 to 5 million years ago. He was unspecialised as to diet, walked upright and almost certainly used tools, but seems not to have fashioned them. Probably became extinct in the face of competition from* Homo habilis *about 2 million years ago. A closely related species, A. robustus, was more heavily built and somewhat specialised in his teeth and masticatory apparatus for a vegetarian diet. He survived until about 1,5 million years ago. Both stood about 152 cm tall and weighed around 27,5 kg and 36 kg respectively.*

Homo habilis *Probably looked much like A. africanus except for a larger head to accommodate*

HOMO HABILIS

his larger brain: upwards of 640 cc as against 440 cc in A. africanus. *He is the earliest representative of the genus* Homo *and probably shared a common ancestor with* A. africanus *some 5 or 6 million years ago. Undoubtedly a maker of stone tools, and apparently ancestral to* Homo erectus.

Homo erectus *Brain-size varies quite a lot, but the average is around 935 cc as against 1 345 cc in modern man. The species is widespread in the MIddle Pleistocene (about 1,5 to 0,5 million years ago), having been found in Java, China, East Africa, North Africa, and possibly South Africa and Europe.*
   Fossils such as the skull '1470' from East Rudolf (Kenya) present problems: at 1,8 million

HOMO ERECTUS   HOMO SAPIENS

years old it belongs in the time-range of H. habilis, *but with a cranial capacity of around 810 cc
it looks well on the way for inclusion in the*
erectus *group!*

Homo sapiens *The species to which all forms of
living man belong. It also includes a wide range of
fossils including 'neanderthal man' and two that
may be in the order of 250 000 years old (Swans-
combe and Steinheim in Europe). The brain-size
is large (1 100 cc to more than 1 600 cc), the
face is vertical (in* erectus *and* habilis *the lower
part of the face projects markedly, and the effect
is heightened by the absence of a chin), and the
skeleton is adapted for a fully erect posture and
striding gait.*

Signs of Man

A number of stone tools have been found at
Sterkfontein and Swartkrans, and to discover who
was the maker of these it is necessary to look more
closely at the relative ages of the australopithecine
cave fillings. On the basis of faunal studies
Makapansgat and Sterkfontein are grouped together as being broadly the same age, and are older
than Swartkrans and Kromdraai; there is nothing in
the fauna from Taung that requires that it should be
older than Swartkrans and Kromdraai. At Sterkfontein there are three breccias of different ages (see
glossary). The youngest, or Upper Breccia, belongs

to the Florisian faunal stage and need not detain us. Of the other two the older (Lower Breccia) known as Sterkfontein Type Site (see glossary), has yielded the fauna on which the Sterkfontein faunal span (or Makapanian) is based plus all the undoubted *A. africanus* material from the site. The remaining breccia (Middle Breccia) on the evidence of its bovid remains is younger than the Type Site breccia, bearing a closer resemblance to Swartkrans. The oldest and youngest breccias include a number of species similar to living forms that are bush-loving and water-dependent, such as roan antelope, reedbuck, buffalo, nyala, sable antelope and bushbuck, whereas in the Middle Breccia the incidence of such types as springbok and gazelle indicate a more open environment. The Middle Breccia, in a locality known as the Extension Site, has yielded a number of undoubted stone implements, and a few teeth which have been variously attributed to *Australopithecus* or to a more advanced hominid. It seems that the Lower Breccia once filled the cave so that for an unknown but possibly very long time no more material was able to enter the cave. A collapse of the floor onto a lower cave re-opened the upper part, and a new cycle of sedimentation gave rise to the Middle Breccia. In the interval between them tool-makers had entered the Sterkfontein valley.

Like the Sterkfontein Type locality, Makapansgat has yielded abundant remains of the gracile australopithecine but as yet no associated stone tools. Taung is also devoid of stone tools, but can be shown on geological grounds to be contemporary with, or more recent than high-level gravels containing simple stone tools in the adjacent Vaal River Valley.

At Swartkrans investigations have proceeded further than at any of the other sites. Here the form of the cave and the history of its filling have been well worked out. Breccia accumulated in a vertical shaft leading to an 'Outer Cave', until the shaft became choked. Subsequently a slight floor subsidence and the opening of a new shaft on the surface, south of the original shaft, resulted in the entry of a newer set of sediments, filling an 'Inner Cave' and the remainder of the 'Outer Cave'. So Swartkrans too has an Older and a Younger Breccia, and on faunal evidence the time difference between the two seems likely to be considerable; 69 per cent of the species from the Older Breccia are extinct, as against 40 per cent of the species in the Younger Breccia. The Older Breccia has yielded fossils representing at least eighty-five individuals of the robust australopithecine *A. robustus*, part of a skull and mandible belonging to a member of the genus *Homo*, and certainly one and possibly seven simple stone tools. The Younger Breccia has yielded a mandible belonging to the genus *Homo* and a number of stone tools, including a cleaver of Acheulian type.

Evaluation of these South African discoveries becomes clearer when viewed against the background of events in East Africa, where finds are more numerous and are well dated by the potassium/argon method.

The principal East African sites are shown on the map (fig. 4). From Lothagam and Kanapoi specimens resembling *A. africanus* are dated to about 4 million and 5 million years ago respectively. Neither site contains any stone tools. At Olduvai Gorge a number of well-preserved archaeological sites have produced stone tool assemblages associated with a particularly rugged form of *A. robustus* and an ultragracile creature with a brain size of 680 cc. This latter creature, represented by several specimens, has been regarded by some anthropologists as belonging to the same genus as modern man, but to a new (extinct) species, *Homo habilis*. Others regard it as a large-brained *Australopithecus*. Such differences of opinion remind us of the problems of taxonomy (naming) and phylogeny (evolutionary history) referred to earlier. In terms of brain size *Homo habilis* certainly occupies an intermediate position between *A. africanus* and *Homo erectus* of the Middle Pleistocene. The dating of these Olduvai fossils is fixed between 1,9 and 1,7 million years, though the robust australopithecine may have survived for a long time after this.

In sites just east of Lake Rudolf, dated to about 1,8 million years ago, we have a similar association of artefacts with a larger-brained (800 cc) gracile hominid, and a robust australopithicine. The discoverers of these fossils think it unlikely that three species of hominid would exist side by side and have proposed that the robust and gracile australopithecines are simply male and female of the same species. This is an attractive idea, but it is one that cannot easily be applied to the South African situation. If *robustus* and *africanus* were male and female of a single species, we would have to explain why in the two older sites of Sterkfontein (Type Site) and Makapansgat only females got into the deposits, while at the later site of Swartkrans eighty-five males and no females fell foul of leopards. This seems about impossible. The most acceptable explanation of the South African situation would be one in which *A. africanus* was the only hominid in the Transvaal at the time of formation of Sterkfontein (Type Site) and Makapansgat breccias. A long time later, perhaps a million years or more, when the Older Breccia at Swartkrans and the Middle

million years ago

PLEISTOCENE

PLIOCENE

A

H. sapiens
H. erectus
H. habilis
A. africanus
common ancestor
?
A. robustus
Ramapithecus

B

H sapiens
H. erectus
H. habilis
A. africanus
?
A. robustus
Ramapithecus

C

H. sapiens
H. erectus
H. habilis
Homo
?
gracile ♀   robust ♂
Australopithecus
Ramapithecus

Breccia at Sterkfontein accumulated, *A. africanus* had become extinct in South Africa whereas an early representative of *Homo* and *A. robustus* had appeared on the scene, immigrants from East Africa. Swartkrans Older Breccia has all the appearance of being the South African equivalent of Bed I Olduvai, perhaps 1,5 to 1,9 million years old, and the Swartkrans fauna would be in accord with such an age.

Where does this leave Taung? At face value it would appear that Taung was the sole example of the survival of a gracile australopithecine into the period of stone-tool-making, but this may not be the case. A new assessment of the fossil's brain-size has demoted him. Instead of a rather large-brained *A. africanus*, it is now thought that he may be a young specimen of *A. robustus* in which the craggy features of adulthood had not yet developed. This is awkward for the taxonomists but removes a difficulty

15 *Three interpretations of the evolution of the hominids (the line leading to man). Any of the populations indicated would be likely to have displayed considerable variation and new species or genera deriving from them would be likely to arise from a section of a population rather than the whole population. This is thought to be particularly likely in the case of the mid-Pleistocene hominids, where more sapient groups formed part of the population alongside the extreme* erectus *types. The situation finds a parallel during the Late Pleistocene, when neanderthal man seems to have represented an extreme form of* Homo sapiens *alongside more familiar-looking peoples.*

for the prehistorian. Against this background it also seems wiser to regard the teeth from the Sterkfontein Type Site as belonging to the genus *Homo* rather than to *Australopithecus*.

The possible relationships of the fossils just discussed are represented in figure 15. Basically three possibilities suggest themselves. In 'A', *A. africanus* is in the direct line of descent of man. In 'B' the *africanus* and the human lines spring from a common ancestor in the mid-Pliocene or earlier. They remain morphologically very similar except that the human ancestor develops a much larger brain and more elaborate cultural behaviour leading to persistent tool-making. In both 'A' and 'B' the *robustus* line is established as a separate line at an early date and persists into the early Middle Pleistocene. In 'C' the human and australopithecine lines divide early in the Pliocene and the robust and gracile individuals represent sexual differences within a single species of *Australopithecus;* a view not supported by the South African evidence.

Life in the Lower Pleistocene

The earliest stone tools in South Africa are probably the handful from the Older Breccia at Swartkrans and those in the high-level gravels of the Vaal River. They are of great interest as representing early tool-making in the south, but because they are so few, and are found in such uninformative circumstances, they have little to tell us of the behaviour of their makers. However, the similarities in age and in the associated hominid fossils suggest that the behaviour patterns of the South African early men 1,5 to 1,8 million years ago would have been similar to those of their East African contemporaries. It is to East Africa that we must turn for additional information.

The best archaeological sites and the clearest expressions of early tool-making are found at Olduvai Gorge, dated 1,8 million years ago and later. But from the range of activity represented, and on purely theoretical grounds, it could be expected that tool-making goes back much further. In the Omo River valley in Ethiopia there is scanty evidence for simple stone tools as early as 3,0 million years ago, and these may represent some of man's earliest and sporadic experiments in fracturing stone.

From Olduvai we get a picture of activities involving a surprising range of tool types (fig. 16): cobbles and chunks that show signs of use, pieces from which flakes have been struck to produce a tool with a sharp cutting-edge (choppers), polyhedral and spherical stones shaped by use and perhaps originally a source of flakes, stone flakes prepared and used as knives, scrapers and points, and a few rare pieces extensively flaked to provide a pointed tool with a working edge on either side (the ancestor of the handaxe). These features are repeated at a number of sites of broadly the same age, and the name 'Oldowan' culture has been coined for this stage of human technology. There is clear evidence that particular raw materials were selected for particular tools: coarser-grained rocks for the heavier tools such as choppers, and finer-grained rocks for the small, sharp-edged tools. The range of tools suggests a variety of clear-cut activities. Though many of these may have been concerned with cutting meat from dead animals, some undoubtedly related to the working of other materials at a simple level, such as the trimming of sticks to be wielded or thrown at small game.

The repeated occurrence of tools and bones concentrated on living sites suggests the use of a 'home base' by a social group. The carrying back of food to this home base points to food-sharing, and this practice has been highlighted by some anthropologists as an important feature distinguishing human primates from non-human primates (apes and monkeys). The latter 'browse' individually while on the move, and the only food-sharing is between mother and infant or young juveniles. But the real significance of the behaviour may be otherwise. Carnivores such as wild dog, hyena and lion share meat. Whether earliest man scavenged or hunted his meat the operation must often have been dangerous, and pregnant females or females with infants would have been safer left out of it. Leaving the women and children to collect food near the home base while the men hunted or scavenged in groups could have had an important survival value for the group, but it would require food-sharing as inevitably as in a wild-dog pack. The behaviour which distinguished man from the non-human primates might rather be seen as his persistent predilection for meat as a regular, if small, part of his diet.

Meat is a high-protein food and success in obtaining it would have conferred distinct advantages on the species. If the development of special patterns of behaviour perhaps involving division of labour between male and female, accompanied by the acquisition of technological skills, was an essential part of man's success it is not hard to see hand, brain and posture combining to raise him rapidly above the level of his non-human primate contemporaries.

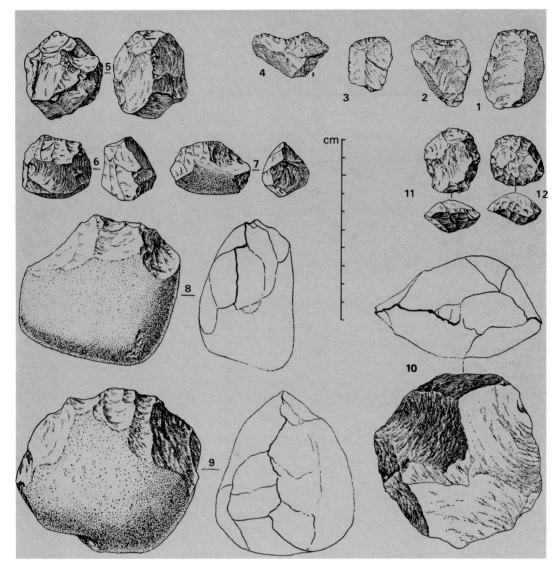

16 Oldowan tools from Bed 1, Olduvai Gorge. 1–4, flake tools; 5, polyhedron; 6 & 7, small chopper-tools; 8 & 9, large chopper-tools; 10–12, discoids. The range of sizes and shapes of tools (not all illustrated) suggests a variety of regular and relatively specialised activities were established by 1,8 million years ago.

The Lower Pleistocene saw the emergence of an impressive array of predators and scavengers to take advantage of the incredibly abundant supply of game. Unique among the scavengers was man, or proto-man. He was the only primate to take to meat as a regular and important part of his diet, and he was the only professional scavenger who could approach his work on two feet instead of four, with his hands free to wield the weapons and tools that he had fashioned.

A. robustus must have had a common ancestor with man and although he went far enough along the line to learn to walk upright, his fate was sealed when he ignored meat in favour of plant foods. He side-stepped the stimulus to develop culture and a bigger and better brain. His way of life may have been very much like the baboons and he may have failed because his bipedalism robbed him of the baboon's agility. He also lacked the baboon's intimidating fangs. If *A. africanus* did not evolve into *Homo,* and the South African evidence suggests he did not, his demise is less easy to explain. He was bipedal and his hands were free for work. He was not a specialised vegetarian. Possibly *africanus* represents a segment of a species that stuck with a mid-Pliocene pattern of behaviour whilst another segment of the species took the line to man; in other words he failed to develop those special features that made for a really efficient primate meat-eater. If this were so he may none the less have been similar enough to proto-man in his needs to have competed, and competed unsuccessfully.

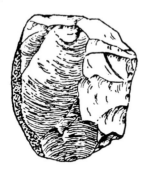

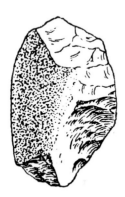

Methods of Dating

We have spoken of the principles of relative dating and have referred to the absolute ages of some geological events. It is appropriate to glance briefly at the principles of dating that enable us to provide a time-scale for the story of man.

Radiometric Dating

Many kinds of atoms have unstable nuclei which decay spontaneously. They are said to be radioactive, and the process of decay is radioactivity. A result of the decay process is that the 'parent' atom changes and produces a different atom (or atoms) termed a 'daughter' atom. Calculation of age depends on the fact that at the time of formation of a mineral or rock containing the radioactive element no 'daughter' atoms are present. From the moment of formation radioactive decay begins to produce 'daughter' atoms. Because the decay rate for the various radioactive elements is known, and because the relative proportions of 'parent' and 'daughter' atoms can be measured, the time that has elapsed since formation can be calculated.

Most radioactive dating methods are suitable only for very ancient rocks far older than the emergence of man. One, however, the potassium/argon method, can be used for dating rocks of any age down to about 50 000 years ago. With younger rocks it is less reliable. Unfortunately the method is applicable only to certain minerals formed during volcanic eruptions of which none have occurred in Southern Africa within the Tertiary and Quaternary periods. There have, however, been numerous eruptions throughout the Tertiary and Quaternary in East Africa and it has been possible to date the major stages of human evolution in that area. Another radioactive method, protactinium/thorium, is applicable to a mineral found in ocean floor sediments and can give dates back to about 150 000 years ago. It may seem strange that this should help in any way with the story of man. What it does is to provide dates for climatic changes which are recorded in deep-sea sediments. These in turn may be correlated with climatic events on the land, thus helping to date the climatic framework within which man evolved.

A more directly useful method is one based on radioactive carbon. The radiocarbon method was discovered in the late 1940s and can be applied to organic remains (charcoal, wood, shell, bone, etc.) up to about 45 000 years old. Beyond this difficulties inherent in the method render the dates less certain and they are best regarded as an indication of the minimum age of the sample.

Climatic Dating

Much information about global temperature fluctuations has come from the study of the fossilised remains of tiny marine animals (the single-celled forams that comprise the planktonic life of the oceans), recovered in cores of sediment from the ocean beds. The plankton species that live in the surface waters respond to temperature change in several ways. The oxygen isotope proportions in their shells vary; regular changes take place in the shapes of the shells of some species; and of course the frequencies of 'warm' and 'cold' species change with any prolonged change in surface-water temperatures. Because the surface waters of the oceans reflect global temperature changes associated with major climatic shifts (glacials and interglacials), and because the surface-water plankton that do not get eaten end up as corpses on the sea bed, the ocean-floor sediments preserve a sensitive record of long-term temperature fluctuations that have occurred at the surface. The top few centimetres of the deep-sea cores can be dated by the radio-carbon method. The deeper (older) parts can be dated by the protactinium/thorium method back to 150 000 years ago. Because sedimentation rates appear to be fairly constant over the dated part of the samples it is possible to estimate reasonable dates for the older parts of cores. Although correlation with glacials and interglacials is not simple the ocean record is favoured because it probably provides a more accurate record of global temperature changes. Long, unbroken records can be recovered, and dating is more secure than the dating of terrestrial climatic events.

One of the effects of the formation of the Pleistocene ice-sheets was to lower the level of the oceans by as much as 100 m or more below the present level. Melting of course restored the level. But it has been shown that these downs and ups of the sea were superimposed on a steadily declining sea-level. Thus the sea never got back after a glaciation to the level it attained before that glaciation. This is represented diagrammatically on page 15. The result has been a series of marine beaches higher than the present, and progressively higher as we move back through earlier interglacials. Since the effects were world-wide the raised beaches provide a useful basis for correlation and relative dating. They fit into a framework of dating by making it possible to correlate events in non-glaciated parts of the world with glacials and interglacials. Any radiometric dating of the glacial/interglacial succession, on dry land or from deep-sea cores, may be extended with care

The approximate pattern of high and low sea-levels through the Pleistocene. The chronological scale must be regarded as very approximate. The elevations of the earlier low sea-levels are not known. The Würm sea dropped to at least 100 m below present sea-level.

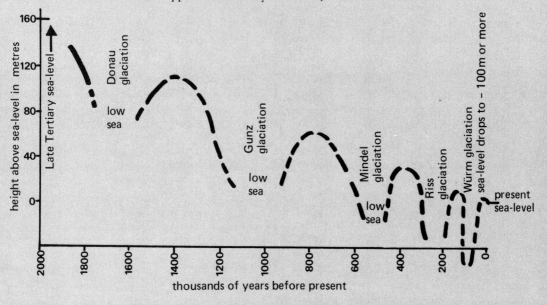

to appropriate high-level beaches.

High-level beaches are recorded in various places and at various heights around the shores of Southern Africa, but have been little studied. However, at three caves on the south coast, Die Kelders, Nelson Bay Cave and Klasies River Mouth, Middle Stone Age deposits rest directly on old high beach deposits of the last interglacial. Since they appear to have got there soon after the sea retreated, an age of at least 70 000 years or more is likely for these deposits.

Faunal Dating

In Europe the deposits of the glacials and interglacials provide a convenient relative chronological framework for associated archaeological materials. In Southern Africa the climatic oscillations were far less severe and produced different and not well-understood effects. As a result we are lacking a comparable framework for ordering Pleistocene events. The deposits in which artefacts and associated fossils occur are small-scale and scattered. Ordinary stratigraphic correlation is out of the question. Radiocarbon dates can reach back only to around 45 000 years ago and other radiometric means of dating cannot be used for lack of suitable materials. In such a situation one of the few ways of dividing up the 2 to 3 million years in which we are interested is on the basis of fossil animal (mostly mammal) remains.

Faunal dating is possible because with the passage of time some species, or whole groups of related species (genera) have become extinct, while new species and genera have arisen to take their place. The creation of a relative chronology out of this situation depends on the combination of several things. The ordinary rules of stratigraphy are fundamental in sites with several layers. Where human artefacts are present these may provide a broad basis for correlation of layers from one site to another. But above all we rely on the skill of the palaeontologist in being able to recognise, often from fragmentary material, what species or genus a particular fossil belongs to. Teeth, preferably whole tooth-rows, are usually the most easily diagnosed, followed by horn-cores and certain of the post-cranial bones of the skeleton. Ribs and vertebrae, and the shafts of bones lacking their ends are not very helpful. Some parts of the skeleton of an extinct animal may not be distinguishable from the same parts of its living descendant and although the palaeontologist may suspect that he is dealing with an extinct form he has no alternative but to list it as 'not distinguishable from

. . .'But despite the difficulties an immense amount has been learned about the fauna of Southern Africa from the late Tertiary to the present.

Radiocarbon dating is a great help in putting things in order within the past forty millennia. What we find within the datable range is that sites belonging to the Holocene (approximately the last 10 000 years) have a completely modern fauna, with no extinct species. The only exceptions are three species (quagga, Cape lion, and Burchell's zebra) which have become extinct in the past 150 years. In deposits which date between 10 000 years and the limit of radiocarbon, and those which lie beyond the reach of radiocarbon but are associated with Middle Stone Age artefacts, we have something different. These deposits contain a full range of modern fauna plus a few extinct species and two extinct genera. These include a giant buffalo (*Pelorovis*) with horns measuring 3 m from tip to tip, a giant hartebeest (*Megalotragus*), two large zebra (*Equus*) species, a smaller antelope of the hartebeest/wildebeest variety, a kudu, a springbuck and a reedbuck. In addition to the short-list of extinct forms the period is also characterised by the first appearance of the modern African elephant and of the modern bushpig and warthog. Prior to this there was a variety of extinct pig and elephant species. This stage of faunal evolution is called Florisian, after the site at Florisbad where it was first clearly recognised, and probably evolved about 100 000 years ago.

At the other end of the time-scale a group of caves in the Transvaal give us a good picture of the fauna of the Highveld early in the Pleistocene. Three of the caves, Sterkfontein, Swartkrans and Kromdraai, lie about 35 km west of Johannesburg and the fourth, Makapansgat, is near the town of Potgietersrust 250 km to the north. All the caves show every sign of being very ancient. Their fillings of breccia (a mixture of soil, rock and bone) are consolidated to the hardness of concrete. The caves themselves had become completely filled and almost eroded out of existence. For these reasons alone they might be taken to be very ancient.

Apart from the remains of a very early man-like creature (*Australopithecus*) they have yielded fauna dominated by extinct species and genera. In a list of 150 species only 46 are given as living species. A number of genera have left no living descendants at all. As one palaeontologist has put it, 'A modern field naturalist transported back to the days of the ape-men and asked to identify the mammals he saw could not be expected to put up a very impressive score. With the usual pass mark of 40 per cent he

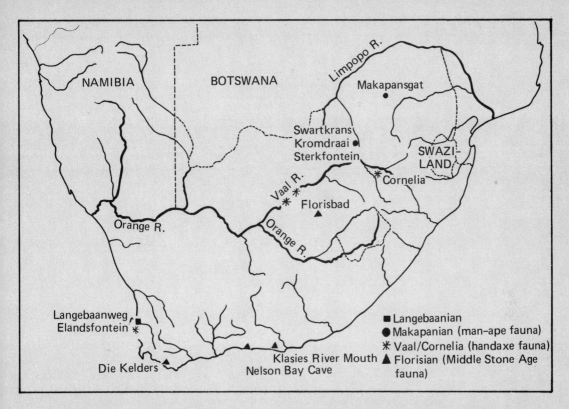

The principal sites on which the major faunal stages are based.

would fail dismally'! The sites are of slightly different ages, and although the fauna as a whole are referred to as Makapanian they are often divided into a Sterkfontein Stage and a later Swartkrans Stage.

In East Africa where ancient lake silts and volcanic ash form deposits hundreds of metres thick it has been shown on clear stratigraphic grounds that australopithecines and fauna of Makapanian type underlie levels containing handaxes of the Acheulian culture. In Southern Africa the sequence must have been much the same, for in the Vaal River gravels, and in old lake sediments at Cornelia in the north-eastern Orange Free State, as well as at Elandsfontein in the south-west Cape (see page 45) handaxes are associated with fauna intermediate in appearance between the Makapanian and the Florisian. The fauna, variously referred to as the Hand-axe fauna, the Vaal/Cornelia, or the Cornelian fauna, seem to contain the full range of living species with the exception of modern elephant, bushpig and warthog. There were also five extinct species of elephant, four extinct genera of pigs, the three-toed horse (*Hipparion*), a short-necked, ant-lered giraffe (*Libytherium*), a giant baboon (*Simopithecus*) and a large sabre-toothed cat. There are a number of survivors from the ape-man fauna but

they are on the decline, and the proportion of extinct species is reduced to about 50 per cent.

Deposits older than the early Pleistocene are extremely rare in Southern Africa. None the less the site of Langebaanweg in the south-west Cape has yielded tens of thousands of fossils without a single living species being found. It has produced the only example of a fossil bear so far found south of the Sahara. Comparisons with East Africa indicate that this Langebaanian fauna must be in the order of 3 million years old, and represents a late stage of the Pliocene Epoch.

Six faunal divisions for a 3-million-year period (page 46) may not seem very helpful, but in the absence of more sensitive means of dating its value should not be underestimated. Also, it is expected that as the evolutionary histories of such groups as the elephants, pigs, and carnivores become better known it may be possible to use them for a much finer indication of relative age.

Names of Faunal Stages		Principal Sites	Approximate Order of Age	Associated Archaeology	
Recent		too numerous to list	up to 10 000 years ago		Iron Age to 2 000 Later Stone Age industries
Florisian or Florisbad faunal span		Florisbad, Vlakkraal, Kalkbank, Cave of Hearths, Wonderwerk, Klassies River Mouth, Swartklip, Melkbos, Nelson Bay Cave, etc.	10 000 to around 125 000 years ago		Albany and Robberg industries, etc. Middle Stone Age
Cornelian or Vaal–Cornelia faunal span		Vaal River Younger Gravels, Cornelia, Elandsfontein	up to 1,5 million years ago	Early Stone Age	Acheulian industries
Makapanian	Swartkrans faunal span	Swartkrans, Kromdraai	perhaps between 1,0 and 2,0 million years ago		Oldowan
	Sterkfontein faunal span	Sterkfontein and Makapansgat	2,0 to 3,0 million years ago		pre tool-making in Southern Africa
Langebaanian		Langebaanweg	probably between 3,0 and 5,0 million years ago		

Archaeological Dating

It is also possible to use artefacts as fossils for the relative dating of the deposits in which they occur. But there are important differences. The number of species of animals is always far greater than the number of human artefact types. Animals evolve by a slow process of gradual change and diversification, and the process is generically controlled. Artefacts may change by gradual improvement, the discovery of new materials, or by fashion, but the process is subject to the whim of the makers. There tend to be periods of rapid change separated by periods of stability and until the history of change is fairly well known, artefacts can provide only a coarse guide to relative age. Where fauna and artefacts occur together in a deposit the relative chronology will be much more certain. But it is well to remember that none of the relative chronological methods can in themselves tell us the age of things. If a radiometric date has been obtained for a particular fauna or artefact assemblage in one place it may, with caution, be extended to similar assemblages

The five faunal stages before the Recent are our principal guide to the age of associated artefacts or human remains in Southern Africa. Approximate ages are suggested on the basis of correlation with sites in East Africa dated by the potassium/argon method.

elsewhere. But allowance must be made for the fact that evolution may take different directions and progress at different rates in widely separated areas.

Finally, for the latest periods of prehistory in Southern Africa there is an additional contribution that artefacts can make to dating. Within the past 1 000 years, and perhaps much more, traders have come to the east coast of Africa in search of ivory, ambergris, slaves, leopard skins, gold, and even iron. We know little of what was given in return, but it did include glass beads, porcelain, and occasionally objects of brass. Where the place and time of origin of such objects can be determined they provide an additional source of dating.

3

A Prehistoric Dark Age

The Problem

Fitting together the scraps of information from South and East Africa we can say that the first South Africans, about 1,5 million years ago, were probably not very different from the gracile australopithecines, whose features are rather well known. They differed in the size of their brain and in the development of their material culture. At 600–800 cc their brains were nearly twice what the man-apes possessed, and they had begun to fashion flaked stone tools to meet their unsophisticated but constant needs. The Oldowan culture so well documented at Olduvai Gorge in Tanzania is man's first recognisable industry and marks the beginning of the Early Stone Age. Although not very visible in South Africa it is probably represented in the few tools from the Older Breccia at Swartkrans, and in some of the more ancient spreads of gravel in the Vaal River valley. This was in the time-range generally referred to as the Lower or Early Pleistocene. Considering the almost unimaginable remoteness of the period we have been able to learn a remarkable amount about the creature and his ancestry and the way in which he lived; a point to which we shall return later.

At the other end of the time-scale, from about 10 000 years ago, when the last cold spell of the Pleistocene was giving way to the warmer conditions of the Holocene (see glossary), we have an even clearer picture of man and the way he lived. Skeletal remains, often complete skeletons, are abundant and these show us that in the interval between the early Pleistocene and the Holocene the biological evolution of man had moved right up to date. The skeletal remains of the Later Stone Age are those of modern man, *Homo sapiens*. Alas, the stages by which the transition took place are almost completely unknown. Through the long millennia of the Pleistocene, man progressed in South Africa from small-brained, culturally limited, manually imperfect creatures still testing the advantages of recently acquired erect postures to become by at least 10 000 years ago fellow men of a kind no stranger than the many and varied races inhabiting the world today. In the stone tools littered across the countryside and lying buried in the fillings of caves and rockshelters we can see several stages in the transformation of technology from simple Old-

47

owan to the sophisticated tool-kits of the Later Stone Age. But throughout this long period of change the actors remain tantalisingly out of view, and we are desperately short of detail.

Stone Ages and Cultures

The period under discussion is divided by archaeologists into two main parts, the Early Stone Age and the Middle Stone Age, to which it would be as well to give some definition. Time deals harshly with organic remains such as wood, fibre, skin, shell and bone, and for the major part of pre-history the evidence for human activity and cultural development lies almost exclusively in the bits and pieces of stone that helped our ancestors cope with life. These bits and pieces reveal two important things: the shapes and sizes of artefacts, and the techniques of stone-working used in their manufacture. Using this information plus the evidence of stratigraphy and faunal and radiometric dating (see pp. 42–6), the 2,0 million years of human activity in Africa have been divided up into three great parts, the Early Stone Age, the Middle Stone Age and the Later Stone Age. The brief Iron Age which follows need not concern us yet. Within these major 'Ages' the archaeologist again makes use of the characteristics of the surviving evidence to establish entities which he calls cultures. So, within the Early Stone Age we have the Oldowan and the Acheulian cultures; within the Middle Stone Age a number of names have been proposed including Stillbay, Pietersburg, Mossel Bay and Alexandersfontein. In the Later Stone Age we have the Wilton culture and the Smithfield culture, each regarded as having a number of differing regional variations.

It is important to be clear just what these cultures amount to. Usually the name of a culture is the name of the site or locality (type site) in which the first characteristic assemblage of artefacts was found. Thus at the time they were found the artefacts from the little seaside resort of Stillbay on the south coast were unparalleled elsewhere and so the name was taken to characterise associations of those particular types of artefacts. Wilton is the name of a farm in the eastern Cape where 'Wilton' artefacts were first found, and so on. The archaeologist's 'culture' is a concept based on artefacts as virtually the sole surviving expression of something originally much more complex. By comparing assemblages of artefacts from a large number of sites he will single out those which he sees as stemming from a common tradition and he may draw a distribution map of the territory over which they occur. With the help of dating techniques he may be able to define the time during which his culture flourished.

There are, however, two serious drawbacks to this concept of cultures. First we know that artefacts are only one expression of a society, and that there are others of equal and sometimes of greater importance. Language is an obvious one, and is one most effectively used in the divisions and subdivisions of peoples today. Political alliance, kinship, religion and economy are others. We know that simple tools such as knives, choppers, scrapers, spears, digging-sticks and awls are technological responses to the need to perform certain tasks which are often universal, and similarities in tool types may reflect nothing more than the best solution to the problem concerned. They are unlikely to be limited to people of a particular political, social or religious persuasion, and therefore might have little meaning in terms of real groupings of people. None the less the occurrence of certain technological features over a continuous stretch of country, in contrast to different ones in an adjacent territory, when both are contemporary and the environments are similar, is likely to have some meaning. Perhaps it defines the extent of a major language grouping, and if it does we are unlikely ever to isolate smaller ethnic units archaeologically other than the smallest coherent group: a family or extended family.

The second weakness is that too much emphasis on 'cultures' tends to lead to a pigeon-hole mentality in which everything has to be fitted into one culture or another. This leaves little scope for the idea of evolving cultures: of gradual or rapid cultural change, or the derivation, by divergence, of two 'cultures' from one. Pigeon-holes are separated from one another by partitions; contemporaneous but different cultures may be separated from each other geographically, but a culture that reaches its zenith, declines, and in its decay gives rise to something new doesn't fit too easily into a pigeon-hole framework.

Culture names can be useful as devices for focusing the attention on a particular area or a particular bracket of time or in a general way to some technological phenomenon, but we should recognise that in themselves they tell us little of interest about people. With this in mind we may attempt a short summary of the main features of the Early, Middle and Later Stone Ages as technological stages.

The Early Stone Age

It is predictable that man's earliest essays into tool-making should be essentially simple and it is not surprising that the Oldowan cannot be recognised by the presence of any unique stone-working technique or any special tool-types. Rather its recognition depends on an absence of those special features which distinguish later cultures, combined with evidence of an early Pleistocene date. The earliest flaking techniques are basically simple and appear to involve no more than the use of one stone as a hammer to detach flakes of stone from another piece held in the free hand. Two objectives were involved: the detachment of flakes of stone which could then be used for cutting or scraping other materials, and the detachment of flakes with a view to producing a sharp working edge on the parent piece. Within the limits of this rather simple approach to stone-tool-making a number of classes of tools have been described for East Africa including a variety of forms of chopper, pieces flaked to a discoidal shape, others so extensively flaked as to merit the description polyhedron, flakes with their edges trimmed to form a working edge and triangular slabs with a corner flaked to provide a narrow but strong sharp chisel-like edge (chapter 2, fig. 16). The working edges of the choppers sometimes show a chipping or scaling of the edge confined to one face, suggesting that the piece was used with a scraping action. On others chipping occurs on both faces and the flaked edge may be battered as if the piece had been used for chopping. The polyhedrons appear to be choppers that have been extensively flaked to provide several chopping edges, which have been all but battered out of existence, sometimes to an extent that renders them almost smooth. Whatever the chopping activities, they sometimes involved under-stones or anvils which show extensive signs of repeated and apparently heavy blows. At Olduvai Gorge, where the deep deposits contain a long sequence of stratified sites, we find that in the later Oldowan sites (Developed Oldowan) more care seems to be lavished on the shaping of many of the tools. More flake-tools are present and certain of the choppers have been flaked in such a way that two cutting edges converge to a crude point, heralding the evolution of one of the typical tools of the Acheulian culture, the handaxe (fig. 1).

1 Handaxes from South Africa. Plan-form and size vary enormously.

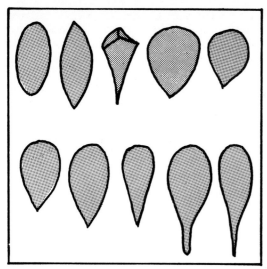

2 *Diagrammatic shapes of some handaxes recorded from Africa. Many of the shapes recur with what appears to be deliberate design, which may relate to function or be mere fashion.*

Apart from the scrappy evidence that occasional stone-flaking may extend back to 3,0 million years ago in the Omo River basin in Ethiopia, there is no reason to suppose that tool-making became formalised to the extent seen in the Oldowan culture until around 2,0 million years ago, and the oldest dated sites are those of Olduvai Gorge and Koobi Fora, both of which are dated to around 1,8 million years ago. How long it took for the Oldowan to evolve into what we call the Acheulian is not very certain for we have few radiometric dates for the Acheulian and only one for an early Acheulian occurrence in East Africa. The latter, however, is a satisfactory dating and indicates that by 1,5 million years ago development of stone-working had taken an important step forward; a step given recognition in the archaeologist's scheme of things by the designation of Acheulian culture.

The Acheulian is named after the site of St. Acheul in the Somme valley in France. Here, well over a hundred years ago, handaxes, called by the French *bouchers* or *coups de poing*, had been found in the Somme gravels. To all intents and purposes the African specimens are the same, so the French type-site name is adopted. But although there is a unifying similarity throughout Africa, Europe, the Near East, and a large part of India, there are also some differences and the local expressions tend to carry as a prefix the regional name; hence European Acheulian, Moroccan Acheulian, East African and South African Acheulian. Over most of Europe handaxes were made of flint, but flint does not occur in Africa, and its near neighbour, chert, only occurs in South-

3 *Cleavers from South Africa.*

cm

ern Africa in small pieces not suitable for the manufacture of large tools. Thus in Southern Africa a wide variety of hard rocks were used, as locally available. Quartzite is one of the most widespread and commonly used materials, but where necessary other rocks, such as quartz, diabase and indurated shale were employed. Often, as in the Vaal River valley and in some of the south-west Cape sites, these rocks occur as rounded, water-worn cobbles, or small boulders, and were worked by the same technique as the European flint, that is by removing flakes from the rock until it assumed the right shape. But unlike flint such rocks also occur in the form of very large boulders in stream beds, or as fallen blocks where the solid rock outcrops. In such situations it was discovered in South Africa, as in other parts of Africa, that a really heavy blow with another large stone, or perhaps swinging the core, held in both hands, against a rigid anvil, could detach a very large flake of a size and shape that needed only the smallest amount of trimming to convert it to a handaxe or cleaver.

Handaxes and cleavers in the Acheulian of Africa show an amazing variety of shapes, and the shapes are often repeated with a frequency that suggests that they were deliberately fashioned that way (fig. 2). The earlier handaxes, as seen in the older sites in East Africa and, for example, in the gravels at Three Rivers Estates near Vereeniging, have a very simple appearance and rarely show signs of the removal of more than about ten flakes in the course of their shaping. But they are a distinct advance on the simple chopper-tools of the Developed Oldowan, and already reveal the basic form that was to characterise handaxes for approximately 1,4 million years. The essentials are an elongate form, commonly pear-shaped or triangular, terminating in a point with a cutting edge on either side. The butt-end opposite the point may be left rounded and untrimmed, as if to clasp in the hand. With the passage of time this tool became more refined. The cross-section became much thinner and more symmetrical and the lateral edges straighter and sharper. This was accomplished partly by perfection of the technique for obtaining large flat flakes as blanks for handaxes or cleavers, and partly by more extensive retouch, or secondary flaking, probably using batons of wood or bone as hammers, rather than another stone. Dr. Revil Mason has observed that up to sixty flake-scars may be counted on some of the Later Acheulian handaxes from the gravels at Riverview Estates on the Vaal River. Whilst the description 'large tool with two cutting edges approximately in the same plane, converging towards a

point at one end' provides a reasonable general definition for handaxes it is not a perfect one. The 'point' is rarely, if ever, very sharp and does not often give the impression that its function was piercing. Indeed in many handaxes the point or tip is rounded, and some handaxes are almond or oval-shaped, trimmed to a cutting edge all round.

The other great fossil of the Acheulian, the cleaver (fig. 3), is basically a handaxe in which the point or tip is replaced by a broad, axe-like cutting edge (fig. 4). The sides of the cleaver apparently were not required for cutting purposes and trimming is normally to give the tool its desired shape. The cutting edge is not produced by secondary flaking but by the natural edge of the flake from which it is made. Such

4 Some outline shapes of cleavers. As with the handaxes these variations may reflect fashion, function, or in some cases the technique of manufacture.

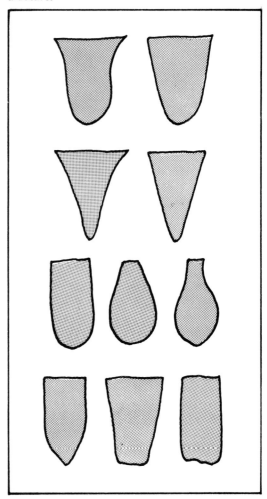

5 *Acheulian disc cores are roughly circular in plan and bi-conical seen from the side (like two saucers placed face to face). They could be direct ancestors of the cores used in Middle Stone Age times.*

edges, where the two faces of the flake meet, can be very sharp indeed, but sharp, thin edges are also brittle and will not stand up well to rough usage.

Flake tools are present in the Acheulian, most commonly in the form of scrapers, but include some which seem to be designed for piercing, and others for gouging. The edges of the scrapers are often carefully and evenly trimmed to a concave or convex line but there appears to be no attempt to achieve regularity of shape or size as in many later industries. This has been taken to indicate that hafting was not practised, and that all the tools were hand held.

The one remaining aspect of the stone technology of Acheulian times that should be mentioned relates to the cores from which flakes were derived. Flakes are, of course, produced in the process of shaping handaxes and cleavers and other large tools. But often large pieces are found from which flakes have been removed, but not, apparently, with a view to converting the piece to a tool; rather the intent seems to be the deliberate production of flakes to be used as tools. The remaining chunk, not being readily classified by the archaeologist as a tool, is referred to as a 'core' and is regarded as a waste product. But we have to admit a very great difficulty here, for in many cases a 'core' may equally well be a chopper or

even a pick, or the rough-out for a handaxe. If the specimens have been preserved in a very fresh condition, in a cave or in very fine sediments, a distinction may be possible on the basis of wear on the edges of tools, which should be absent on the edges of a discarded core ... unless the core has been picked up and pressed into use, on the spur of the moment, as a chopper or a scraper! With the tools of the Early Stone Age we have to admit that we are working almost completely in the dark, and whilst we may sort things into what appear to us to be meaningful categories, and give them names, we can only guess at their purpose and the materials on which they were used.

Within the class of cores, however, there are one or two items of interest. For the most part cores are unprepossessing irregular-shaped objects which staunchly defy classification, but in some instances pieces are found which seem to be made repeatedly to a pre-determined form. The first of these are discoid in shape, having the form of a shallow double cone (fig. 5), flakes having been removed either side of the equator and often right the way round. Often the form is rather crude and irregular, but occasionally very regular specimens are found. Archaeologists seem not always to be sure whether these objects should be classed as tools or as cores but either way the form and pattern of flaking of many of them must have resulted in the production of fairly regularly shaped flakes, often triangular in form.

The second type of core conforms to a very specific pattern in which the piece is deliberately prepared for the production of a single large flake of pre-determined shape and size. They are called Victoria West cores after the small town in the Karoo where they were first found, and they are of two kinds. The first can sometimes be quite massive, weighing up to 30 kg; in length they vary from around 15 cm up to 45 cm. In plan they are a rather asymmetric pear-drop shape. Viewed from the side they are even more asymmetric. The surface from which the desired flake was to be struck was flaked to a low dome whereas the lower part of the core was deep and steeply flaked. When properly prepared a heavy blow at the right point on one side would detach a large flake approximating in size and shape to the low-domed surface. Such flakes required relatively little trimming to convert them to handaxes or cleavers. Because the point of impact which detached the flake lies about midway on one edge of an elongate flake they are commonly called side-flakes, or side-struck flakes.

The second kind of Victoria West core is basically

the same, but with a circular plan form (fig. 6). The flakes removed tend to be longer along the axis of the detaching blow and are spoken of as end or end-struck flakes. A more widely used term today to describe the Victoria West technique of flake production is 'Levallois technique' after a site near Paris where it was first recorded.

Part of the interest of the disc and Levallois cores' lies in the tenuous thread of connection they provide between the Early Stone Age and the Middle Stone Age. Whilst we might argue on grounds of logicality that the South African Middle Stone Age is the natural evolutionary product of the South African Early Stone Age we can scarcely claim to have any evidence to prove it. There are no *typological* links in the form of characteristic tool-types of the Acheulian surviving into the Middle Stone Age, but one of the characteristic features of the Middle Stone Age is the use of Levallois technique and disc cores in the production of flakes for tools. The presence of both these techniques in the local Acheulian at least removes the need to look further afield for the origin of an important technological feature of the Middle Stone Age.

6   A Victoria West II or Levallois core. The required flake has been removed from the shallow-domed upper surface. The specimen is smoothed by prolonged exposure to the weather.

The Middle Stone Age

How is the Middle Stone Age distinguished from the Early Stone Age? In the simplest terms handaxes and cleavers are absent, tool-types not present in the Acheulian make their appearance, and the Levallois technique reaches altogether new levels of refinement. In the Early Stone Age the Levallois technique of flake production was used to obtain very large flakes for the manufacture of handaxes and cleavers. In the Middle Stone Age such large flakes seem not to have been required and the Levallois cores and disc cores are very much smaller and more delicate, commonly around 76 to 130 mm in diameter, but sometimes even smaller. The earliest stratified Middle Stone Age industries also give us the first clear evidence of a stone-working technique aimed at producing very long, parallel-sided flakes termed *blades*. The dorsal (or outer) surface of the blade often shows a pattern of longitudinal scars left by the previous removal of blades from the core, while the cores themselves develop a fluted appearance. The same technique might be used to secure long triangular flakes such as occur in some industries, particularly on the south coast (fig. 7).

The large, heavy tool element of the Early Stone Age is virtually absent from the Middle Stone Age and industries of this stage are often characterised as 'flake-tool industries'. In the production of a Leval-

53

7 Middle Stone Age artefacts from the Orange Free State. 1-3, fluted cores for the production of elongate flakes, or blades; 4-6, blades, or flake blades (true blades should display more parallel scars on their upper surfaces); 7 & 8, triangular flakes likely to have come from a discoidal core.

lois flake the core is trimmed to the desired size and shape, and often at the point where the detaching blow is to be struck a series of very small flakes is removed at right-angles to the 'equator' of the core, providing a faceted striking-platform. Part of this platform comes away with the flake, and the piece is then referred to as a 'faceted platform flake' (fig. 8). On the basis of the long stratified succession at the Cave of Hearths (fig. 9), Professor Mason has indicated that the practice of faceting platforms increased in popularity with the passage of time. This is best interpreted as reflecting an increasing interest in controlling the size and shape of flakes. Indeed the same series of specimens also shows that the mean lengths of flakes decreased with time and that they became more uniform in size. Unfortunately lack of similar long successions has so far prevented us from discovering whether similar trends are to be found in other parts of South Africa in the Middle Stone Age. Perhaps when the details of Klasies River Mouth Cave (fig. 10) become available it will be possible to examine such details for the

8

8 The platform of a Middle Stone Age flake, showing the facets prepared on the platform prior to the striking of the flake from its core.

southern coastal region.

It would be unwise to attempt too bold a characterisation of the flake-tool component of Middle Stone Age industries, for they have been too imperfectly described. The whole concept of the Middle Stone Age in South Africa was established in the 1920s on the basis of collections of artefacts lying on the surface or eroding from geological deposits. Often the collections were small and almost inevitably the collectors took only those pieces that had some aesthetic appeal. The search was directed in particular at pieces known as 'points' about which we shall say more presently. Although within the past quarter century upwards of twenty Middle Stone Age cave sites and several open sites have been investigated in South Africa, Swaziland, and Lesotho, detailed and definitive reports have appeared for only a handful in the Orange Free State. For the Transvaal sites a good deal of statistical information has been published showing that scrapers form an important element among the flake-tools. Unfortunately few pieces are illustrated and the statistics do not provide a good picture of the degree of regularity in the sizes and shapes of the scrapers. No other kinds of flake-tools are referred to.

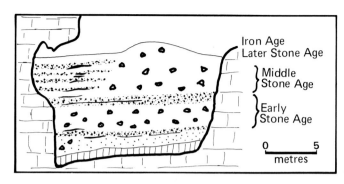

Iron Age
Later Stone Age
} Middle
Stone Age
} Early
Stone Age

0   5
metres

9

9 Diagrammatic drawing of the layers cut through in excavating the Cave of Hearths. Few caves have such a long and complete record of human habitation.

10 The succession of industries at Klasies River Mouth is built up from information from several caves. The earliest phase of the Middle Stone Age may date from an early part of the last interglacial period, more than 100 000 years ago. In the interval since then the vegetation of the area has undergone a number of changes. Note the absence of any industries between the end of the M.S.A. (at least 20 000 years ago) and the L.S.A.

CAVE 1	CAVE 1a	CAVE V	CAVE X	VEGETATION DEDUCED FROM ANIMAL REMAINS
			L.S.A. with pottery	
L.S.A. 2 525 2 795 4 695 4 755		L.S.A. 2 285 4 110		
M.S.A. phase IV				
	M.S.A. phase III	} greater than 38 000 B.P.		more open grassland
	'Howieson's Poort'			
M.S.A. phase II	M.S.A. phase II	} dates range from 26 800 to greater than 38 300 B.P.		increased forest or bush cover
M.S.A. phase I				forest/grassland macchia mosaic comparable to present
	beach at 6 – 8 m above sea-level			

10

55

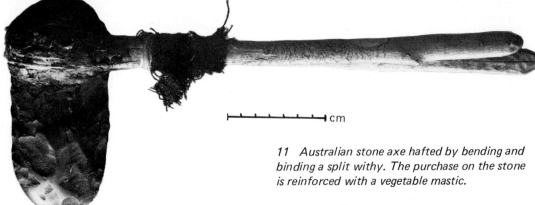

11 Australian stone axe hafted by bending and binding a split withy. The purchase on the stone is reinforced with a vegetable mastic.

But flake production in the Middle Stone Age was certainly more controlled and regular than in the Early Stone Age and this reflected in the residual cores as well as in the flakes themselves. On these grounds alone we would expect to find a greater degree of uniformity in the flake-tool classes, and this is certainly seen to be the case for several sites in the Orange Free State, from which rather more specimens have been illustrated. Our interest in the regularity of these flake-tools lies in the evidence they may embody for an important technological advance from the Early Stone Age; one which may indeed have underlain the transition. It is tempting to speculate that one of the factors setting off the Middle from the Early Stone Age was the development of efficient means of hafting stone tools, and here we have to fall back on our knowledge of hafting practices among recently living Stone Age peoples, in particular the Australian aboriginals, on

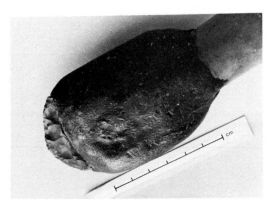

12 The blade of this Australian adze would be classed as a scraper in most archaeologists' typologies.

13 Steep scraper hafted in vegetable mastic to a wooden handle (now missing) and probably used as an adze for light wood-working. From Touw River Cave a little east of George.

56

a few examples from the Later Stone Age of South Africa, and on some plain assumptions about how things are likely to have been in the earlier stages of prehistory.

It is hardly necessary to seek proof that the earliest stone tools were not hafted. For many millennia they reflected no more than the realisation that fractured stone yielded sharpness and hardness appropriate to a momentary need to cut, pierce, chop or scrape. It is not until the production of handaxes and cleavers transformed the Oldowan to the Acheulian that the artefacts themselves raise the question whether hafting was employed or not. The very name 'handaxe' reflects the assumption of early workers that these tools were simply held in the hand. Many of them not only 'feel right' in the hand but are hard to imagine as having been hafted in any way. But this is not true of many of the flatter, or more regularly shaped and symmetrical handaxes and cleavers. They could have been simply hafted by binding in the manner of some Australian axes (fig. 11). Flake tools are abundant in the Early Stone Age, as the evidence of well-preserved living sites in east and central Africa, and one or two less informative sites in South Africa show. But whilst hafting cannot be ruled out, the lack of regularity in size, shape and disposition of retouch on scrapers (the most abundant class of flake-tools) has led several workers to suppose that they were not intended for hafting. As one of them has put it, 'This indicates . . . that the original shape of the flake or nodule before its use as a tool was largely immaterial to the user provided that it could be conveniently held and was a shape and size suitable for the purpose for which it was required.' If handaxes and cleavers were attached to wooden handles by binding, and wielded in use, it is hard to explain why they should have disappeared in the Middle Stone Age, for there is nothing in this later age that would serve the same function if attached to a wooden handle. Perhaps this is an argument against handaxes having been hafted; but we are very much in the realms of speculation. A more profitable approach would be through a study of the microscopic wear on the edges in an attempt to discover the mode of use and the kinds of material they were used on. If the actions were cutting or scraping, the weight of such heavy tools as handaxes and cleavers might have been compensated for in later times by the leverage possible through a strong handle firmly attached to a lighter stone 'bit'.

The size and form of many Middle Stone Age scrapers are not particularly different from specimens which in Australia are attached with vegetable mastic cement to wooden handles and used with a chopping action as adzes (fig. 12). That the same technique of hafting was known at a later date

14   Middle Stone Age 'points' may have been spear- or even arrow-heads, or knife blades, but they were almost certainly hafted in a fairly sophisticated way. Their forms and techniques of manufacture may be helpful in the future as indicators of chronology.

57

15 An Australian stone point of a kind similar to some South African Middle Stone Age points, hafted as a spear-head.

in South Africa is shown by a variety of specimens dating from the Later Stone Age in which the mastic and handle have been preserved (fig. 13). These include scrapers of basically similar form to Middle Stone Age scrapers, though smaller. All of which encourages us to suppose that the character of South African Middle Stone Age industries may owe much to the invention of hafting stone 'bits' to wooden or bone handles with a vegetable mastic.

We have referred to a Middle Stone Age artefact called a 'point'. If anything can be said to represent a 'zone fossil' of the Middle Stone Age it is these points. They are made on flakes, usually triangular, and generally derived from true Levallois cores or from radially flaked discoidal cores. The striking-platforms, where preserved, are commonly faceted indicating careful preparation for a flake to suit the purpose. Transformation into a point is effected by secondary flaking of one or both faces of the flake (unifacial or bifacial working) to give it the desired shape and finish. Great variation in shape, size and finish is to be found in this class of tool (fig. 14) and it still remains to be ascertained what factors underlie such variation. What is pertinent to our discussion is that these artefacts are commonly supposed to have been the heads of spears (and perhaps even arrows) and to have been hafted in the manner of recent specimens from Australia

16 Australian triangular stone flake, identical to many Southern African Middle Stone Age flakes, hafted as a knife.

and some of the Pacific islands (fig. 15). Parallels of this kind are suggestive, but they do not constitute proof, and it is as well to note that similar flakes, with or without retouch, were hafted in various parts of the world as knives (fig. 16). But whether as knives or spears hafting with mastic is involved, and the symmetry of the Middle Stone Age specimens, which was clearly carefully contrived, suggests that they too were hafted by a similar technique.

All things considered there is a good deal of circumstantial evidence that even if hafting was not an invention of the Middle Stone Age it was at least brought then to a level of perfection that permitted fundamental changes in the use of stone. Indeed the emergence of the Middle Stone Age may stem directly from such a technological advance. Although proof of hafting may have to await a lucky find in a dry cave site or a waterlogged spring deposit, such as Florisbad, a careful study of the specimens themselves might provide further circumstantial evidence.

17 Australian triangular flake hafted like a pick; probably a club for killing wounded or trapped game.

The Later Stone Age

By about 8 000 years ago all trace of the Middle Stone Age has vanished and we find ourselves dealing with stone industries characterised by the archaeologist as Later Stone Age. Traditionally in South Africa these have been assigned to two major cultural complexes, the Smithfield and the Wilton, of which we shall have more to say later. We refer here to the Later Stone Age simply to round off this rather summary account of the major divisions of the Stone Age in order that we can discuss in a more meaningful way the changes that led up to it.

Just as the Middle Stone Age was characterised partly by a general reduction in the sizes of artefacts, compared with the Early Stone Age, so too is the

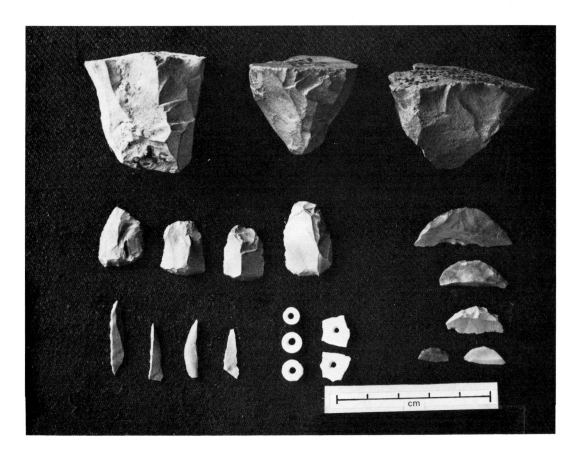

18 *A group of Later Stone Age artefacts. Top row: three cores; centre left: four small convex scrapers of the kind used as adze blades; lower left: four backed blades, possibly arrow-head parts; lower centre: three finished and two unfinished ostrich eggshell beads; right: five segments, possibly parts of knives or arrow- or spear-heads.*

Later Stone Age compared with the Middle. Like most generalisations this one is open to criticism, for there are exceptions. But it is true for many Late Stone Age industries that the stone tools and the waste flakes associated with them are markedly smaller than in most Middle Stone Age industries. The exceptions we may comment on later. The items which are notably absent are the disc and Levallois cores, and the faceting of platforms so often associated with them, and the characteristic, though not abundant, unifacial and bifacial points. Flaked stone tools are commonly made on small flakes struck from irregular-shaped cores or on small, ribbon-like blades struck from cores which sometimes as a result resemble small fluted cones

(fig. 18). In particular many of these Later Stone Age industries contained small blades blunted by steep flaking along one edge (backed blades) and other pieces with a similar blunting retouch along a curved edge (segments or 'crescents') (fig. 18). In addition to flaked stone some use is made of 'peck-ing' and grinding to shape stone, and bone tools become common. The numerous rock paintings and engravings seem to belong mostly to this period, and beads and pendants are abundant.

The Problem of Transitions

Thus it was not unusual to think of the Early Stone Age as a large-flake and core-tool tradition, the Middle Stone Age as a flake-tool tradition with Levallois technique and unifacial and bifacial points as specially characteristic, and the Later Stone Age as a microlithic tradition based on small flakes and micro-blades. Until very recently it was thought that certain industries could be recognised that provided a logical transition from Early to Middle and Middle to Late; these were referred to as the First

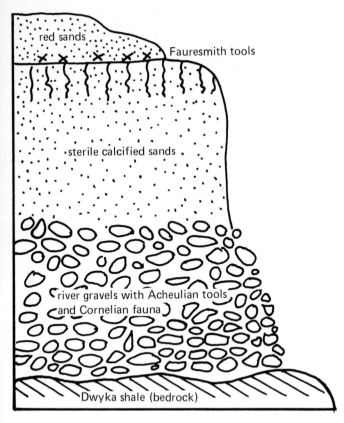

red sands

Fauresmith tools

sterile calcified sands

river gravels with Acheulian tools
and Cornelian fauna

Dwyka shale (bedrock)

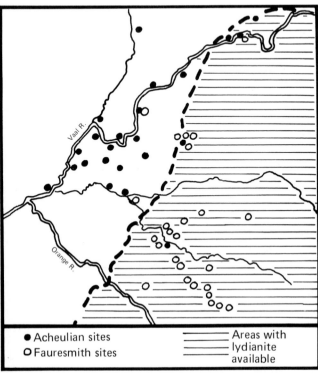

Vaal R.

Orange R.

● Acheulian sites
○ Fauresmith sites

Areas with
lydianite
available

*19 Stone tools assigned to the Fauresmith cul-
ture are commonly found on the surface of pale
sands hardened by a heavy lime content, overlying gravels containing Acheulian tools and Cornelian fauna. The time interval represented by
the calcified sands is quite unknown. Middle
Stone Age tools are sometimes found overlying
the red sands.*

Intermediate cultures and the Second Intermediate
cultures.

The first of these concepts arose from the discovery of artefacts found at the little town of Fauresmith in the Orange Free State in the 1920s. The artefacts comprised rather small handaxes, together
with various flake-tools, large elongate flakes
(blades), and flakes with simply faceted platforms.
In a number of places such assemblages were found
in and on calcified sand bodies, which overlay the
gravels of the Vaal River in which 'normal' Acheulian tools and 'Cornelian' fauna were found (fig.
19). They therefore appeared to be both chronologically and typologically 'intermediate'. A shift towards a greater use of small flake-tools was also
stressed. These features were considered distinctly
different from the Acheulian and the term Fauresmith was coined as a culture-name. But there are
snags. None of the Fauresmith sites is datable either
radiometrically or faunistically. It may merely be
said that some Fauresmith sites are later than some
Acheulian artefacts, without saying how much
later, or how old are the underlying Acheulian tools.
Or, indeed, what interval separates the Fauresmith
from the ensuing Middle Stone Age.

The emphasis on the use of small flake-tools was a
mistake, for at the time the Acheulian was known
only from collections from river gravels or exposed
open sites, in neither of which were flake-tools very
prominent. More recently the careful investigation
of Acheulian sites in archaeological context at one
or two places in South Africa (Amanzi Springs,
Doornlaagte, Muirton) and several in East Africa
has shown that small flake-tools were always important, and sometimes dominated an industry.

*20 Sites on which the Fauresmith was first iden-
tified in the area in which it finds its classic expression, together with Acheulian sites in the
vicinity. The Fauresmith sites are seen to lie mostly in areas where indurated shale (lydianite) is
available. It is thought that the Fauresmith is
really a localised variant of late Acheulian which
takes on a distinctive character because of the
raw material (lydianite) used for tool-making.*

Certainly no distinction is possible on the relative proportions of small flake-tools to large cutting- or chopping-tools. Recent careful reviews of the evidence relating to Fauresmith tend to agree that there is no real justification for separating 'Fauresmith' industries off from Acheulian, and that if any distinction is to be made it should not extend beyond the designation of 'late Acheulian'. It has been suggested that such differences as might be sustained between 'classic' Fauresmith assemblages and Acheulian material from the adjacent Vaal River gravels could as well stem from differences in available raw materials as from any more profound reasons. The Acheulian sites in the Vaal Valley lie on areas of Ventersdorp lava and in the gravels themselves, where quartzites, amygdaloidal lavas and diabasic rocks were used, whereas the Fauresmith sites are restricted to the Ecca-Beaufort series in which indurated shale was often the only suitable material available (fig. 20). The recognition of Fauresmith industries outside of the area of such rocks is certainly far less convincing.

If there is no clear justification for separating the Fauresmith from the late Acheulian, then we have no convincing evidence for the transition from Early to Middle Stone Age: a fascinating problem for the future.

It is unlikely that anyone today would subscribe to the theory that the Middle Stone Age in South Africa arose as the result of the arrival of immigrant peoples bearing the new culture and rapidly supplanting the culture and populations of the Early Stone Age. Nor would there be much enthusiasm for the suggestion that a whole technology diffused into South Africa from the north, replacing the Acheulian. It would, however, be less wise to deny the possibility of the diffusion of an idea relating to hafting, especially if it were a distinctly advantageous idea.

The transition seems to have been at least as early in South Africa as in Europe. Radiocarbon dates indicating ages greater than 45 000 and 50 000 years for apparently evolved expressions of the Middle Stone Age have been obtained from Border Cave near the south-east border of Swaziland (fig. 21), Bushman Rock Shelter in the eastern Transvaal (fig. 22), Ha Soloja in Lesotho (fig. 23) and Montagu Cave in the south-west Cape (fig. 24). At Die Kelders (fig. 25) and Nelson Bay Cave (fig. 26) on the south coast (fig. 27), Middle Stone Age occupation seems to follow fairly soon after a high sea-level belonging to a late stage of the last interglacial some 70 000 or 80 000 years ago. (For figs. 22–6, see pp. 70–1.) At Klasies River Mouth it appears that the

INDUSTRIES REPRESENTED	C14 DATES B.P.
Iron Age	500
?	13 300
pre Early L.S.A.	38 600 36 800 36 100
post Final M.S.A.	greater than 40 000
Final M.S.A.	greater than 48 700
Full M.S.A.	

21 The succession of industries found in the Border Cave. The terms are those of the excavators. The 'Final M.S.A.' is believed to be the industry described by an earlier worker as containing 'slender ribbon-like blades, numerous backed blades, butt-end scrapers and small pressure-trimmed triangular "arrow-heads", and almost purely Levallois in character'.

Middle Stone Age commences early in the last Interglacial. These are all fully fledged Middle Stone Age industries and the implication is that the technological innovation occurred upwards of 70 000 to 80 000 and perhaps 125 000 years ago.

Just as the Fauresmith was thought to represent a culture occupying a transitional position between the Early and Middle Stone Ages so the Magosian and Howieson's Poort cultures have long been held to represent the essential link between the Middle and Later Stone Ages. Both cultures showed a blending of Middle Stone Age features (disc cores, faceted platform flakes, unifacial and bifacial points) with those generally considered to be Later Stone Age (small blades and blade cores, backed blades and segments) and were assigned to a Second Intermediate stage. A decade ago only five radiocarbon dates had been processed for industries belonging to this stage. One of these, at about 31 000 years ago, from a site in East Africa, was considered to be unacceptably early, and was discounted. The other four dates from Zambia and Rhodesia ranged from around 16 000 to 9 500 years ago; a time range

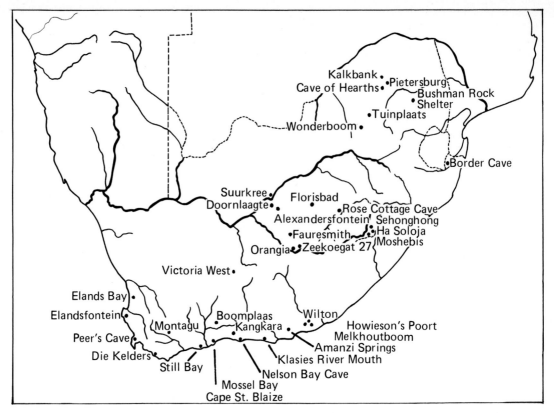

*27 The location of the principal sites mentioned
in this chapter.*

which seemed to fit perfectly with what was then
known of the dating of the Middle and Later Stone
Ages.

However, from the mid-1960s a flow of new
radiocarbon dates progressively complicated the
comfortable picture of the Late Pleistocene/Early
Holocene date which was essential for industries
leading to any form of Wilton-like development
about 8 000 years ago. At about the same time new
excavations at the Wilton type site (fig. 28), at
Melkhoutboom nearby (fig. 29) and at Nelson Bay
Cave on the south coast (fig. 26) gave definition to
two new industries underlying the Wilton and bearing no resemblance to either Howieson's Poort or
the Magosian. But let us look first at the curious way
in which these latter two industries have sunk into
the depths of antiquity far away from the Wilton
which they were thought to have spawned.

The radiocarbon date of 18 740 B.P. (Before Present) published in 1968 from a re-excavation of the
Howieson's Poort type site was considered to be
surprisingly old, compared with the Zambian and
Rhodesian dates, but still acceptable. A second date

of 19 600 was published in 1974. The first real shock
to traditional thinking came in 1969 with the publication of findings in the Bushman Rock Shelter in
the eastern Transvaal (figs. 22, 27). Although the
shelter was not excavated to bedrock, approximately a metre of Middle Stone Age deposit was
found underlying about 1,5 m of Later Stone Age
filling. Radiocarbon dates indicated an age in excess
of 51 000 years for the Middle Stone Age tools, and
whilst these do not include backed blades and segments and seem, therefore, not to be Magosian or
Howieson's Poort, the date was far older than anything previously published for the Middle Stone
Age.

At about the time that the Bushman Rock samples were being processed, the laboratory in Pretoria was also examining samples obtained during
excavations in Rose Cottage Cave in the eastern
Orange Free State in 1962. At this site (fig. 30) three
successive stages of South African Magosian were
overlain by near-sterile sands above which were a
'Pre-Wilton' and a Wilton deposit. The Wilton industry was normal for the area and the date of 6 850
obtained for it is interesting but not remarkable. Of
far greater interest is the 'Pre-Wilton' underlying it.
B.D. Malan, the original excavator of the site, de-

Excavated layers	Industry	Stages of development of Wilton	Dates B.P.
1 2a	WILTON	death/birth	
2b 3a		post/climax	• 2 270
3c 3d 3e 3f		climax	
3g 3h 3i		formative	• 4 860 • 8 260
4a 4b	ALBANY		

28

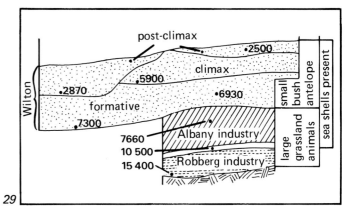

29

28   The Wilton Large Rock Shelter is important for its long succession of deposits of the Wilton culture. Janette Deacon's careful study of the artefacts suggests that the history of this culture can be traced through various stages from near its inception to the time of its disintegration, perhaps in the face of the beginnings of pastoralism in the area. It suggests a relatively stable population in the area for some 6 000 years.

29   The succession at Melkhoutboom Cave. The transition from Late Pleistocene to Holocene, as at other sites, is marked by a change in fauna from large, gregarious plains animals to solitary bush-dwellers. Contact with the coast begins with the Albany industry.

30   Rose Cottage Cave was a key site in the dating of the so-called 'Magosian' phase of the Middle Stone Age and for its very early dating of the Pre-Wilton industry with its microlithic cores and tiny ribbon-like blades. The date of 6 850 for the Wilton, while comparable with dates in the Cape Folded Mountains, is interestingly early for the Orange Free State. The period of depopulation reflected in sites on the Orange River may not have extended to the mountains and their foothills.

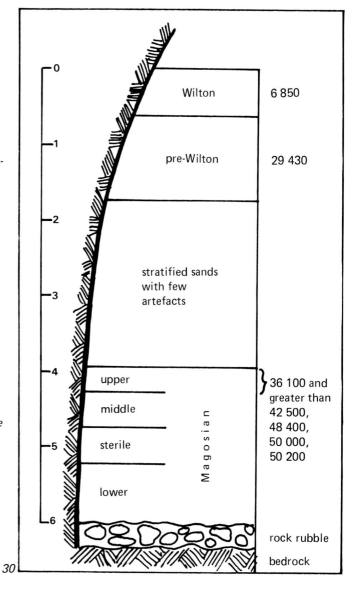

30

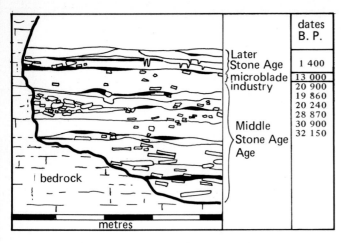

	dates B. P.
Later Stone Age	1 400
} microblade industry	13 000
	20 900
	19 860
	20 240
	28 870
Middle	30 900
} Stone Age	32 150
Age	

31 *The microblade industry at Sehonghong appears to be the same as the Pre-Wilton at Rose Cottage Cave, and helps pin down the dating of the industry. The Middle Stone Age industry contains well-made segments and backed pieces.*

scribed this industry in 1947 in the following words: 'extremely rich in debitage of a microlithic industry which it is difficult to analyse by virtue of the almost total absence of recognisable tools. This industry contains no trace of the Levallois technique. Microlithic cores abound ... The most common artefacts ... are extremely small, slender blades, many of which show some damage along one or both edges ... (and) rare endscrapers such as characterise the microlithic industries of the Later Stone Age in South Africa'. This totally new and puzzling industry would have been expected a decade ago to belong around 8 000 or 9 000 years ago. The uppermost South Africa Magosian 2 m below it would have been expected to be about 9 000 to 10 000 years old. In the event the early part of the 'Pre-Wilton' industry turns out to be in the order of 29 000 years old and the uppermost Magosian at least 50 000. These extraordinary dates were published in 1972, just two years after closely similar dates had been obtained for a Howieson's Poort industry sandwiched between Acheulian and Wilton layers in a cave near Montagu at the western end of the Little Karoo (fig. 24). The industry at Montagu is said by the excavators of Howieson's Poort to be virtually the same as that from the latter site. The original Howieson's Poort radiocarbon dates were apparently contaminated with younger carbon.

At Klasies River Mouth (fig. 10) an apparently similar industry is dated by radiocarbon to greater than 38 000 years whilst other evidence suggests that its true age may be in the order of 60 000 to 70 000 years. At this particular site the Howieson's Poort 'transitional' industry is overlain by Middle Stone Age industries of a conventional kind which, on traditional thinking, ought always to *underlie* industries of the Howieson's Poort and Magosian type. Unfortunately we know of no other good example of this interrelation between conventional Middle Stone Age layers and Howieson's Poort, although the same situation was claimed in 1935 for the Cape St. Blaize cave and in 1941 for Peers Cave near Cape Town.

The association of Levallois (Middle Stone Age) technique with segments and backed pieces is recorded also from Lesotho where it is dated to around 31 000 B.P. at Sehonghong (fig. 31) and greater than 43 000 B.P. at Ha Soloja (fig. 22). Interestingly, at the former site the Rose Cottage Cave 'Pre-Wilton' industry is also present, above the Middle Stone Age layers, and apparently survives until about 13 000 years ago.

All this amounts to a very complicated and not very satisfying picture. Basically there are two problems. First, with the exception of the Montagu Cave none of the sites or industries mentioned has received full publication so that it is impossible to make precise comparisons between one site and another, either in terms of selected industries or successions of industries. Secondly, and even more serious because the problem will remain even when fuller descriptions of the sites are available, the phases of human activity represented by these industries are virtually undatable because almost without exception they lie beyond the effective range of the radiocarbon dating method. No amount of 'scissors and paste' work will reduce this difficult and mostly very recent information to a simple and comprehensible pattern.

But two things of immediate interest do emerge. The first is that whatever they eventually prove to consist of, and however they may be related to each other, the South African Magosian and the Howieson's Poort have nothing directly to do with the origin of the Wilton and related industries. The second point of interest that has certainly been visible for a long time but which has perhaps not received quite the emphasis that it merits is the strength of the blade elements in the Middle Stone Age.

Technological Considerations

Stone blades with carefully prepared striking-platforms were stressed as part of the lowest Magosian industry in the Rose Cottage Cave. In Lesotho at

Ha Soloja 3,25 m of deposit, the upper part of which is greater than 43 000 years old, contains a Middle Stone Age industry throughout, described by the excavator as a 'sophisticated blade industry', while the nearby site of Moshebi's contains two successive Middle Stone Age industries both with a strong blade element. The blades in the lower deposit average about 150 mm in length and those in the upper industry about 70 mm. Although the descriptions are less specific it is clear that blades are at least present in the Pietersburg industry of the Transvaal, and in the recently re-described Mossel Bay industry from the Cape St. Blaize cave. The well-illustrated Middle Stone Age industries from upwards of a score of sites in the south of the Orange Free State display a significant and persistent percentage of blades and blade cores. The excavator believes that three successive stages of the Middle Stone Age are present and that the blades of the earliest stage are the largest, often 120 mm or more in length. The absence of adequate descriptions for the south-west and eastern Cape, Natal, and much of the interior makes it impossible to say whether or not this same blade element occurs in other areas or whether true flake industries akin to the Mousterian of Europe are represented.

What is quite clear is that from a very early stage there is an important difference between the Southern African Middle Stone Age and the equivalent European Middle Palaeolithic. The early and persistent appearance of blades (despite their production by a different technique) combined with bifacial foliate points (fig. 14), and in at least some industries tools with a blunting retouch (backing) along part of the margin, presents us with something much more like a mixture of European Middle and Upper Palaeolithic in a time-range which is substantially earlier than the European Upper Palaeolithic. If we can accept this it makes it considerably easier to see the Howieson's Poort and Magosian in Southern Africa for what they undoubtedly are: merely particular expressions of the Middle Stone Age, localised, perhaps, in time and space. Just how localised we shall not know until more sites have been carefully investigated and a more precise knowledge of relative and absolute chronology is obtained. There are still many gaps in the record, and our view of events in this difficult period must of necessity be provisional. But if we accept the existence of an important blade element in at least a major part of the Southern African Middle Stone Age, probably from its inception, it may go a long way towards explaining subsequent developments.

We referred above to certain newly discovered industries underlying the Wilton at several sites in the south and south-east Cape, and bearing no resemblance to the Howieson's Poort or Magosian. The first of these has been named the Albany industry after the Albany district in the eastern Cape. At present it is an ill-defined and imperfectly understood entity consisting mainly of large flakes and scrapers which, in the sites where the industry is known, are predominantly of quartzite. Since other kinds of raw material were also used and were more extensively used in the levels overlying and underlying it at Melkhoutboom, it looks as if there was a deliberate preference for quartzite. Though why this should be is one of the enigmas of prehistory. As yet the industry is known only from a small number of sites in the southern mountains and on the coast, with one outlier on the south-west coast at Elands Bay (fig. 27). Although most of the radiocarbon dates place it between about 8 000 and 12 000 years ago it begins 2 000 years earlier at Boomplaas (fig. 32). Certain industries that fall within the same time-range in the Transvaal (Early and Middle Smithfield) and that are presumed to occupy the same time-range in the northern Cape and Orange Free State (Smithfield A), display somewhat similar typological trends compared with what precedes and follows them. They appear to represent a northerly equivalent of the Albany industry, although it should not necessarily be supposed that there is any real connection between them.

The large cave at Nelson Bay on the Robberg Peninsula (fig. 26) was occupied from the latter part of the last interglacial period, almost continuously until a few centuries ago. At the beginning of its occupation, as today, it was probably a coastal cave. But with the onset of the last glaciation the sea-level began to fall, exposing a wide coastal plain in front of the cave 60 to 70 km wide at times and supporting a typical African plains fauna. The sequence of deposits in this cave enables us to view the food residues and artefacts of its various inhabitants through times when it was an inland cave overlooking a vast undulating plain with herds of wildebeest, springbok, blesbok and quagga, through the gradual encroachment of the sea until it lapped the rocks just below. The Wilton and Albany industries are both represented and it is with the appearance of the Albany industry some 12 000 years ago that we find the first remains of marine animals– seals, dolphin, fish and shellfish – indicating the close proximity of the sea. Below the Albany industry lay another, of previously unknown type, which has been named the Robberg industry. Its time-range at Nelson Bay Cave is from 12 000 to around 19 000

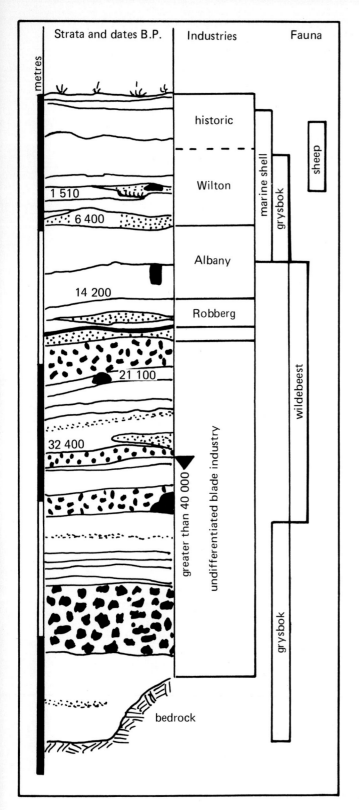

The figure contains the following labels:

Strata and dates B.P. | Industries | Fauna

metres

historic

Wilton

1 510

6 400

Albany

14 200

Robberg

21 100

32 400

greater than 40 000

undifferentiated blade industry

marine shell

sheep

grysbok

wildebeest

grysbok

bedrock

years ago. No description of this industry has as yet appeared and we know no more than that it is 'characterised especially by distinctive artefacts which superficially may be classified as either small carinate scrapers or bladelet cores'. If these pieces are in fact bladelet cores the blades from them must have been very small indeed, and it is tempting to equate the industry with the 'Pre-Wilton' from Rose Cottage Cave described above (fig. 30) and recorded also at Sehonghong in Lesotho (fig. 31).

At Sehonghong a single date of 13 000 years is associated but at Rose Cottage Cave the dates carry back to around 29 000 years. Between this industry and the underlying Middle Stone Age in Nelson Bay Cave there are sterile deposits indicating a period perhaps as long as 20 000 years when the cave was not occupied.

Prehistoric Populations

No attempt has been made in the foregoing pages to examine in detail the archaeological evidence. To do so would require the whole of a very long book. We have, however, attempted to summarise the salient features in order to provide some indication of the nature of the evidence, and in reality the inadequacy of the evidence available in any attempt to talk about the peoples who inhabited South Africa during this immense period of time when so many important things were happening. Like it or not, we must now attempt to use this evidence to say something about the peoples involved.

We have remarked that it is unlikely that either *Australopithecus* or *Homo* evolved in Southern Africa from earlier Tertiary ancestors. *Australopithecus* probably spread into Southern Africa, ultimately from East Africa, and clearly did so quite a long time before we find our first unequivocal remains of true man at Swartkrans. What is less certain is whether or not man the toolmaker evolved from *Aus-*

32 Boomplaas Cave. An almost unbroken sequence, possibly covering 80 000 years. Grysbok suggest closed bush cover, while the wildebeest point to more open grassland. It should be noted that an important faunal change occurs within the period of the Albany industry, suggesting that culture-change is not always linked to environmental change. The blade industry below the Robberg remains undiagnosed because the samples are too small. Work is continuing at the site.

tralopithecus in Southern Africa. By and large the evidence is against it and it is more likely that the transition took place in East Africa, with a division of the lineages leading to *Homo* and *Australopithecus* taking place early in the Pliocene. In this view *Australopithecus africanus* might be seen as a rather successful bipedal primate with a strong predilection for meat, which he most likely obtained partly by collecting 'small fry' and partly by group co-operation and tool-wielding to drive predators from their kill. The earliest men can have appeared little different, but it seems that they adopted a practice that was to have far-reaching consequences for their descendants. That practice was the breaking of stones to enable them to deal more successfully with the carcases they won from four-footed hunters, and perhaps also in the shaping of sticks to be wielded in the daily search for food. If a more successful, tool-making competitor to *A. africanus* arose in East Africa this in itself may have influ-

enced the spread of the latter and ultimately his extinction. At any rate the most probable interpretation of the evidence is that early, tool-making hominids spread into Southern Africa from the north about 1,5 to 2,0 million years ago, and perhaps a million years after the arrival of *A. africanus*. The first phase of the peopling of Southern Africa is therefore one of immigration followed by subsequent expansion, and this is reflected in the numbers and distribution of sites (fig. 33).

Distribution maps reflect the activities of archaeologists sometimes more than of prehistoric

33 Generalised distribution of Lower and Middle Pleistocene sites. Map D includes industries other than Fauresmith thought to belong to the same evolutionary stage. The stippling in Map A shows the area blanketed by wind-blown sands of Tertiary age. In this area surface water is scarce, as is raw material for stone tools.

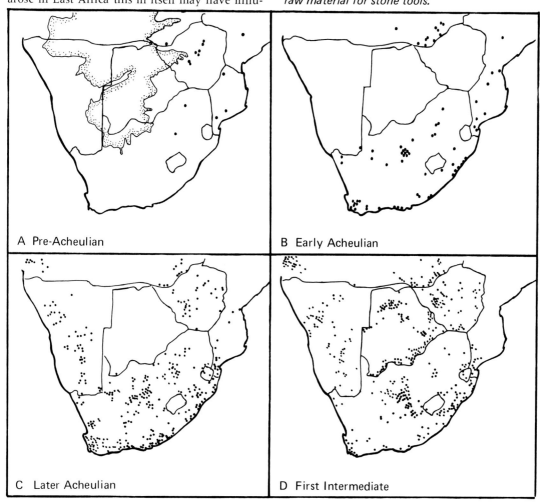

A Pre-Acheulian

B Early Acheulian

C Later Acheulian

D First Intermediate

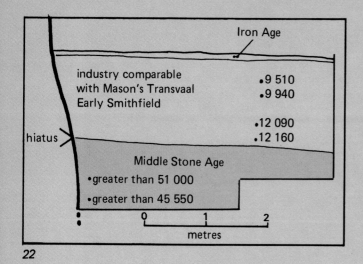

industry comparable
with Mason's Transvaal
Early Smithfield

Iron Age

•9 510
•9 940

•12 090
•12 160

hiatus

Middle Stone Age

•greater than 51 000

•greater than 45 550

0   1   2

metres

22

22 Bushman Rock Shelter. The deposits have not yet been excavated to their full depth, but the site makes an important contribution to the dating of the Transvaal Middle Stone Age. The industries dated between 9 000 and 12 000 years ago are apparently comparable to industries known from Rhodesia, the Orange Free State, and the southern Cape coast. They represent a very imperfectly known period in the prehistory of Southern Africa.

23 Ha Soloha, Lesotho. The deposits contain Middle Stone Age artefacts throughout. The site is important for the early dates it provides for an industry described as a sophisticated blade industry with segments and backed pieces.

24 Section drawing showing the layers exposed by excavation in the Montagu Cave. Layer 1 contained Later Stone Age tools. Layer 2 contains several Middle Stone Age levels with tools almost identical to those from Howieson's Poort near Grahamstown. These levels are dated from about 23 000 years ago to more than 50 000. Layers 3 and 5 contained Acheulian tools and are separated by a sterile deposit (layer 4). Montagu is one of the very few caves anywhere in the world to have yielded signs of occupation in the Early Stone Age.

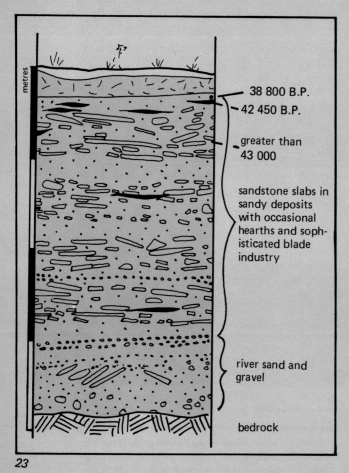

38 800 B.P.

42 450 B.P.

greater than 43 000

sandstone slabs in sandy deposits with occasional hearths and sophisticated blade industry

river sand and gravel

bedrock

23

	Layer and Industry	Dates B.P.
	1 Later Stone Age	
		• 7 100
		• 23 200
		• 50 800
	2 Howieson's Poort	• 45 900
	3 Acheulian	
	4 sterile	
	5 Acheulian	

24

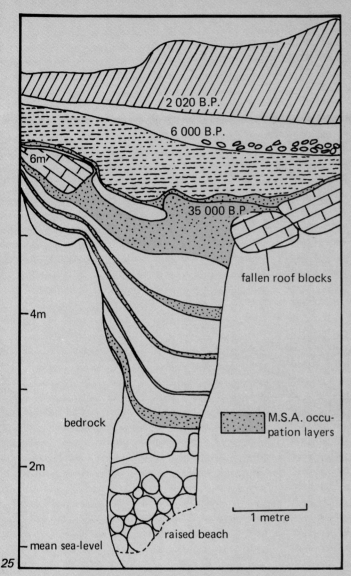

2 020 B.P.

6 000 B.P.

6m

35 000 B.P.

fallen roof blocks

4m

bedrock

▓▓▓ M.S.A. occu-
pation layers

2m

1 metre

mean sea-level

raised beach

25

25 At Die Kelders a series of Middle Stone Age
occupations follows fairly soon after a high stand
of the sea during the last interglacial. The cave
then remained unoccupied from about 35 000
years ago until a little over 2 000 years ago when
it was occupied by people herding sheep and using
fine pottery. The M.S.A. hunters took large numbers of mole-rats from the nearby sand-dunes.
They also hunted eland and small, solitary antelope.

26 The succession at Nelson Bay Cave, Robberg
Peninsula. Excavations were carried out in two
separate areas which have not yet been linked, resulting in a gap in the record between about 6 000
and 3 000 years ago. The site is important for the
information it will eventually yield on the Robberg and Albany industries, and for the picture
it gives us of the exploitation of the great coastal
plain exposed during the last glaciation.

Industry	Dates B.P.	Salient Features
Post-Wilton	1 930 2 540 2 925	marine foods domi-nate the food debris
unexcavated		
Wilton	6 020 8 120 8 570 8 990	percentage of small bush-loving antelope increases sharply
Albany	10 150 10 540 11 540	first marine fauna first bushbuck last eland & warthog
Robberg	11 950 18 100 18 660	fauna typical of open grasslands (eg. wilde-beest, hartebeest, springbok, giant buf-falo, quagga)
sterile (hiatus in occupation)		
M.S.A. with segments but no blades	? 100 000 or more at base	
		beach at 12 m above sea-level bedrock

26

The delicacy and symmetry with which these 'points' were worked in the Middle Stone Age suggests they were hafted as knives or spear-heads with the aid of a vegetable gum mastic. The very small specimen is of a size appropriate to an arrow, and suggests that the bow may have come into use much earlier than was previously thought.

A 'Strandloper' pot from Danger Bay near Sal-danha Bay. The complete pot was discovered by Mr J. Rudner in 1952 among the sand-dunes and shell-middens of the area. The pot has a conoid base, contracted neck and internally reinforced lugs. There is no decoration, but there is a red ochre burnish. The elliptical shape of the top is unusual.

A spouted 'Strandloper' pot from Jeffreys Bay, found by I. and J. Rudner in 1951 and recon-structed from shards found among shell-middens on the beach. The pot is elliptical in section and is decorated on the shoulder with two horizontal rows of impressed oval dots. The base is globular and there are no lugs. It had a red ochre burnish in its original state.

high. The technological transition from Early to Middle Stone Age must reflect some advantageous change in the system by which man exploited his environment or it would not have happened. We have suggested that the change might be related to the invention of hafting or the improvement of existing simple methods of hafting. It is tempting to see at least some Middle Stone Age points as spearheads, and it may be that this conferred sufficiently increased success in hunting to lead to a significant increase in population. We can imagine that the invention or adoption of the bow and perhaps later the development of the use of poisons in hunting conferred similar advantages and were also followed by population increases. But if the population of the Early Stone Age was really so much lower, it must have been for reasons other than shortage of food supply. Among contemporary hunter–gatherers the woman cannot cope with more than one child plus all the paraphernalia she must carry in the course of collecting food or moving camp. If a new baby arrives while another is still being nursed (sometimes to the age of four or five years) the new-born infant is likely to be killed. Apart from any deliberate limitation of population by such drastic means, the mortality rate was very high, for instance, among australopithecines. Although early man joined the food debris in the leopard lair at Swartkrans far less often than did *Australopithecus*, he must have had many other hazards to survive.

A final word before leaving the question of population size or density. We have suggested that the very small number of sites for the Early Stone Age may in part result from destruction of the evidence or even simply failure to have found it. But another factor is worthy of consideration: the original visibility of sites. Most Acheulian sites have been recognised and recorded on the evidence of handaxes and cleavers which are large unmistakable objects. But there is evidence from East Africa that not all Acheulian sites include handaxes. The content and character of sites quite certainly varies, for a number of reasons. We assume that Early Stone Age man was a hunter and the chance preservation of wooden spears at Lehringen in Germany, Clacton in England and Kalambo Falls in Zambia certainly points to this. It is none the less possible that Acheulian culture contrasted with Oldowan culture reflects improved equipment for scavenging as much as specifically for hunting. If this were correct it would be possible to argue that the gathering of vegetable foods and small easily-taken animals such as caterpillars, tortoises, snakes, lizards, rats and mice might on occasion have sustained the group for long periods and that for much of the group's existence little in the way of durable archaeological evidence might be produced.

Patterns of Behaviour

In the matter of behaviour our knowledge is severely limited. The only way to calculate group size is to make the assumption that the kind of ratio between camp-size and number of inhabitants that exists today was the same in the remote past. But then calculation can be made only where the whole of an ancient campsite has been exposed by excavation. In the few such instances known from East Africa the figures suggest small groups of four or five adults and larger groups of twenty to thirty: possibly single family and 'local group' units. On one of the East African sites there was evidence of raw material having been carried from sources up to 50 km distant. The quantities of artefacts and unmodified stone (1 000 kg) carried into this site imply either a protracted continuous occupation or repeated return to the same site. If the imported raw material reflects group mobility then perhaps it is more likely that the site was regularly re-visited. If so this is an interesting insight into the territoriality of these early men. The immense concentrations of artefacts through 3 m of accumulated hillslope rubble at Wonderboom near Pretoria, in the gravels of the Vaal at 'Power's site' and in the silts on the edge of an ancient 'pan' at Doornlaagte near Kimberley, also suggest the repeated use of highly localised campsites over long periods of time. Looking at the locations of Acheulian sites throughout Southern and East Africa there seems to be a clear preference for the margins of lakes or pans and for the sandy beds of seasonal streams. The attractions might have been fresh water, the more abundant and varied vegetation found in such situations or the fact that watering places are good hunting or scavenging places.

Despite the great length of time through which the Early Stone Age persisted, and despite a considerable degree of variability within artefact categories (e.g. handaxes and cleavers), there is little to suggest true regional or chronologically discrete groupings such as we find in the Middle Stone Age. This has been suggested to reflect a different kind of social organisation in the Lower and Middle Pleistocene, in which groups 'may have been linked by marriage, exchange, etc., to other groups through a vast web of contacts that extended over large areas'. This is not to imply a highly organised 'web of kinship' but rather perhaps the kind of free flux or movement of members between groups that one finds in chimpanzee populations, or the less marked movement of males between gorilla groups. The effect would be to keep societies or groups 'open' and inhibit differentiation. Such a conclusion may explain the uniformity of technology over vast periods and areas in the Early Stone Age. Yet even in the Acheulian we may see the beginnings of regional division. One example of this may be recorded in the development of the 'Victoria West' cores in a restricted area between the lower reaches of the Vaal and Victoria West and eastwards to Venterstad, with possible outliers further east. Although suitable raw materials occur elsewhere the technique seems not to have spread beyond the region indicated, though it was undoubtedly also invented independently elsewhere, such as in Morocco and in Europe.

When turning to the post-Acheulian populations of the late Middle and Upper Pleistocene we find that the same problems and limitations occur. The same arguments about population density and size of group must be used, and we find the same paucity of informative sites. In the southern Orange Free State two sites have preserved apparent Middle Stone Age settlement structures. One of these (fig. 35), known as Zeekoegat 27, is no more than an approximately circular scatter of dolerite cobbles and blocks of sandstone, some of them 30 to 45 cm in maximum diameter, together with many smaller pieces. As a structure it presents some difficulties, for the artefacts are not so much concentrated within the circle as among the blocks comprising it. This makes it difficult to view the stones as an an-

34 Numbers of known sites for stages of the Stone Age, plotted against time. The relatively few sites for the immensely long period of the Early Stone Age may be partly due to poor preservation but almost certainly also reflects a very small population.

chorage for some kind of screen or thorn-bush surround. The alternative suggestion made by the excavator that the stones anchored the guy-ropes of a large skin tent is not easily refuted, but does not have a very convincing ring. It is doubtful if even twice the weight of stones would hold a tent of that kind in a stiff breeze, and it is almost inconceivable that hunter–gatherers would burden themselves with such a weighty piece of apparatus. Perhaps the most informative feature of the site is its size. If, as the excavator believes, little has been lost by erosion, the area – about 152 square metres – might be appropriate to a group of about a dozen people.

The other site, Orangia I, is architecturally much less equivocal, and contains a number of well-preserved structures (fig. 36). These are thought to fall into two categories: elongate curved alignments which might have anchored windbreaks to shelter working areas, and screened sleeping-hollows. Some of the sleeping-hollows were cut up to 60 cm below the original surface, and lined with stones. These are extremely interesting features, and not a little puzzling. The sleeping-hollows are not more than a metre in diameter and we must suppose they were either individual hollows, or that their occupants slept very intimately! The grouping of the structures and the clustering of the artefacts around them gives the impression that they form a unit whose limits are contained within the excavated area (6 m x 9 m), but at a few metres distance and about a metre lower, in an eroded area, was a scatter of about twice as many artefacts. Unfortunately we are not told if there was any evidence to suggest that the eroded part of the site had contained any similar structures. If the density of artefacts over the eroded area was comparable to that in the preserved part of the site it might, like Zeekoegat 27, represent occupation by a group of little more than a dozen people.

Possible windbreaks are known from one of the Oldowan sites at Olduvai Gorge 1,8 million years ago, and another at the Acheulian site of Kalambo Falls in Zambia. But fire, which is widely attested in

34

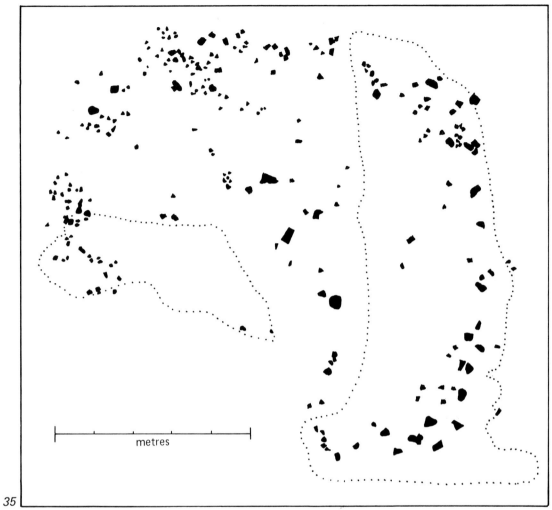

the Upper Pleistocene, is well documented from only one Acheulian site in sub-Saharan Africa (Kalambo Falls). Several carefully investigated Early Stone Age sites which should have preserved evidence of fire had it existed failed to do so, and it must be concluded that prior to the Middle Stone Age fire was available only in the presence of

35 The roughly circular scatter of boulders and cobbles at Zeekoegat 27 is associated with Middle Stone Age tools. The areas outside the dotted lines were exposed by erosion; those within remained buried. The stone tools (not shown) were scattered among the stones of the circle rather than within them.

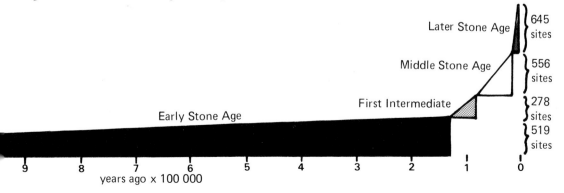

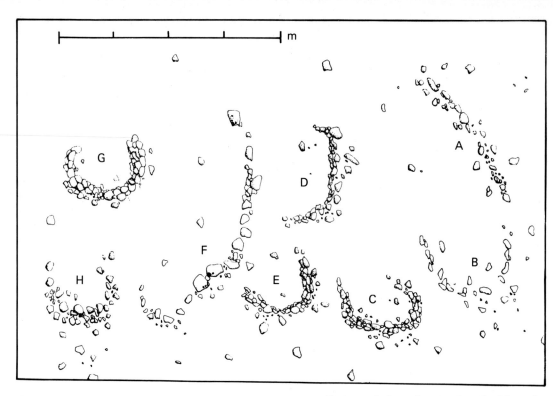

36 *The group of structures at Orangia I. It has been suggested that A/B, F and possibly D may mark the positions of screens sheltering working areas, while C,E, H and G were probably sleeping-hollows.*

natural conflagrations. The presence or absence of fire may have had much to do with the use of caves as dwelling places, for only six caves or rock-shelters have yielded evidence of Early Stone Age occupation in South Africa, as against at least twenty-seven in the Middle Stone Age and upwards of fifty in the Holocene.

Although almost 600 sites must be on record for the Middle Stone Age in South Africa, almost all of these represent small or large surface collections of artefacts with no precise information as to the sizes of the sites, and their ages are completely unknown. Of the relatively small number of sites more carefully investigated, only a handful have received anything like detailed and informative publication, and it is impossible to write with much confidence about the amount and nature of variation. Nevertheless there are sufficient good indications from widely separated areas to suggest that within this time period there is a great deal more variation than in the preceding Early Stone Age. The 'sophisticated blade' industries of Lesotho may well have some affinity with the industries described from the area of the Orange River dam scheme, but there appears to be nothing comparable in the south-west Cape. The triangular flakes with an apparently deliberate 'step' at the end opposite the point, presumably to facilitate hafting, from sites on the south coast have not been mentioned for other areas. The large segments found with the Middle Stone Age material in Nelson Bay Cave, and at Montagu, seem not to occur in the Transvaal, and there is great variety in the forms and techniques of manufacture of unifacial and bifacial points that will almost certainly prove to be in part regionally based when their study has been carried further. Some differences may prove to relate in part to the nature of available raw material, or the form in which it is available, and in the virtual absence of even relative dating it is impossible to say to what extent time-linked changes are involved. But we have a clear impression that the technological change from Early to Middle Stone Age is accompanied by other and more profound changes. The increase in the number of sites should reflect an increase in population, and the most likely cause of such an increase would be improvements in food-getting techniques and other factors creating greater security which permitted and led to changes in social organisation. This last factor would be essential if we are correct in supposing that it was social behaviour rather than food supply that held down population in the Early Stone Age.

Linguists have proposed that language as we know it has developed over about 50 000 years, and some prehistorians see a link between this and the relatively rapid development of culture during the Upper Pleistocene. It is a situation that is somewhat similar to the rapid expansion of the brain and the development of culture in the Pliocene and early Pleistocene.

The development of the brain and man's first material culture must have proceeded in unison, each stimulating the other and making for a relatively rapid development of both; a process involving what is known as feedback. It is hard to imagine that culture could have survived and evolved through the 2 million years of the Oldowan and Acheulian without some form of rudimentary language. If language took a significant step forward in the Upper Pleistocene it did not do so at the touch of a magic wand, but as part of a complex feedback system. As parts of such a system it is tempting to see technological advances, expansion of the brain, and the development of more complex language which this facilitated, together with concomitant developments in social organisation all operating in concert to produce the growth of complexity apparent in the Upper Pleistocene. Certainly it is in the Middle Stone Age that we find our first unequivocal evidence of hunting.

From an early stage in his development man must have been capable of securing small ground game such as hares, tortoises, rock-rabbits, snakes and lizards. But when we find the bones of larger game animals there must always be an element of doubt as to whether they were hunted or scavenged, especially in the earlier periods. The best guide to an active role on the part of man is when particular animals occur with a higher frequency than one would expect if man was merely taking advantage of what died naturally or was killed by four-footed predators.

Although we have a list of species found in the Kalkbank site in the Transvaal we are not told how many of each are represented. The list is typical of the open plains country in which the site is located, but the list itself need reflect no more than successful scavenging. At Die Kelders and Klasies River Mouth, however, the figures are altogether more informative.

The sites are at opposite ends of the Cape Folded Mountains and the settings are generally similar except that at Die Kelders there is an extensive area of sand dunes immediately west of the site. In both cases the occupants were actively pursuing the Cape fur seal. Both sites reflect a relatively higher frequency of eland (compared to other animals) than would be expected and the figures show a clear selection for this rather docile animal at Klasies River Mouth. By and large the Die Kelders people concentrated on small ground game (hyrax, hares and mole-rats), and the hunting of small, solitary antelope. The emphasis on hares and mole-rats undoubtedly reflects the proximity of the sandy terrain, absent at Klasies River. The Klasies River occupants were altogether more active and aggressive hunters. The high figures for Cape buffalo and the extinct giant buffalo clearly indicate systematic hunting, but there are interesting differences in the ages of animals represented. In both cases newborn or foetal animals are most abundant, but above this age group there is no clear selection in the case of the Cape buffalo; animals of all ages are fairly uniformly represented. In the case of the giant buffalo juvenile and young adult animals are underrepresented but the figures pick up quite sharply again in the fully mature age group. Richard Klein, who studied the bones, suggests that the Klasies River hunters concentrated their attacks on adult females in advanced pregnancy, or while giving birth. In any case their willingness to tackle either species of buffalo points to a high degree of competence in hunting. The presence of small numbers of bushpig and warthog lends strength to this contention, for these too are dangerous animals to hunt.

The greater security afforded by the use of fire, caves and rock-shelters, as well as the value of fire as a tool in the shaping of wood, must have facilitated development. The improvement of the spear would have permitted a significant shift from scavenging and gathering to an altogether more aggressive hunting behaviour. Whatever it was, the faint hint of regionalisation visible in the Middle Pleistocene shows considerable signs of having crystallised in the Upper Pleistocene into several regional sets.

People on the Move

The appearance towards the end of the Upper Pleistocene of even more dramatic developments in the micro-blade industries at Rose Cottage Cave and Sehonghong, and the Robberg industry a little later in the Cape Folded Mountains and the adjacent coastal plain, followed by the Albany industry, all seem to point to an increasing tempo of cultural change. To what extent these too will prove to be local phenomena, only time and intensified research will tell.

In the southern mountain districts and the adjacent coastal plain suggestions have been made that cultural changes and the distribution of population were linked to climatic changes and to the dramatic geographical changes resulting from the emergence of the coastal plain during the last glaciation, and its progressive and rapid drowning from about 18 000 years ago. A hint of this is seen in the appearance of the Howieson's Poort at Klasies River Mouth coinciding with a change from bush to more open vegetation.

A feature of great interest, though of uncertain significance, is an apparently widespread hiatus in the occupation of caves in the southern mountains and adjacent coastal plain immediately prior to the late Upper Pleistocene (fig. 37). In at least half a dozen caves in which both Middle Stone Age and later occupations are present there is a complete break of anything from 20 000 to 50 000 years. In at least five others occupation commences only in the late Upper Pleistocene or later. The only known exception is at Boomplaas, where the break (probably about 18 000 years ago) seems to be only a short one. Below this the indications are for essentially continuous occupation back to an estimated 80 000 years ago.

The hiatus falls within the time period of the last glaciation, and the end of this episode was marked in Southern Africa by an increase in temperature about 10 000 years ago. But there is no evidence of very severe frost conditions in the Cape Folded Mountains or the adjacent part of the coastal plain during the Upper Pleistocene and it is not easy to believe that non-occupation resulted from adverse climatic conditions. Whilst acknowledging the reality of fluctuations in temperature and rainfall in Southern Africa during the Pleistocene we have expressed the view that these seem unlikely to have had very far-reaching effects on man except in very marginal areas, but the Cape mountains and the plain to the south are not marginal occupation areas. In view of this we have to look for some other explanation for the apparent absence of habitation at this time.

It is a period when, for much of the time, the sea had retreated to a far lower level than at present, and a very large coastal plain became available for occupation. About 20 000 years ago, when the sea stood 140 m lower than at present, the plain in the extreme west near Cape Town was 16 km wide, expanding to 160 km at Cape Agulhas, and narrowing again eastwards to 70 km at Robberg and 64 km at Klasies River (see chapter 1, fig. 4). At Klasies River Mouth the Middle Stone Age inhabitants were systematically exploiting marine resources despite the fact that the shore was probably already some distance from the cave and over a hundred metres below. They also hunted a wide range of medium and large game animals. There can be little doubt that a combination of coastal plain and sea-shore would offer a more secure and varied food supply than a combination of coastal plain and Cape Folded Mountains. We are unable to say at present precisely what effect on vegetation, and therefore on fauna, the climatic fluctuations of the Upper Pleistocene would have had, so that little precision can be woven into the discussion. But the absence of occupation from so many tested sites in the southern region in the time bracket from 10 000 or 18 000 years ago to 30 000 or more years ago suggests very strongly that in the main the population was elsewhere. It is suggested that in large measure they had migrated southwards with the retreating shore, though by no means abandoning the plains. Such an explanation does not account for all the evidence, for Middle Stone Age occupation seems to be present at varying times in the early and middle part of the Upper Pleistocene. But if we knew in more detail the contours of the immediate off-shore regions, knew more precisely the fluctuations of the sea-level, and knew more certainly the chronology of the Middle Stone Age deposits concerned, apparent inconsistencies might well disappear.

After this hiatus, occupation, or re-occupation, commences around 18 000 or 19 000 years ago with the Robberg industry in at least four cave sites (Boomplaas, Kangkara, Nelson Bay Cave, and Melkhoutboom). In the case of Nelson Bay Cave, Melkhoutboom and Boomplaas the faunal remains indicate open grassland species such as wildebeest, quagga, blesbok/bontebok, and springbok. In the case of the first of these sites this need mean no more than that the wide grassy plain before the cave had not yet been drowned by the sea. In the other two cases it points to an environment different from that of today, where there is no niche for the grazers. The appearance of people at these sites might be taken to reflect the rather rapid encroachment of the sea between 20 000 and 15 000 years ago, bringing the sites within the landward margin of their territorial range. But the sea was still quite distant, for there is no sign of marine food remains in the deposits. Such a situation does not involve any known climatic (and therefore environmental) change and there is no obvious phenomenon with which to link the appearance of the Robberg culture. If we are correct in

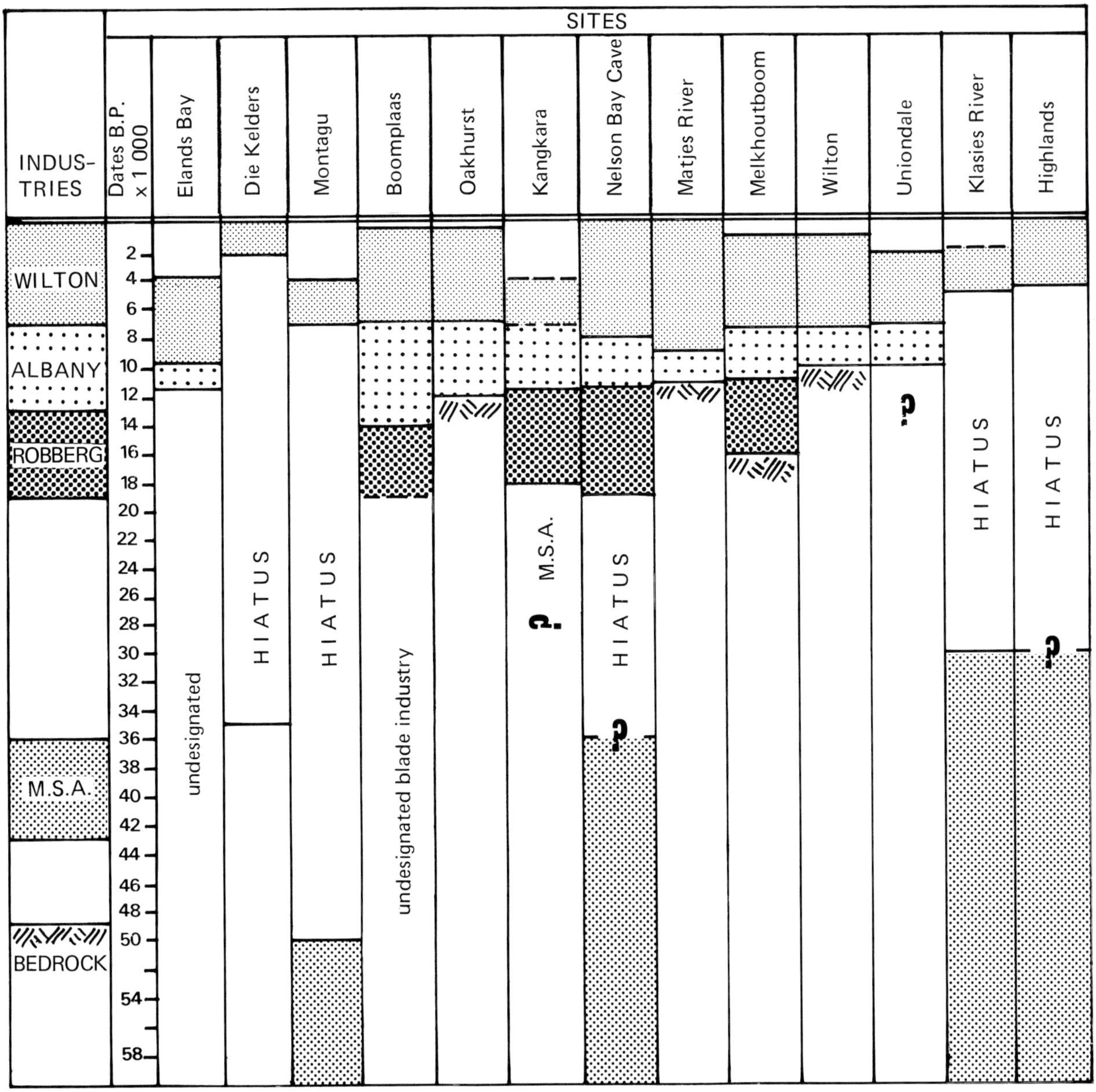

Figure: Chart showing SITES across top (Elands Bay, Die Kelders, Montagu, Boomplaas, Oakhurst, Kangkara, Nelson Bay Cave, Matjes River, Melkhoutboom, Wilton, Uniondale, Klasies River, Highlands) against INDUSTRIES (WILTON, ALBANY, ROBBERG, M.S.A., BEDROCK) and Dates B.P. ×1000 (scale from 2 to 58).

Elands Bay: undesignated
Die Kelders: HIATUS
Montagu: HIATUS
Boomplaas: undesignated blade industry
Kangkara: M.S.A. ?
Nelson Bay Cave: HIATUS, ?
Matjes River
Melkhoutboom
Wilton
Uniondale: ?
Klasies River: HIATUS
Highlands: HIATUS, ?

thinking that we are dealing with populations spreading northwards then we must suppose that the Robberg industry developed at some unknown date on the now submerged Late Pleistocene coastal plain. Perhaps when the Boomplaas research project has progressed further we shall have a better idea about this, for the break below the Robberg industry appears to be a short one and is preceded by a long succession involving a blade industry (or industries) of different character. This solution might be a nice, tidy, and simple one virtually untestable without some deep-sea archaeology, but it would

37 Of thirteen cave sites which have been investigated on the south Cape coast or the nearby Folded Mountains, no less than five show an hiatus in occupation between the Middle and Later Stone Ages. Four other sites were occupied for the first time at the end of the Pleistocene and the histories of four sites are not known for the period prior to the Late Pleistocene. It seems that this region must have been very sparsely inhabited throughout much of the Upper Pleistocene. The chronologies indicated are in several cases approximations or guesses.

79

be wise not to overlook the existence of what sound like remarkably similar industries in the same time-range far to the north in the Orange Free State and Lesotho. We can only reserve judgment until more evidence is available.

If the Robberg industry presents us with an enigma it is no greater than that of the Albany industry, which immediately succeeds it. Around 11–12 000 years ago (14 000 at Boomplaas) the Albany industry crops up in no less than nine of the recently investigated sites in the mountains and on the coast. The industry is quite different from the Robberg industry and must represent a remarkably rapid evolution from it, which cannot be documented on the available evidence, or else be a new intrusive culture. As with the Robberg industry, the Albany does not seem attributable to any particular local climatic or environmental stimulus. Certainly the sea had now moved close in, and the fact is recorded by the abundance of shellfish, fish, seal bones and marine bird bones in the Albany levels at Nelson Bay Cave. Small quantitites of shell even reached Melkhoutboom and Boomplaas, 45 and 70 km respectively from the coast. At Nelson Bay Cave the open grassland animals are gone by now, although the presence of eland and warthog indicate more open conditions than at present. But again this probably reflects the drowning of the coastal plain rather than climatic and vegetational change, for at Elands Bay, Boomplaas, and Melkhoutboom the large grazers still persist. Indeed it is *within* the Albany layers at Boomplaas that grassland is lost to encroaching shrub and bush cover, as is documented by the replacement of wildebeest by grysbok in the deposits.

It is tempting to regard the Albany industry, like its predecessor the Robberg, as a local south-coast phenomenon. But with both we have the same problems of finding a point of origin, and of the existence of industries with at least some parallel features (large flakes and scrapers) far to the north, in approximately the same chronological position.

Compared with the Lower and Middle Pleistocene, the Upper Pleistocene and Early Holocene see a far greater variety of discreet industrial entities, and a much more rapid rate of change. Historically this is interesting and it is an important part of the task of archaeology to document the changes. But the interest lies not in the study of the artefacts themselves, or in the technological fashions they reveal, but in the people who made them. The first step to getting the people right is to identify their responses to their environments, physical and social, and then to try to understand the nature of

changes and the reasons for them. The artefacts with which this chapter has been all too largely concerned provide the most obvious indication of periods of stability and periods of change. To put flesh on the picture requires food residues in the form of bones and, still better, of plants, for it is in the changing patterns of the utilisation of the resources of the environment that we are likely to come closest to the kinds of social organisation that developed to meet man's needs.

In this chapter we have been concerned with an immense period within which human artefacts alone indicate that important changes were taking place. Whether on the coast or in the interior, faunal remains indicate that Upper Pleistocene man was a successful hunter of 'large grassland animals (as well as small creatures) and it has been suggested this required 'large local-group organisation, low population density, large territorial range and the absence of fixed territorial boundaries'. The proposed overall low population density for the Lower, Middle, and Upper Pleistocene would certainly facilitate the last three of these requirements, and the hypothesis of low population may be supported by the abandonment of the sites indicated (fig. 37) as the territory expanded with the retreat of the sea.

These hazy glimpses of human populations in the landscape are possible in the south of the country because of a great deal of recent fieldwork of a very high quality, and because fortune has favoured us with some long sequences and with good preservation of fauna. It is an encouraging indication of what may yet be achieved in other areas. In the interior of the continent the story is less clear and will remain so until the completion of work on a number of sites.

The Evolution of Man

We started this chapter by saying that for the beginning of the Pleistocene we have a vivid picture of the appearance of a very close relative of man in *Australopithecus*. In fossils of the same age or a little later in East Africa and at Swartkrans we have a less perfect record of what our first tool-making ancestors were like, and apart from the larger brain the differences from *Australopithecus africanus* seem not very striking. At the other end of the time-scale with which we have been dealing we are face to face with modern man. What happened in between? The evidence is distressingly scanty and it is for this reason, and because it seemed sensible to sketch in the chronological and cultural framework first, that

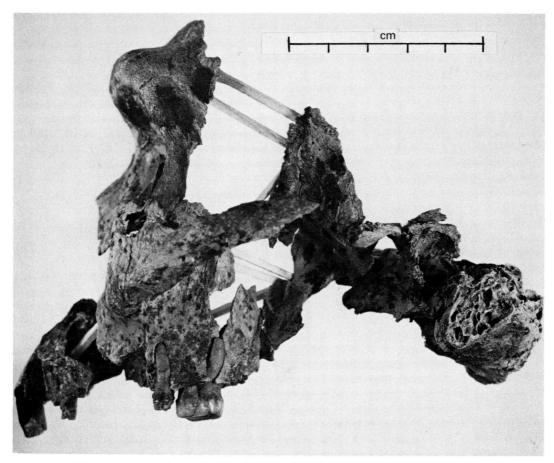

cm

we have left the question of the evolution of the toolmaker himself to the last.

For the enormous period of the Acheulian the only human fossil we have from South Africa, securely associated with cultural remains, is a fragment, from the Cave of Hearths in the Transvaal, of the lower jaw of a twelve-year-old child, retaining three teeth. Certain features of the mandible, including its robustness and the presence of a slight bony chin, have led to the suggestion by Professor Tobias that it belongs to a population that was transitional between *Homo erectus* (formerly known as Java Man, Peking Man, or *Pithecanthropus erectus*) and an African branch of modern man, labelled by some as *Homo sapiens rhodesiensis* (after the skull found in 1921 at Broken Hill [Kabwe] in Zambia). We have nothing that certainly represents *Homo erectus* unless it be the skull and mandible from the Older Breccia at Swartkrans (fig. 38) and the mandible from the Younger Breccia of the same site. However, we must await final judgement on these specimens. It should, however, be noted that the Swartkrans Older Breccia fossils would be among

38 Not much to look at, but this fragmentary skull from the Older Breccia at Swartkrans is currently South Africa's oldest man. Features distinguishing it from the robust and gracile australopithecines are the quite sharply rising forehead, above the brow-ridges; the marked projection of the nose-bones; and the fact that the base of the brain-case descends almost to the level of the teeth. It probably represents a stage of human evolution older than that of Homo erectus.

the oldest examples of the group if they were so assigned.

For the late Middle and Upper Pleistocene we are not very much better off. There is a well-preserved skull-cap (the Saldanha skull) and a mandible fragment, possibly belonging to the same individual, from the rich fossil site of Elandsfontein in the south-west Cape. The site is an area of extensively wind-eroded sand in which fossil animal remains and Acheulian artefacts occur on the floors of troughs between mobile sand dunes (see page 83). Whilst the bulk of the fauna is Early Stone Age,

Middle Stone Age elements and artefacts are also represented. The human remains were found exposed on the surface and there is no sure way of knowing whether they belong with the earlier or later material. On balance, however, it seems likely that the later date is correct since the skull is almost the twin of the much more complete specimen from Broken Hill (now Kabwe) which has been shown to belong to an early stage of the Zambian Middle Stone Age. These large-brained (1 300 cc) men with huge, rugged faces and strongly developed ridges above the eyes have often been compared with the neanderthal sub-species of *Homo sapiens* in Europe. Some have even claimed them as late-surviving representatives of *Homo erectus*. But many of the 'classic' neanderthal features are not present in the African fossils and brain-size and dating alone would seem to remove them from the *erectus* group. Current opinion favours them as a variant form of *Homo sapiens* within the Upper Pleistocene of Africa.

Certain other fossils are also firmly of Upper Pleistocene (Middle Stone Age) date or are generally accepted as such. The Klasies River Mouth site yielded two lower jawbones, one small and robust, and the other slender with smaller teeth. Unless the differences are attributable to sex difference, as one author thinks possible, the mandibles may indicate two distinct types (races or sub-races) within the Middle Stone Age. At Tuinplaats about 130 km north of Pretoria roadworkers in 1929 uncovered a skull and some limb bones in a quarry dug for road metal. The bones came from a lime-rich soil horizon overlain by about 50 cm of reddish soil. From the same horizon as the bones came Middle Stone Age artefacts and a fragment of an extinct buffalo. Although it cannot be demonstrated that the remains

were not buried into the Upper Pleistocene stratum at a later date, the skull shares features with others for which a similar age seems fairly certain. These are a skull from the Border Cave, and one from the lowest levels of the Florisbad site.

The Border Cave skull was found in the course of casual digging but the site has been carefully investigated subsequently on at least two occasions, and there seems little doubt that the skull derives from the Middle Stone Age levels. The one remaining skull, Florisbad, is the most securely dated (to older than 44 000 years) but its features are thought to be somewhat distorted by a genetically induced deformity. The forehead is unusually broad and flattened, with a correspondingly broad face giving it a somewhat grotesque appearance. But despite this it is believed that the skull belongs to the same kind of population as that from Border Cave. Several other skulls or skeletons at one time thought to belong to the Middle Stone Age are either now shown to be later, or are so dubious as to be generally discounted.

None of the skulls described above can be closely dated. All are thought to be post-Acheulian, though probably older than 40 000 years. If we could see these individuals walking about today Florisbad might give us something of a shock on account of his physical deformity, and Saldanha man and his Zambian counterpart would probably strike us as distinctly odd-looking, with rather massive faces and decidedly beetling brow ridges tending to accentuate the lowness of a truly low, sloping forehead. You might decide not to start a conversation. But the remaining two, from Tuinplaats and Border Cave, would probably pass unnoticed in a crowd. And yet it is likely that the Saldanha type and the Tuinplaats type represent no more than extremes of variation within an essentially *Homo sapiens* stock. Having said this it is necessary to add that while neither of these groups resembles the recent or Holocene populations of South Africa, the type represented by the Tuinplaats/Border Cave group could well be ancestral to the modern Negroes and to the Khoisan (Bushman and Hottentot) populations.

The problem posed at the beginning of the chap-

39 Two views of the position of Homo erectus *in the evolution of man. The one sees him as an unsuccesful descendant of* Homo habilis, *becoming extinct in the Middle Pleistocene. The other view sees H. erectus as part of a very varied Mid-Pleistocene species contributing in part to the make-up of modern man.*

H. sapiens

H. sapiens

H. erectus

H. erectus and other less specialised forms

H. habilis

H. habilis

Fossils at Elandsfontein are found on and below the floors exposed between modern, shifting dunes.

ter, alas, remains unresolved. We can only assume that the men who made the Acheulian tools in South Africa were, as were their Acheulian or Middle Pleistocene contemporaries elsewhere in Africa, Europe and Asia, members of the species *Homo erectus*. Opinions differ as to whether *H. erectus* was in the direct line of descent of modern man (fig. 39) and South Africa at present has nothing to contribute to the resolution of the problem. The few fossils we have are much later in time than the known examples of *H. erectus* and belong to a more advanced being. We do not know when, or by what process the transition to *Homo sapiens* of the Upper Pleistocene took place; we only see him in an ill-defined time range without any clear ancestry. Within this population the type represented by Saldanha man was probably a specialisation that led nowhere, and it disappeared before the Holocene. We should not think of the process in terms of the extermination of a discrete group, but rather of a blending back into the wider population of which it was part. In all probability Saldanha man's genes contributed in some measure, as did those of Tuinplaats man, to later populations. But the stages of development that led to the varied populations of the Holocene will not be known until more fossil evidence is found.

Oldowan man crossed the Limpopo as an immigrant but it is not necessary to suggest the same for Acheulian man. Whether the subsequent story is one entirely of indigenous development or whether new arrivals came from the north we cannot say. All we can say is that there is nothing in the archaeological record that requires the arrival of new populations within the Pleistocene.

4

A Way of Life Perfected

Sources of Information

When we move out of the Pleistocene into the Holocene we enter a completely different world. Even making allowances for the thinness of the evidence, Pleistocene man seems alien and remote. The picture we have of Southern Africa in the past 8 000 years presents us with something altogether more familiar; something we can come closer to understanding. There are many reasons for this. The time period lies well within the effective range of radiocarbon dating. Events can be dated, trends identified and information otherwise irretrievable can be salvaged. Gaps in the sequence of deposits in caves and rockshelters can be accurately measured in such a way that it is possible to determine whether they are merely of local or of wider significance. The number of sites available for study is immensely greater (see chapter 3, fig. 34) and this wealth of material has attracted a commensurate amount of attention.

Not only are more sites available, but time has dealt less harshly with them and organic materials are frequently well preserved. The only organic artefact from the Lower Pleistocene of South Africa is a splinter of bone, polished at the tip by use, from the Extension Site at Sterkfontein. From the Upper Pleistocene there is a fragment of a wooden throwing-stick from Florisbad. From the time with which we are now concerned we have tools, weapons, clothing, utensils and jewellery represented in wood, mastic, bone, ivory, shell, leather and plant fibres. Food is represented not only by the skeletal remains of animals, but by plant remains as well. Many thousands of paintings and engravings widely distributed throughout the country (see p. 89) illustrate aspects of the lives of the peoples of these times.

There are difficulties about using the paintings and engravings, primarily because they are mostly undatable. In the late eighteenth and early nineteenth centuries there are records of 'Bushmen' still painting in the southern mountain ranges. As late as the 1860s a Bushman, shot during a retaliatory commando attack for cattle raiding, was found wearing a leather belt from which were suspended ten antelope-horn paint containers with pigments in them. In the eastern Cape, the Drakensberg mountains and Lesotho, horses and Europeans are

depicted indicating a date no earlier than the early nineteenth century. In the south-west Cape, European trek scenes are depicted in the mountains, as well as a mid-seventeenth-century galleon. But there are no such indications for the Transvaal or most other areas. Occasionally paintings have been found on pieces of stone buried in the fillings of caves and rockshelters, but few have been dated. Of those that have, five on the south coast (Klasies River Mouth, Matjes River, and Robberg peninsula) are dated to between 1 925 and 5 600 years ago, one at Boomplaas in the Cape mountains is dated to 6 500 years, while a site in Namibia has yielded several dated to around 27 000 years ago. But, in many thousands of paintings, there seem to be no extinct animals represented, so it seems that the paintings belong in the main to the Holocene. Whilst they represent a rich and entrancing storehouse of information it is one that is not easily tapped.

Turning to more conventional archaeological remains we find an unfortunate unevenness, geographically, of research on Holocene sites. Far more is known of the occupation of the southern mountain ranges and the adjacent coast than of the interior and the north. The discovery of handaxes in the Vaal gravels, in the search for alluvial diamonds, fol-

lowed by the discovery of the australopithecines in the 1920s and 1930s tended to concentrate research in the Transvaal on Lower and Middle Pleistocene sites. The emphasis shifted in the early 1960s to the study of early farming sites, and the Holocene hunters have taken third place. A few sites, mostly unpublished, give us a picture of the artefact content, and a few radiocarbon dates, but little more. In the southern Orange Free State, excavations carried out in the 1960s in the areas to be flooded by the Orange River Dam Scheme provide our first clear picture of the stone tool traditions of that area, together with some radiocarbon dates. To the east, in the southeast highlands of Lesotho, the preliminary results of a major research project give us a tantalising glimpse of valuable information still to come. To the west, around Kimberley, research on Holocene sites has only recently begun and it is a great pity that the information from that area is still so limited, for we are much in need of knowing what was happening on those vast inland plains, so hot in summer and so cold in winter.

That the southern Cape has received most attention is not entirely fortuitous, for at opposite ends of

1 *The principal localities mentioned in this chapter.*

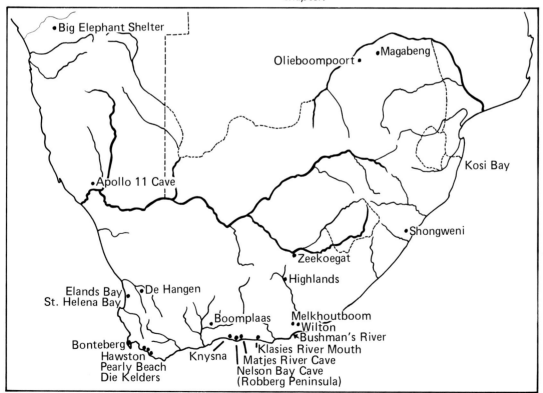

the region are two of South Africa's oldest museums: the Albany Museum at Grahamstown and the South African Museum at Cape Town. It was at the University of Cape Town too, that the first teaching and research post in archaeology was created decades ahead of any other South African university. The early work of Goodwin and Van Riet Lowe, and Stapleton and Hewitt, indicated the possible rewards for research in this area and the challenge has been well taken up. One major project in the eastern Cape has been effectively completed though not fully published. Others along the south coast and in the south-west Cape are still in progress and only partial and provisional results are available. But between them they give us an unparalleled insight into the past of South Africa. Much of what follows in this chapter is based on this southern region research, for the simple reason that it is so much more informative than anything that is available for most other areas. A decade hence it may be possible to draw a more balanced picture.

People in a Landscape

Our concern is with the evolution of Southern African society and in our search for the threads it is necessary to examine several kinds of evidence. We have suggested that population expanded during the Upper Pleistocene and that man assumed a more positive and effective role as a hunter. Regionalised societies were developing, perhaps with accelerated development of language going hand in hand with increased biological and technological evolution. It might not be stretching the evidence too far to suggest that the tendency to regional differentiation visible at this time also marks the development of separate languages. If this view is correct then the results should have become still more clearly fixed in the Holocene, and ought to be there for us to see today.

Unfortunately, within the past 2 to 2,5 thousand years the economic and social systems of the Holocene hunters have been disrupted first by the spread of peasant farming economies from within Africa, and more recently by the incursion of European colonists from without. In the absence of writing there was little hope that the African farmers should have recorded the effects of their contacts with the hunters. In the case of the Europeans the possibility was there but the record was not made. The few scrappy records we have indicate that at first the hunters tended to keep out of sight and to retreat in the face of European colonisation. But

soon, as the colonists took over or disrupted their traditional hunting and gathering territories, conflict arose. The hunters took to raiding the farmers' livestock and the farmers took to hunting the hunters. A few more intellectually inclined travellers left valuable snippets of information about dress, weapons, musical instruments, and food, but nothing systematic. By the time ethnology had developed as a subject, late in the nineteenth century, it was too late; the hunters had all but vanished except in the unwanted remoteness of the Kalahari and in small pockets elsewhere. The great expeditions of the time went to other, more remote areas less disturbed by colonisation.

From the late fifteenth century Portuguese merchant venturers, seeking an ocean route to the land of Prester John, and to the spice lands of the East, called at various points on the coast of Southern Africa and Namibia and left us the earliest reports of the people they met. By the middle years of the seventeenth century the contrast was clearly drawn between the long stretch of country from Namibia to the Indian Ocean inhabited by yellow-skinned hunters and herders with no knowledge of metals, and the south-east coast where the people were more swarthy and better fed, and not only kept cattle and hunted but used iron and copper, grew crops and lived in settled villages (fig. 2). This economic distinction between hunter, herder, and mixed farmer provides our first introduction to the complexities of Southern African society immediately prior to European incursions.

The Evidence of Language

The other comment that was made about the dark-skinned farmers of the south-east coast was that they spoke a language 'not so badly pronounced' as travellers had met in more westerly parts. The languages of the hunters and herders incorporated a number of 'clicks' which made the tongue sound so foreign to many of the early travellers that they must often have doubted whether it was a language at all. It merely served to confirm their view that these outlandish people scarcely merited inclusion within the ranks of mankind. The contacts established by the sixteenth- and seventeenth-century sailors, mostly between St. Helena Bay and the Bushman's River, were almost invariably with pastoralists whose cattle and sheep they needed to replenish their depleted meat supplies. Thus it was that, because of their staccato, clicking speech, the herders were given the

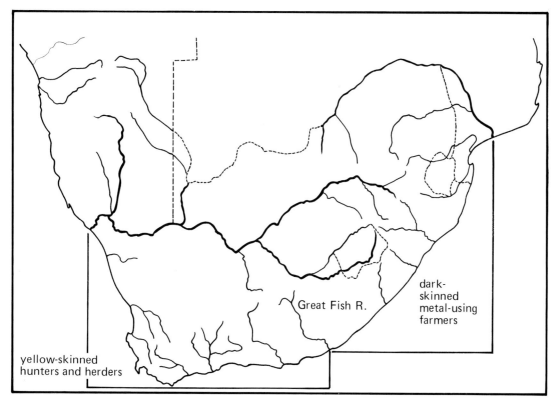

yellow-skinned hunters and herders

Great Fish R.

dark-skinned metal-using farmers

2 *Distribution of Khoisan hunters and herders and Bantu farmers as revealed by sixteenth- and seventeenth-century sailors' records.*

nickname of 'Hottentot'. The hunters who were met with occasionally on the coast, but more often inland, first acquired the names Bosjesmans, Bosmanekens or Bosiesmans from the seventeenth-century Dutch settlers. Whether the name derived from the environment into which the hunters so often melted or to the little windbreaks of branches in which they sheltered we can only guess. But the names Hottentot and Bushmen are not true names. They have led to much confusion and it is preferable to avoid their use. The herders referred to themselves as Khoikhoin, 'men of men', and the stem Khoi is a better term to describe the herders. The herders themselves spoke of the hunters as San, and this is a more appropriate name than Bushmen. Recent research, however, shows that not all Khoi speakers were herders.

But neither San nor Khoi are recognised linguistic terms, as Professor Westphal has been at pains to stress. To adopt them as language families is an unwarranted oversimplification. Despite the disturbances resulting from the spread of African and European farming, Westphal in 1961 could still assemble field data on no less than four distinct 'Bush' languages, several 'Hottentot' languages, and a previously unrecorded language, Kwadi, which is neither a 'Bush' nor a 'Hottentot' nor a Bantu language (fig. 3). The 'Hottentot' languages can be shown to be clearly related and fall into three groups: Cape 'Hottentot' (including Griqua and Kora), the closely related Nama (including Dama) and the more distinct Tshu-Khwe. But the four 'Bush' languages are seemingly distinct and unrelated to each other. Using written records, compiled in the late nineteenth and earlier twentieth centuries, of now vanished 'Bush' languages, Westphal has outlined the distribution of major language areas (fig. 4) as they might have been towards the end of the nineteenth century. This linguistic evidence is important in the present context for two reasons. It indicates something of the human complexity of the southern part of the continent during the Holocene, and it gives us some idea of the sizes of territories that might have been linked by common linguistic traditions.

As regards the sizes of the areas over which different languages were spoken it is interesting to note that in the areas least affected by European encroachment, and therefore most likely to be representative of prehistoric conditions, the languages

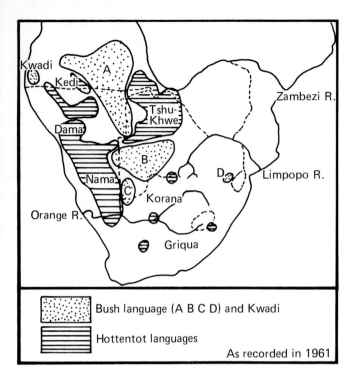

Bush language (A B C D) and Kwadi

Hottentot languages

As recorded in 1961

3 The pattern of non-Bantu languages in Southern Africa today hints at the complexity of human population groupings in the Holocene period.

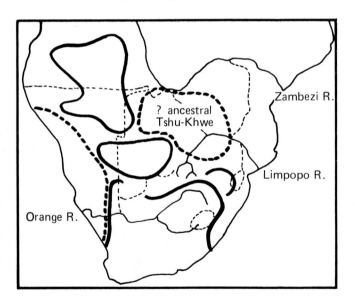

4 A reconstruction from written records of the major areas of Bush languages late in the nineteenth century. It seems likely that the large southern area would be divisible if the evidence had survived well enough.

'Bush' A and B, Nama/Dama, and Tshu-Khwe occupy territories of broadly similar size. In the reconstruction map (fig. 4), with the exception of the southern 'Bush' area, the language territories proposed are only a little larger. The 'Hottentot' languages are omitted from this map as they are believed to have developed in the ancestral Tshu-Khwe area and spread later into territories already occupied by 'Bush' speakers. The southern area is very large. Detail is lacking for the south-east and north-east and it is possible that the area would have been divided into two or more smaller linguistic territories. For each of the areas reconstructed in fig. 4, several languages are recorded and, making allowance for the mass of linguistic evidence that must have been lost completely, we can be fairly sure that the picture would originally have been still more complex.

But it would be wrong to be seduced into thinking that these maps reveal the pattern of prehistoric population networks for the major part of the Holocene. As we shall see in the next chapter the northern and eastern areas had been affected by contact with farmers for many centuries and there may have been far-reaching movements of populations before these surviving patterns developed. Professor Westphal's own assessment of the evidence was that 'the linguistic history of Southern Africa (possibly in the Later Stone Age) was characterised by the presence of a great number of unrelatable and unrelated so-called Bush languages. . . . The Bush languages suggest a sparsely inhabited sub-continent inhabited by several kinds of peoples with several types of distinct cultures, including linguistic cultures. Not much movement and certainly not much rapid movement appears to take place across these cultural borders.'

We need to look deeper than the linguistic evidence of the past eighty or ninety years, and the only way of doing so is through surviving archaeological evidence. Language cannot help us, other than in the ways we have just mentioned, for nothing we dig up can tell us what language its maker spoke. But still our concern is with people; the artefacts, food debris and environmental evidence we discover, interesting though they may be, are but means to an end. The major language group, with all its various dialects, is the unit most likely to be a closed system whose contacts with other major language groups will be minimal. This is the level at which there is the greatest degree of isolation, especially when population is thin on the ground, and it offers the greatest potential for divergent cultural development. If anything in real life ought to repre-

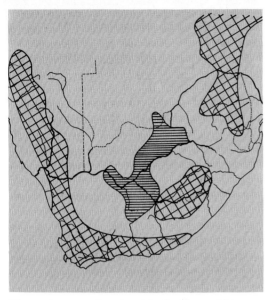

The main areas of rock art in Southern Africa. The areas of painting and engraving are not totally exclusive, though they are predominantly so.

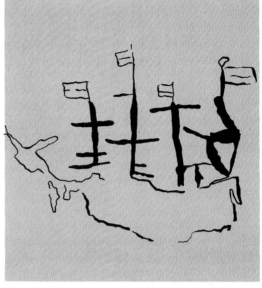

Painting of a seventeenth-century sailing ship, in the mountains north of Cape Town.

Painting of wagon and horse-team from a cave in the mountains 150 km north-east of Cape Town. It is accompanied by numerous other paintings of Europeans, with horses and guns, and possibly dates from the eighteenth or early nineteenth century.

These two antelope are from Tarkastad, north-east Cape. Note the artist's 'palette', the dabs where he tried out his colours.

Below, a recumbent eland; from the Drakersberg.

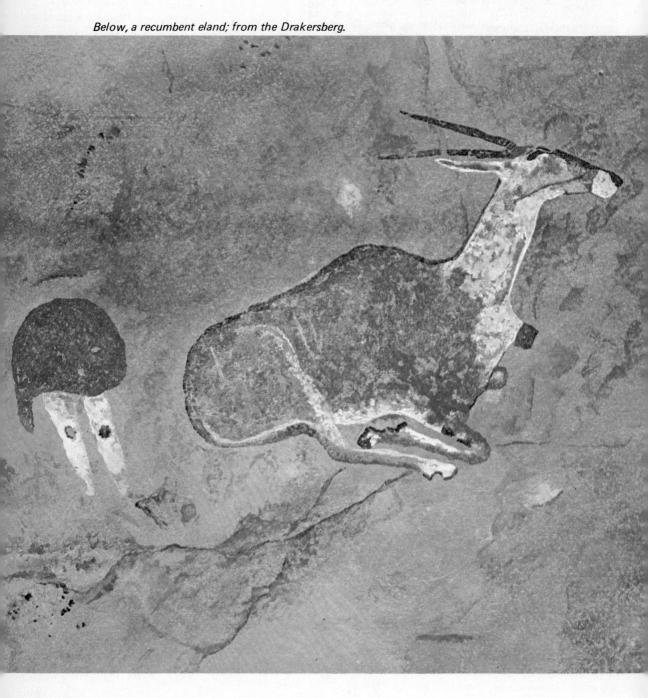

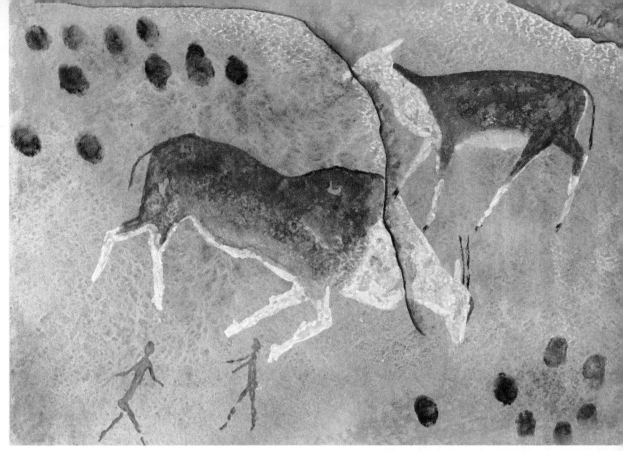

Rock painting from the Drakensberg Mountains, showing a dismounted soldier in uniform shooting at eland. The scene is remarkable for its detail of the uniform and harness, and even the cap lying neglected, in the excitement of the moment, between the soldier's feet.

Small antelope, from the Brandberg, Namibia.

This antelope, probably a klipstringer, is from the Citrusdal area, western Cape.

A kudu cow apparently being **hunted** by bowmen. From Namibia.

sent archaeological cultures it should be these major language groups. Would that it were so simple. Language, as we have remarked, is a major criterion for cultural division, but there is no real reason why the material culture of one language group should be notably different from that of another living in an adjacent area in a similar environment. Nor is there any good reason why material culture should not vary regionally *within* the language group. So it will not help us to make unwarranted assumptions in these directions. We must remember that only a small part of the material things of daily life survive, and this may serve to mask differences that once existed. With these reservations in mind let us examine what archaeology has to tell us.

Old Stones and New Ideas

Ever since Goodwin and Van Riet Lowe published their definitive work in 1929 on *The Stone Age Cultures of South Africa* industries of the Later Stone Age have been thought of as falling into two great families, the Wilton Culture and the Smithfield Culture. The term Wilton was adopted in 1926 from a site on the farm Wilton in the eastern Cape where small tools, particularly segments (fig. 6), were seen to be characteristic of the 'pygmy implements' previously recorded from several parts of South Africa. Indeed, segments in the company of small convex ('thumbnail') scrapers, accompanied by a range of other tools, often including ostrich eggshell beads, bone points, and sometimes pottery, were considered the hallmark of the Wilton 'culture'. The term was rapidly adopted and applied to almost any industry showing this combination of segments and small scrapers, even though the associated artefacts showed much variation from one site to another. Industries seen as belonging to the 'Wilton tradition' were recognised widely in the Southern part of South Africa, in Rhodesia, Zambia, and even as far afield as Kenya. Where associated material differed sufficiently regional prefixes were appended and by 1959 upwards of half a dozen variants were recognised from Zambia southwards to the Cape.

In much the same way the Smithfield culture was born and proliferated. But in this case there was no equivalent of the Wilton shelter to provide a sealed deposit of indisputably associated artefacts. Almost from the start the Smithfield was divided into stages, A, B, and C, thought to be successive.

Smithfield A included large convex and circular scrapers and was said (without a scrap of real justification!) to be associated with the rock engravings of the interior. Smithfield B saw the introduction of concave scrapers and bored stones, scrapers tended to be smaller and more elongate, and the circular scrapers of A disappeared. Smithfield C used a greater variety of raw materials, the tools were markedly smaller, and occurred in caves, whereas A and B had been found only in the open. Bone points were found with C and it was thought to be associated with the rock paintings, particularly in Lesotho and the Drakensberg where the sites were most often found. In the years from 1929 to 1961 a whole range of variants were claimed, mostly in Natal and on the east coast.

The essential factor which was claimed set off the Smithfield from the Wilton was the total absence of segments from Smithfield A and B and their virtual absence from C. The fact that Smithfield C was in so many respects like the Wilton and even, embarrassingly, sometimes produced an odd segment or two led to its being referred to sometimes as a 'crescentless Wilton' (segments were, and sometimes still are called crescents, which is really quite wrong). But the weakness of this great structure of cultures and variants was that it was based too extensively on small, selected collections of surface material. Only the 'finer' pieces were collected, often with no guarantee of true association between individual pieces, and with no reliable guide to relative ages, let alone absolute ages. The whole concept developed during a period that might well be referred to as the pigeon-hole age. If collections were sufficiently alike they were popped into the same culture pigeon-hole; if they were different they were put into separate ones. If the difference was small the second pigeon-hole was labelled 'variant', but if it was great it would be labelled a new 'culture'. The distinction between 'variant' and 'culture' was very much a matter of personal whim. There was no room in all this pigeon-holing for the concept of a culture (like some of the famous civilisations) evolving, reaching a climax, passing into a decline and finally emerging as something different. The result, however, was considered satisfactory because it peopled the landscape with 'cultures' and 'variants' which could be viewed rather as the ethnologist's tribes, hordes, clans or bands – which of course is what we ought to expect. But within the past few years very drastic changes have been introduced to this view of Southern African prehistory.

In part the changes are due to the availability of radiocarbon dates, and in part to the recent and painstaking analysis of carefully excavated material. But in particular it is due to new ways of thinking about prehistoric man, and the phrasing of new questions.

A key development was the re-examination of the Wilton Type-site at the end of the 1960s. Artefacts from fourteen excavated levels were carefully examined not only in terms of the types of tools that occurred together, but also variations in their shapes and sizes, and the preferences shown for raw materials, which were fairly local. The two lowest levels were shown to stand apart in almost every respect from the overlying levels and, as we have noted in the previous chapter, they are assigned to the Albany industry. Above this, individual levels certainly showed variation in the range of artefacts present, and in the frequencies with which certain types occurred. There is little doubt that in an earlier age, had the contents of these levels been found in different sites they would have been viewed as 'variants' of the Wilton culture, made by different but related groups. Such an interpretation makes nonsense of a succession of this kind. It would require a regular group of populations playing 'Box and Cox' in the shelter and such a situation would be quite at variance with what is known of living or historical hunter–gatherer groups. An essential feature of their existence is stability within a territory which is known by them to be capable of supporting the group throughout the year, either with or without seasonal movement.

The alternative explanation proposed, that variations in the tool inventories from level to level reflect variations in activity, is more logical. The range and frequency of tools resulting from any occupation of a site will depend very much on whether it was a short or prolonged occupation, and quite possibly on the season at which it took place. This interpretation sees the levels above the Albany industry as resulting from the repeated use of the shelter by successive generations of people belonging to the same cultural tradition over a period of 7 000 years. The unity of the tradition is indicated by the metrical attributes of the tools, in particular the scrapers, which are the most numerous group. Measurements such as the length and width of the scrapers, and the ratio between width and length reveal *trends* of change best regarded as changes in fashion without any recognisable functional basis. Such a conclusion might be regarded as tenuous were it not for the fact that almost identical trends have been observed through the same time-period in the Wilton levels at Melkhoutboom 50 km to the west.

The contrast between the Albany industry and the lowest Wilton levels is such that it is difficult to see the one as ancestral to the other unless there is a substantial gap in the record, or a very rapid evolution which cannot be seen at Wilton or any other known site. Above this the levels are grouped into a series of stages taken to represent the formative, climax, post-climax, and death/birth stages of an evolving culture. The death/birth stage that gave rise to the Wilton in the eastern Cape (or anywhere else) has not yet been recognised. But the Wilton Large Rock Shelter preserves the ensuing stages well. The formative phase of the new tradition is characterised by a limited range of tool types and a rather low density. Scrapers tend to be small and round, and not to vary much in size. The climax phase sees both the greatest density of artefacts and the greatest variety. The shape of scrapers changes somewhat, and there is a greater variety of scraper shapes. The post-climax phase occupies an intermediate position, resembling the climax phase in some of its characters, and the overlying death/birth phase in others. In the final phase there are fewer tool types and less standardisation in the manufacture of scrapers. Pottery makes its first appearance in this stage and possibly reflects new factors in the economy which contribute to the disintegration of the tradition: a point to which we shall return later.

We have dwelt on the Wilton evidence at some length because prior to its re-evaluation there was a universal tendency to regard archaeological cultures as circumscribed things that either conformed to the agreed description of a culture or were something different, representing different peoples. The analysis presented in the excavation report is detailed and well argued, and encourages us to think much more in terms of stable populations living in well-defined territories over long periods of time. Instead of thinking of cultures as ready-packaged units conjured out of the mists of time, we are led to view them as reflecting dynamic developing human societies. A new culture or tradition is born out of the disintegration of an older tradition. If we can identify the death/birth phase of a culture and fix it in time we are in a good position to ask what it was that brought about the demise of one tradition and its replacement by another. When we can provide answers to such questions for each of the major cultural transitions in Southern Africa we shall take a big step forward toward writing a history of Southern African society instead of sketching in a series of vignettes.

Another advantage of thinking of the evidence in these terms is that it leads us away from seeing cultures as dots on a distribution map to viewing them as entities which, to a great extent, are the product of their environment. Archaeological remains are most likely to be properly understood when viewed in relation to associated food remains, plant and animal, within a particular environment. The lives of hunter–gatherers occupying the great plains of the Kalahari, the Karoo and the grassveld must have been arranged very differently from those occupying mountain lands such as the Drakensberg or the Cape Folded Mountains, or the coastline with its hinterland. We have already remarked that the territorial range and social organisation of peoples hunting large gregarious plains animals are likely to be different from those of hunters in the thickly bushed kloofs of the mountain ranges, and both might be different from coastal dwellers. The search for the elements that give a society stability, expressed most clearly in the climax phase of its culture, must be conducted within the framework of the resources available in its territory, and the same is true for the causes of change.

A Regional Reconnaissance

After a long period in the Upper Pleistocene when there appears to have been no stable settlement in the eastern Cape, the first occupants were the people associated with the Robberg and Albany industries. Whether they came from the north or, as seems more likely, from the south-west, they were people accustomed to hunting large plains animals. When they first settled in the area plains animals were still to be found and the remains of wildebeest, hartebeest and zebra (or quagga) are all well represented at Melkhoutboom. In the small sample from Wilton, the presence of wildebeest and Vaal rhebuck suggests that grassland was more extensive than at present. We have too little information to say just what was happening to the environment of the eastern Cape at this time. Clearly there were important changes between the late Upper Pleistocene and the Holocene and probably the transition there to the Wilton tradition reflects an enforced adaptation to a new type of environment and subsistence as the herds of grazers diminished and finally van-

Excavations in progress at the Bonteberg shelter on the Cape Peninsula in 1962. Analysis of food remains showed that rock lobster formed a regular part of the diet of the inhabitants. The site also yielded what may be some of the oldest pottery from South Africa.

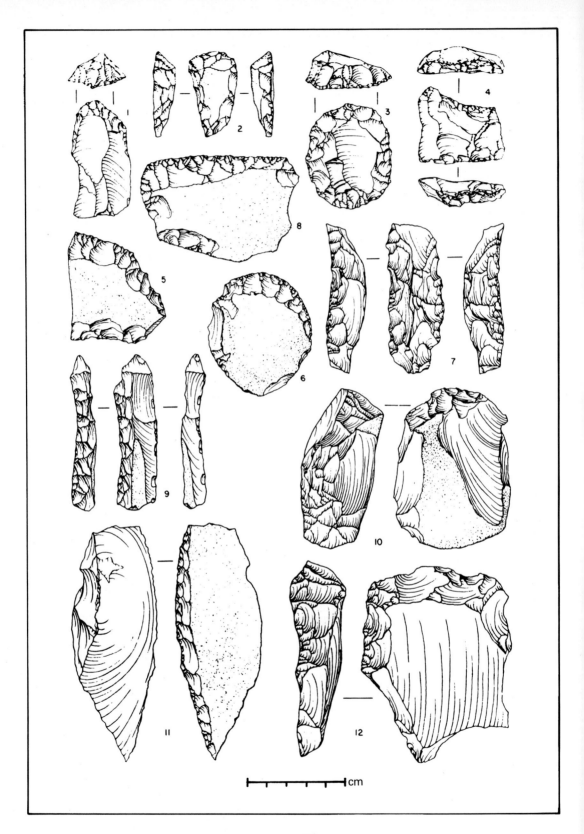

96

ished. The whole of the south and south-west Cape must have experienced the same kind of environmental change, and the indications are that broadly similar responses resulted. We shall return to this question below when considering subsistence patterns in more detail.

Along the east coast the continental shelf is very much narrower and the lowering of the sea during glacial episodes would not have drastically changed the landscape as it did in the south. Temperatures would certainly have been lowered at such times but we have no evidence as to how this might have affected the habitat between the escarpment and the sea. The rainfall is generally high and probably remained so. The vegetation between the escarpment and the coast today is a mixture of forest, scrubforest, and bushveld with extensive grasslands on the higher ground. Perennial streams dissect the area. In all probability this region would not have experienced very marked changes, the greatest perhaps being the extension or contraction of grassland areas. The territorial range would have been extended a few miles seaward at times of low sea-level, but populations would always have had available, within a modest seasonal round, a variety of environments to exploit. It is a region which has been little explored archaeologically and we have little but speculation to guide us. But in all probability the patterns of exploitation would have been much the same in the Holocene as in the Upper Pleistocene. The chief factor in any change was probably technological innovation.

About the only site in this eastern region which sheds any light at all on the problem is the recently excavated cave of Shongweni about mid-way between Durban and Pietermaritzburg. About 1,0 m of deposit is divisible into lower and upper occupation units spanning the periods 23 000 to 12 000, and 4 000 to 1 000 years ago respectively. We shall refer to this site again a little later. At the moment our interest lies chiefly in the evidence provided by shell fragments and beach pebbles that the coastline, about 35 km away, lay within the area exploited by the occupants of the cave. The very low density of artefacts suggests that the cave was used as a stopping-off place rather than a base camp. None of

5 A selection of stone tools typical of the industry formerly known as Smithfield A. in the Orange Free State. The industry is dominated by rather large varieties of scrapers and appears to be a Free State equivalent of the Albany industry in the southern Cape, dating to around 10 000 to 12 000 years ago.

the 755 stone artefacts in the lower level showed any signs of Middle Stone Age technique or typology. Indeed they are a most uninformative collection. The faunal remains from both upper and lower units show no divergence from what is known of the fauna of the area in the nineteenth century. Slender though the evidence is it suggests that exploitation patterns were the same in both the late Upper Pleistocene and the Holocene.

When we cross the Great Escarpment into the inland plateau we enter the territory *par excellence* of the Smithfield culture. In these vast plains and rolling hills, caves and rockshelters are much less frequent than in the mountains and the deeply incised river valleys that flow from them. Few have been examined, and the scattered surface sites, preserving nothing but stone, and undatable, are of little help. But a careful appraisal of the results of research in the eastern Cape and the southern Orange Free State, referred to at the beginning of this chapter, sheds some interesting light on the Holocene prehistory of at least the south-east corner of the plateau, and on the vexed question of the Smithfield culture itself.

An intensive study by Hilary and Janette Deacon of half a dozen sites in the eastern Cape, including the key sites of Wilton and Melkhoutboom, shows that segments, which are one of the distinguishing characteristics of the Wilton culture at its height, do not occur with the same frequency at all times. They are most common in deposits dating between 3 000 and 7 000 years ago. They are relatively scarce in the earliest stages of the Wilton, and tend to disappear after the climax phase. This has rather important implications for the Smithfield culture.

In his study of sites in the upper reaches of the Orange River Sampson gave a much sharper definition to the range of industries subsumed under the heading 'Smithfield'. A combination of stratigraphy, radiocarbon dates and typological comparisons led him to propose six phases for his local Later Stone Age succession. In fact phase 1 (fig. 5) does not belong in the Smithfield milieu, and should be included in the imperfectly understood industries of the end of the Pleistocene. The excavated sites representing the other phases show a strong element of backed blades and segments (fig. 6) not normally associated with the Smithfield. Taking a recent critical look at this situation and at the relevant radiocarbon dates, the Deacons have come up with some interesting observations. The first is that the Smithfield, as known from the type area southwards, can no longer be sustained as a separate cultural tradition: Sampson's phases 2, 3 and 4 look

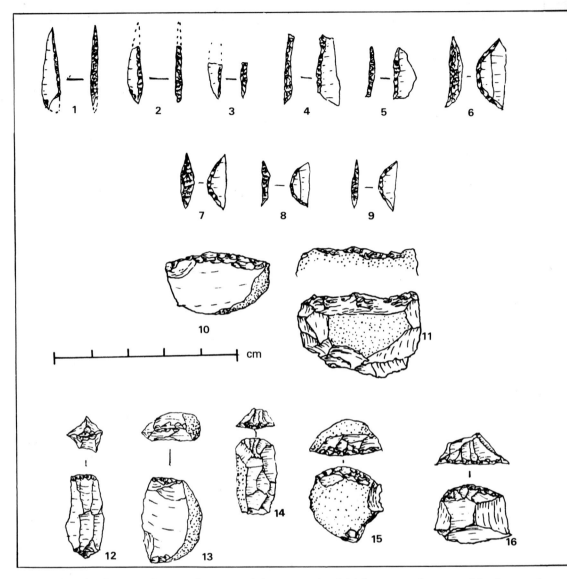

remarkably like the post-climax Wilton. Certainly the industries are not identical, but the fact remains that they are so similar that they really ought to be thought of as stemming from a common tradition, whatever name may be chosen for it.

The second observation is that no Smithfield sites have been identified anywhere within the range of 9 500 to 4 600 years ago (fig. 7), and within this time period no sites of any kind have been found in the drier areas of the inland plateau: specifically in the southern part of the Orange Free State, and in the eastern Cape north of the folded mountains. The absence of sites in this dry corner of the inland plateau is taken to reflect a period when climatic conditions reduced an already marginal area to a state in which hunter–gatherers could no longer obtain a satisfactory living. We must suppose that the temperature rise at the end of the Pleistocene resulted in a population drift from this very large area to regions that offered an easier and more secure existence. This is most likely to have meant a move southwards into the Cape Folded Mountains or eastwards to areas of higher rainfall, for the areas to the west were probably even less attractive. About 4 500 years ago improved conditions attracted new groups to settle in the area. At present we are no more able to say whence these groups came, than we can say where the ancestral groups retreated to at the end of the Pleistocene. There is, however, a clue. The people who re-settled the lands of the

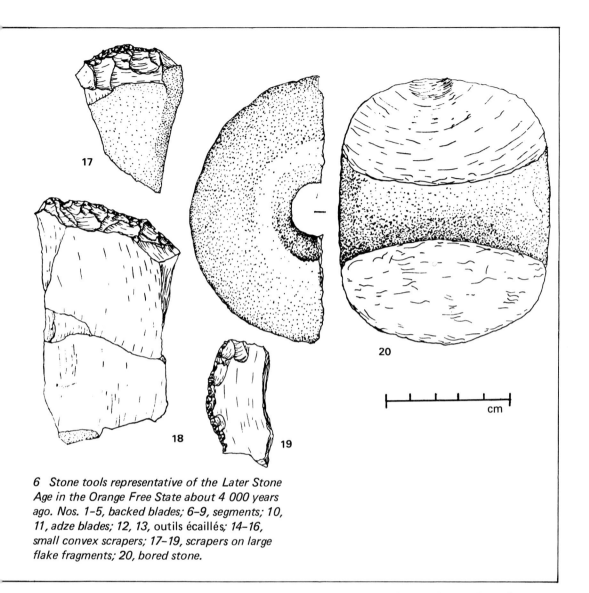

6 Stone tools representative of the Later Stone
Age in the Orange Free State about 4 000 years
ago. Nos. 1–5, backed blades; 6–9, segments; 10,
11, adze blades; 12, 13, outils écaillés; 14–16,
small convex scrapers; 17–19, scrapers on large
flake fragments; 20, bored stone.

upper Orange (fig. 1) came from an area in which
they were accustomed to using pebbles of agate or
chalcedony. In the earlier stages of their settlement
they clung to the use of agate, which could only be
obtained from patches of gravel along the banks of
the Orange. It was carried to sites as much as 60 km
from the river despite the fact that an equally good
raw material, indurated shale, was certainly used
from the outset, but they persisted in their use of the
agate, particularly for small convex scrapers, which
were only slowly abandoned in favour of the more
elongate forms for which the indurated shale was
more suitable.

If the Smithfield industries of the southern parts
of the plateau are more correctly regarded as an extension of the southern Wilton tradition the same is
not necessarily true of areas farther north. The archaeological evidence for the Holocene in the
Transvaal is not extensive and only very provisional
remarks are possible. Mason, in 1962, proposed a
three-fold division of 'Later Stone Age' industries
into Earlier, Middle, and Later Smithfield, following
the 1929 A,B,C, classification of Van Riet Lowe, now
invalidated by Sampson's work in the Orange Free
State. At Uitkomst dates of 9 000 and 9 800 years
ago for a Middle Smithfield occurrence tend to confirm the relationship to Albany suggested by the
presence of large flakes and large scrapers. In the
case of the Transvaal and Orange Free State occurrences an interesting feature is the inclusion of

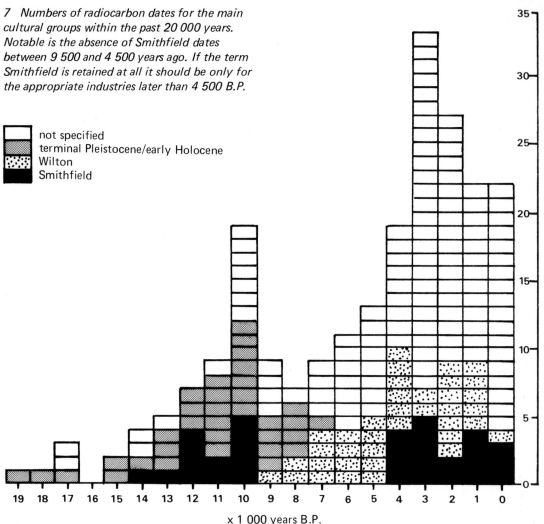

7 Numbers of radiocarbon dates for the main cultural groups within the past 20 000 years. Notable is the absence of Smithfield dates between 9 500 and 4 500 years ago. If the term Smithfield is retained at all it should be only for the appropriate industries later than 4 500 B.P.

□ not specified
▨ terminal Pleistocene/early Holocene
⠿ Wilton
■ Smithfield

number of dates

x 1 000 years B.P.

bored stones in the tool-kit. These were used to weight digging-sticks and suggest an emphasis on the gathering of root stocks or tubers. The associated stone rings (fig. 8) are another and more enigmatic artefact. Neither of these types have been mentioned for the sites in the Cape Folded Mountains and adjacent coastal strip. Similarly early dates have been obtained for what is probably the same kind of industry at Bushman Rock Shelter in the eastern Transvaal (see page 70, fig. 22).

The Later Smithfield of the Transvaal is something altogether different. It approaches much more closely to the old concept of what a Smithfield industry should be: a scraper-based industry lacking in backed tools. Although Smithfield sites are said to be widespread in the Transvaal few have yielded good assemblages from excavated levels. The two main occurrences, and the only ones for

which radiocarbon dates are available, are the caves of Olieboompoort and Magabeng (fig. 1), dated to 870 and 1 020 years ago respectively. What is notable is the complete absence of either segments or backed blades in the Transvaal sites, or indeed pottery, all of which are present in the Orange Free State and the southern Cape within the same time range. Exploration is not sufficiently advanced to allow us to draw any sort of boundary between these two apparently different late Holocene material culture areas, but the evidence does suggest a possible major ethnological division.

Thus far we have considered the evidence, linguistic and archaeological, for major population groupings. But ultimately we are likely to learn more by examining the smaller groupings, within the framework of their territories, which make up the larger. Since the 'Bushmen' represent surviving groups of Holocene hunter–gatherers it is worthwhile to look briefly at what they have to teach us.

Environment and Group Size

Lee and Marshall have described !Kung groups either side of the border between the northern parts of Namibia and Botswana. Plant foods form about 67 per cent of the diet, and of this the nutritious and easily gathered mongongo nuts form about 50 per cent. For most of the year the groups live dispersed in camps by pools not far removed from the sources of the nuts, but in the dry winter season, for a couple of months, they are thrown back on the permanent waterholes, which happen to be further from the groves of nut trees. At this time of year hikes of up to 25 km are sometimes involved in collecting the nuts, and water must be carried. But for the rest of the year they rarely move more than 10 km from their waterhole camp, and except for a few weeks the areas beyond this, though equally rich in plant and animal food, are ignored. Camp may be moved five or six times in the year, but rarely more than 16 to 20 km from the waterhole. The abundance of nutritious vegetable food removes much of the pressure from the hunters, who are described as 'conscientious but not particularly successful'. Many of the smaller and more humble creatures – rodents, snakes, lizards, termites and grasshoppers – are despised by the !Kung. The group size fluctuates considerably from day to day. With men away

hunting or visiting and visitors coming in, the numbers may vary anywhere between twenty-three and forty. The !Kung have found a particularly favourable niche, and whilst the overall population is probably lower, locally the groups of up to forty people are subsisting off a territory of about 250 square kilometres for most of the year. And it is water, not food supply, that inhibits year-round occupation of the same territory. Neither group size and composition nor territory are rigidly defined.

Farther south in the Central Kalahari nature is less generous. The G/wi bands tend to be a little larger, from forty to sixty all told. But like the !Kung they vary continually in size and composition. They are said to be formed of a series of interrelated family circles woven together by a net of kinship ties. In this area food plants and animals are so sparse that the camp must be moved often. Plant foods are still the most important part of the diet, constituting at least 60 per cent even at times of the year when hunting is most productive. At times of plant shortage, in the early summer (September, October, and part of November), the men tend to give up hunting, except with traplines, and help the women with their gathering. At such times the groups split up

8 An unusual feature of the 'Earlier Smithfield' (cf. Albany industry) of the Transvaal are flattish perforated stones with the outer edge ground to a sharp ridge. Often they are too small to have been worn even on a child's wrist.

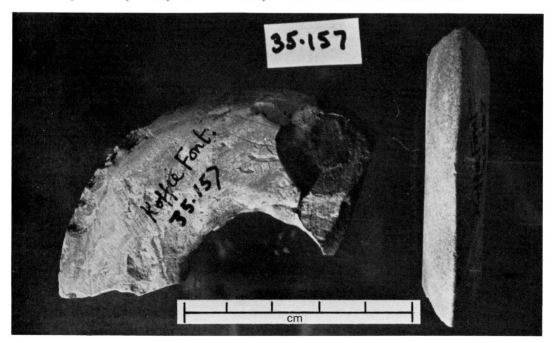

into family units and disperse widely. Rodents, birds, tortoises, snakes, ants and termites are all eaten. Most hunts are limited to day trips by pairs of hunters but occasionally as many as ten or twelve men will set out on a more protracted hunt. The territory is larger, 900 square kilometres for one group of eighty and territorial boundaries are more rigidly defined and respected. Animals are handled carefully so as not to drive them out of the territory.

Immediately we can see from these two examples from adjacent areas of the inland plateau how dramatically behaviour is affected by the particular circumstances of food supply. The size of territory necessary to support the group varies, and so too do proprietary attitudes. The one group leads an easier and more sedentary existence while the other must be more mobile and experience periods of pronounced group fragmentation. Neither group really has the potential for moving seasonally to quite different environmental settings. They are adapted to a single, uniform slice of landscape. The !Kung lead a life of security provided by the mongongo nut, which is available throughout the year, whereas the G/wi experience a two-or three-month period of considerable stress. The switch from bow and arrow to trapline hunting among the G/wi, during the stress months, is clearly reflected in fig. 9 in the complete absence of any of the gregarious plains animals in the months of September, October,

November, and the dramatic increase during that time of the solitary duiker and steenbok. The complete absence of tortoises from the onset of winter to the beginning of summer, presumably when they are hibernating, is a reminder of the possible value of this animal as an indicator of the season of occupation of a site.

Clearly any attempt to understand prehistoric hunter–gatherers of the Holocene will benefit if the archaeologist turns naturalist and looks at his study area in terms of the resources it has to offer at different times of year. Such an approach has underlain several recent research projects in the southwest, south, and south-east Cape. Unfortunately most of these projects are either unpublished or still in progress and only bits and pieces of information are available.

The Cape Folded Mountain belt is an interesting setting in which to conduct this kind of research. Not only does it provide a variety of habitats within the mountains themselves, from high, open ground to densely bushed kloofs and grassy valley bottoms,

9 A record of the number of animals killed by a band of G/wi hunters in an average year, based on field records. Note the sharp increase in duiker and steenbok, taken with traplines during the early summer, and the absence of tortoise in the winter months when this animal is inactive.

Number of Animals Killed by One Band in an Average Year

	J	F	M	A	M	J	J	A	S	O	N	D	TOTAL
giraffe	1												1
kudu		1		1	1						1		4
eland	2	1		1	3	1						1	9
gemsbok	2	4	2	1		4	3	4				3	23
hartebeest			2	1	2	2	2	1				1	11
wildebeest	1		3	2		2	2	1				1	12
springbok	4	2	6	6	4	6	2	4				1	35
duiker	5	4	3	7	2	3	1	2	12	10	12	4	65
steenbok	3	4	3	6	8	2	4	2	8	10	15	3	68
springhare	30	24	28	30	26	22	20	4	3		8	32	227
porcupine			1		1								2
warthog				1									1
fox				4		3	1	3	2	1	4		18
jackal			2			1	2	2	3	4			14
rodents	20	30	30	30	40	20	20	15	15	15	30	30	295
birds	18	22	13	15	6	12	3	12	16	16	20	8	161
tortoises	90	90	80	40							50	90	440
snakes	6	3		8	10	8	2				6	4	47
ants (litres)	0,5	0,5	0,5								0,5	0,5	2,5
termites (litres)	4	2										2	8

but it also offered the hunter completely different environments well within the reach of quite modest seasonal movements. Inland lay the great plains with their herds of antelope and zebra, and in the other direction the sea with its wealth of marine animals. Just how this pattern of variety may have been exploited in the past is the subject of much current research.

Returning for a moment to group or band size, we have noted that the !Kung bands varied a great deal, from twenty-three to forty, and that the G/wi were even larger, reaching sixty or even eighty. The *mean* group size for the !Kung has been given variously as twenty-four and twenty, and whilst comparable figures are not available for the G/wi Silberbauer remarks that the optimum size of permanent groups seems to be between fifty and sixty. For the more southerly regions figures are hard to come by, for few observations were made before the hunters suffered the drastic disturbances of the eighteenth and nineteenth centuries. Schapera, however, reports that groups in the Cape and Namib were much smaller than those in the north. So far as we can tell from contemporary reports of commando raids on the Bushmen of the Karoo, in the eighteenth century, group sizes there varied from five to fifty-five with a mean of about eighteen.

Determining the sizes of prehistoric groups is much more difficult, but some indications are available. Using modern comparative data on floor area and population Parkington has suggested a population of twelve to fifteen people in the cave of De Hangen 220 km north of Cape Town (fig. 1). The estimate is based rather on the area of well-preserved grass bedding (fig. 10), than on the total floor area of the cave, for with caves the occupants have to take what nature offers rather than what they themselves might prefer. But the figure is interesting in view of the information on group sizes in the same general area provided by rock paintings. In fifteen sites in the adjacent mountains Maggs examined twenty paintings which seem to show social groups gathered together in camps, either rock-shelters or in the open, with their bags, quivers, bows etc., hung from the bushes or shelter wall above their heads (fig. 11). The group sizes vary from around five to thirty-five with a mean of thirteen. These highly individualistic paintings occur over a very limited area of 24 by 6 km and if not by the same artist they certainly belong to a localised 'school'. The territory defined is certainly too small to represent the annual 'beat' of a group of this size, but it could well represent the 'core' area used by members or sections of the group, or the whole

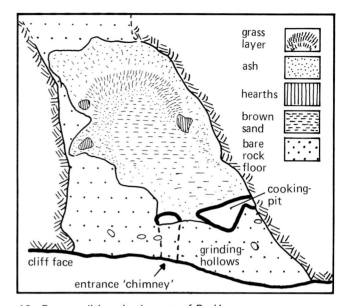

grass
layer

ash

hearths

brown
sand

bare
rock
floor

cooking-
pit

grinding-
hollows

cliff face

entrance 'chimney'

10 Dry conditions in the cave of De Hangen preserved not only wood, leather and twine, but also grass bedding. Grinding of foodstuffs took place on the rock surface near the mouth of the cave, and the natural pit was used as a cooking-place. De Hangen may have been home for a dozen people.

group, during a limited time of the year when the mountains provided a yield that would support them. Similar group sizes are suggested by the Big Elephant Shelter (fig. 12) in the Erongo Mountains of Namibia where the well-preserved internal arrangements point to a group of twelve or fifteen, and by an oral tradition recording the destruction of the last Bushman group of seventeen members in the Longkloof Mountains near Joubertinia in the southern Cape 200 years ago.

Beyond this there is not much to guide us. The evidence, however, suggests that we have to deal with a hierarchy of groups with the family as the smallest and the language family the largest. The natural family of man, wife and children probably rarely exists in isolation, for it is scarcely a viable unit. The smallest group generally recognisable in the archaeological record, the ten to twenty-five group, probably represents the extended family, a two- or three-generation family extended by marriage partners from other groups. But ethnology warns us against viewing these as rigid, unchanging units, and the pattern of flux noted among the G/wi and the !Kung reminds us that other groups joined by a web of kinship populate the landscape. At present we can hardly pretend to be able to define in

any meaningful way any larger, discrete clusterings of groups. Major archaeological discontinuities may reflect boundaries between major language families, but the absence of such discontinuities does not necessarily mean that major groupings did not exist. The distinctions could be masked by the results of parallel or convergent evolution in technology (the evolution of similar artefacts in response to similar problems), as well as through the imperfections of archaeological research.

The Hungry Hunter

A human social group is able to survive only if it achieves a state of equilibrium within its environment. It must be able to obtain enough nourishment to support itself without destroying that on which it depends. A basic requirement for this is that the group should know intimately the re-

11 Paintings such as this one from the south-west Cape provide a vivid impression of the intimacy of a Later Stone Age group 'at home'. Usually the figures are seated, and bags, quivers, bows and sticks are often represented above their heads, as if hung from the branches of trees, or from pegs in the wall of a rock-shelter or cave.

sources of its territory and know to what extent the resources are reliable; what things affect them adversely and what is favourable to them. The strategy of survival normally involves one or more reliable staples which can be supplemented by other kinds of food. The staple is not always the most favoured food in the territory, and it may not even be the most nourishing. It has to be dependable and it has to be capable of sustaining the group. A classic example is the mongongo nut staple of the !Kung.

In practice the hunting of highly mobile game is a precarious way of living. The game is able to range far more widely than man, so there is a high risk that it may not be where it is wanted when it is wanted. It is generally capable of bursts of speed that can take it out of the range of the hunter, and it may be positively dangerous. The rewards, are, of course high. Meat is very nourishing food and it is held in high esteem. But even in landscapes as richly endowed as those of Southern Africa the uncertainties of success probably meant that antelope, zebra, and the large pachyderms never formed the staple diet of prehistoric man.

Immobility or low mobility is a good starting-point, and is a feature of plant-life, or of such creatures as caterpillars, snails, tortoises and certain kinds of shellfish on the coast. It would be easy to construct a scale of food ranked in order of ease of capture, but not all things that are easy to obtain are abundant enough to feed the group for any length of time. It may be, however, that particular areas produce in abundance for short periods regularly and reliably and at different seasons. If so, and this is not

uncommon, the group may sustain itself through the year by moving from one area to another. The movement is never haphazard but is controlled by an intimate knowledge of what is available, where, and at what season. This is not to say that there are not times in the annual cycle when food is scarce, and there may be periods of stress. We have quoted the example of the G/wi. But an understanding of the kinds of strategies possible in a given area, which means a good knowledge of what the plant and animal populations were before farming and industrially based economies altered them, provides a good starting-point for the investigation of the past.

In the south-west Cape such an investigation has grown out of the work by John Parkington in the cave of De Hangen. The cave is formed by the wind erosion of soft parts in a ridge of Table Mountain

12 Plan and section drawing of the three living-units in the Big Elephant rock-shelter in the Erongo mountains, Namibia.

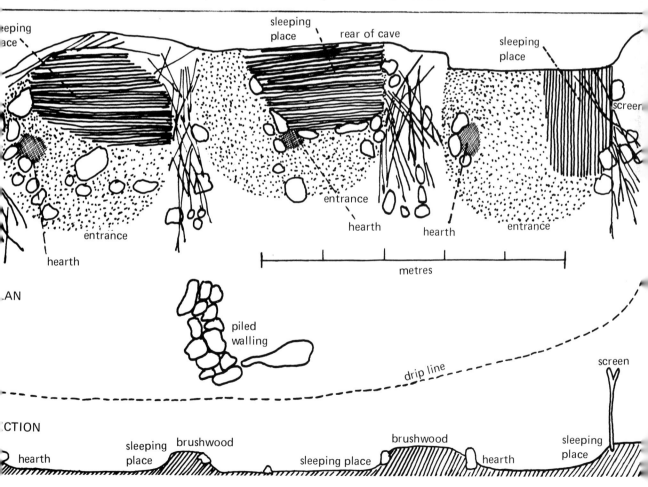

sandstone at the northern end of the Cape Folded Mountains in the south-west Cape (figs. 1 and 10). The mouth opens in the face of a low cliff, about 3 m above its foot, and is entered through a chimney-like opening lower down. On the right-hand side (facing into the cave) is a natural trough-shaped pit whose hearths and food debris declare it to have been a focal point for food preparation. Across the mouth of the cave, where the rock floor comes to the surface, are a number of polished and slightly dished grinding surfaces. The rock floor is uneven and rises to the surface at the front, the back, and on the east side. A broad arc of grass bedding rests directly on the bedrock towards the back and sides of the cave. Within this is a spread of ash, within which three more distinct hearths are visible. A thin layer of brown sand (disintegrated bedrock) partly underlies the ash and partly masks the slope down to the pit. The dry atmosphere of the cave had preserved not only the grass bedding, but an abundance of pieces of wood, bone, shell, ivory, reed, string, leather.

Among the abundant plant remains (bulbs, leaves, seeds and twigs), four species common in the deposit were represented by flowers which could only have been gathered from October to December, indicating a summer occupation of the site. Although a wide range of animal species was present in small numbers two species provide additional support for a summer occupation. Tortoises occur in large numbers, and dassies (hyrax) are also abundant. The pattern of tooth eruption in the dassies indicated that most of them must have been caught in summer, though a few may have been winter deaths. As among the G/wi (fig. 9) the tortoises suggest a summer occupation. Some sort of contact with the coast, 60 km away, is suggested by small quantities of marine shell, presumably brought in as raw material for beads or pendants. These include several halves of black mussel shells wrapped in a large lily leaf, and tied with string

From the point of view of comfort the spring and early summer seems intuitively to be the ideal time to live in this north-facing cave, for the winters are cold, draughty and damp, and the late summer is hot and dry. Abundant among the edible bulbs of the iris family are three species which reach maximum development in early summer (October) and then quickly die off above ground, leaving little or no clue as to the existence of the bulb. Parkington suggests that the edible bulbs and fruits formed the dependable staple of the group, and that in the absence of an obvious winter substitute the group must have wintered elsewhere. There would seem to be little advantage in moving east into the Karoo, where plant foods would be similarly scarce in winter, but a trek to the westward would take them to the sea shore where marine molluscs could replace the plants as a reliable, easily collected staple.

In an attempt to test this hypothesis attention was turned to the coastal cave at Elands Bay. Here conditions are very different. The cave deposits are very deep, covering upwards of 11 000 years, and only the uppermost deposits correspond to De Hangen. The cave is situated part way up a steep, rocky ascent overlooking several hundred metres of intertidal rocks, the home of dense colonies of limpets and mussels. Numerous sea birds nest along the cliffs, and it seems likely that seals occupied a rookery on one of the rocky shelves. Immediately to the north is the outlet of a freshwater vlei (lagoon) stretching inland for 25 km and several hundred metres wide near the mouth. Northwards is a line of coastal dunes behind which the sandveld stretches back towards the mountains. With such a variety of habitats Elands Bay must have been a most attractive area for occupation.

Plant remains are well preserved in the uppermost deposits, but only a handful of bulbs were found, suggesting that the collection of plant foods was a minor activity. On the other hand the range of animal remains is far greater than at De Hangen, and marine forms clearly predominate (fig. 13). Shellfish were eaten in quantity as were sea birds, fish, rock-lobsters and seals. Sea-grass from the vlei took the place of grass for bedding, as in most coastal caves where vegetation is preserved.

An important part of the Elands Bay investigation was the search for information on the season of occupation. Because Parkington's research project, (which involves the study of a number of sites and habitats from the coast to the interior) is still in progress, only preliminary results are available. The most promising guide to the season of occupation so far published seems to lie in the seal remains. A careful comparison of the sixteen mandibles recovered with a large series of known ages in the South African Museum showed that all sixteen belonged to young seals (yearlings), 4 to 10 months old. There are no adults, and no black pups (0-4 months). Since births take place during a short and sharply defined period from mid-November to mid-December the site must have been occupied sometime during the period early March to late August (fig. 14).

Unfortunately the evidence says nothing about other times of year. The absence of black pups may mean simply that seals were hunted selectively; that yearlings were taken shortly before they left

Animal Remains from Elands Bay Cave and De Hangen

MAMMALS	EBC	De H	REPTILES/AMPHIBIANS	EBC	De H
hedgehog	1		tortoise	**	313
other insectivora	**		lizard		*
baboon	3	1	snake		*
jackal	2	1	frog		*
mongoose	1	8			
caracal	2		BIRDS		
seal	24		cormorant (4 species)	147	
dassie	9	64	penguin	37	
hippo	1		gannet	5	
duiker	8	1	albatross	*	
klipspringer		3	petrels (2 species)	*	
grysbok/steenbok	21	6	gulls (2 species)	*	
springbok		1	terns	*	
equid species		1	flamingoes	*	
bontebok	2		pelicans	*	
hartebeest	3		ducks	*	
eland		1	coot	*	
buffalo	1		kite	*	
sheep/goat	1	1	bustard	*	
domestic cattle		1	crows/raven	*	
hare	4	6	francolin/guinea fowl	*	1
dune mole	3				
porcupine	1	1	FISH etc		
unspecified viverrid		2	freshwater fish		*
genet		2	white steenbras	76	
honey badger		1	white stumpnose	23	
gerbil		*	kabeljou	4	
dormouse		*	dassie	10	
shrew		*	elf	5	
unspecified rodents	**		snoek	1	
rat		*	kingklip	1	
cetacean	1		sea barbel	3	
			haarder	4	
			hottentot	2	
			rock lobster	865	
			marine molluscs	very abundant	very rare

* present   ** common

13   The list for De Hangen is complete; that for Elands Bay Cave represents the deposits falling approximately within the time-range of De Hangen (i.e. within the past 1 500 years). It must be noted that even within this time-range the deposits at Elands Bay Cave were much more extensive, and to this extent probably give a more complete view of the meat eaten than do the remains from De Hangen. Clearly the marine environment offered a far greater range of animal foods than the mountains; it may have offered as much or more in the way of plant foods also. The lists do not tell us how much *meat* the inhabitants ate, for we do not know how many people were involved nor what the duration of occupation was at either of the sites. They do, however, give us a good impression of the variety of meat eaten and the relative abundance of particular items.

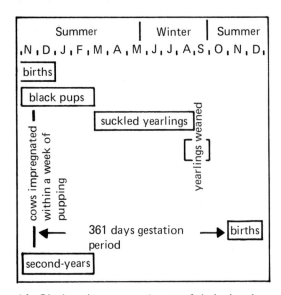

Summary bar chart showing the seal breeding cycle across the months (N D J F M A M J J A S O N D), labelled Summer | Winter | Summer, with categories: births, black pups, suckled yearlings, yearlings weaned, cows impregnated within a week of pupping, 361 days gestation period, births, second-years.

14 *Black seal pups spend most of their time in the rookery, where they are suckled daily by the cows. Yearlings take to the water but return to the rookery each night, and are suckled by the cows which return every few days for this purpose. By August/September the yearlings are weaned because the cows are now in an advanced state of pregnancy, and the yearlings take more fully to the water to feed themselves. By October the rookery is virtually deserted. At the beginning of November the bulls establish bases on the rookery to which the cows come to give birth. Within a few days mating takes place and the cycle begins again. The presence of yearling seal bones only could indicate limited winter occupation of a site, or they could represent the principal casualties washed ashore from offshore rookeries, in an archaeological site occupied throughout the year.*

the rookery because this was the stage at which they yielded the maximum return while still easy to kill. Alternatively, if the rookery was on rocky islets rather than on the mainland, the yearlings might simply represent the washed-up corpses of casualties which always occur among the young seals when they take to the sea. The initial argument for group transhumance between the interior and the coast played on the role of shellfish as an easily collectable staple during the months when plant foods were scarce. That shellfish were collected systematically is indicated by the vast heaps of shells that occur in cave and open sites throughout the length of the coastal strip. But Parkington argued that in the south-west Cape shellfish would be more likely to be collected during the winter months than during summer as the filter feeders (the bivalved molluscs) are sometimes rendered poisonous by tiny marine organisms that occasionally drift inshore in multitudes, colouring the sea quite red. The 'red tides' are most commonly a spring or summer phenomenon, and the shellfish may remain poisonous for up to four months.

However, it is hard to argue for an exclusively winter occupation in view of the large numbers of tortoises which at De Hangen were used to support the notion of a summer occupation. As a matter of fact it is hard to escape the conclusion that whilst the pickings might have been lean enough during the winter months around De Hangen to induce a seasonal migration, at Elands Bay the living might have been good all year round. The hypothesis of an annual 'beat' crossing the grain of the country to take in a variety of habitats from coast to Karoo is an attractive one and we shall undoubtedly know more about is as research progresses. But at present we must admit that the available evidence does not clinch the matter.

At the opposite end of the Cape Folded Mountains, in the eastern Cape, the investigation of several sites within the mountain ranges raises similarly interesting questions as to subsistence and seasonal migration. At Melkhoutboom, H. Deacon has recorded what he describes as a 'dramatic change' from the hunting of large, gregarious grazers to dependence on non-migratory, solitary browsers about 7 500 years ago, corresponding to the replacement of the Albany industry by the Wilton. With this very important change in hunting behaviour he has found abundant evidence at several sites for the systematic collection of a variety of root-stocks (bulbs, corms and tubers). Several species are involved, but the most abundant are watsonias, followed by hypoxis and moraea. Little is known about the use of hypoxis, but both watsonia and moraea are known to be valuable food plants, the former being much sought after by baboons. Watsonias in particular occur abundantly in large stands, and remain visible, and therefore collectable, throughout most of the year. But there seems to be a period of two or three months in the winter when the bulb is providing nourishment for the growth of the plant, and is either unpalatable or less nutritious, or both, and may not have been any use. Certainly in the Cape Point reserve there is a two-month period when the baboons stop eating watsonias.

Deacon is in no doubt that the plant foods, and watsonia in particular, represent the staple element in the diet on which the groups placed their reliance. The response to the stress months when some bulbs were hard to find and others were perhaps not very nourishing, may have lain, as Parkington suggested for the western Cape, in movement to the coast in winter. That this might have happened is suggested by the presence of small but persistent quantities of marine shells in the Wilton levels at both the type site and at Melkhoutboom. The shell represents raw material brought back for the manufacture of pendants (fig. 15), but one way or another it reflects contact with the coastal environment. Of course this does not in itself prove seasonal movement to the coast, for the shell may have been traded up from the coast. But it has been suggested that a tendency for the replacement, with the passage of time, of the marine shell by the local freshwater mussel provides support for the seasonal movement to the coast and reflects the gradual loss or abandonment of the coastal niche. More will be said of this presently.

Towards the end of the Melkhoutboom occupation a new edible bulb species *Cyperus usitatus*, the 'water uintjes' of the early Dutch settlers, makes its appearance. It is also recorded at one or two other late Wilton sites in the mountain region. North of the Cape Folded Mountains, in the dry Cape Midlands area, we have seen that occupation begins late in the Holocene, about 4 500 years ago, after a hiatus of several thousand years. Although the en-

15 *Pendants from Nelson Bay Cave made of sea shell. Similar pendants were found at the inland site of Melkhoutboom.*

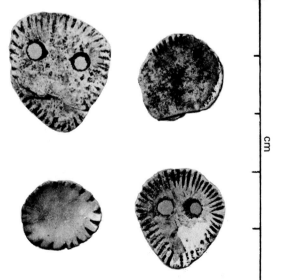

vironmental setting is very different from the Cape Folded Mountains the food remains from Highlands (fig. 1) suggest that the subsistence base was very similar. Some plains animals are found, as one would expect from the setting, but it is the small solitary antelopes that are more consistently represented. Edible bulbs again appear to represent the staple food, though the species are different from those in the mountains. This dry landscape is the ideal home of the ostrich and its eggs were systematically collected, while freshwater mussels and crabs, termites, and ground game added variety to the diet.

The setting of the Highlands site is reminiscent of the territory of the G/wi and, as with the G/wi, it seems unlikely that the Highlands population and others around them had much scope for a seasonal movement to relieve the stress months when bulbs were few and less nourishing. That they did not shift southwards to the Cape Folded Mountains in winter is apparent from the contrasts in the stone implement traditions which, whilst possibly evolving from a similar base, have developed in different directions. Deacon tells us that the tool classes are functionally similar, but that they are very different stylistically. The northern margin of the Cape Folded Mountains is a clear example of the kind of boundary which in all probability separates peoples of distinctly different language groups.

Deacon has suggested that the Wilton groups of the eastern Cape mountains could probably have maintained a year-round occupation from a single site, despite the suggestion of a seasonal movement. It could be argued for these mountain groups, as for the inhabitants of the interior, that they simply tightened their belts and intensified their search for plant foods during the lean months. The hunting of non-migratory, small antelopes is most economically carried out with the aid of traplines, and the process need not be seriously interrupted if the men were required to turn to more mundane persuits for two or three months of the year. Of course, one way to cope with a season of shortage is to store food. The nineteenth-century historian Stow reports that certain bulbs were crushed and dried, and would then keep for a long time. He also reports, though without specific evidence, that some Bushman tribes formerly collected grass seeds to be kept for the winter months, and also that locusts, collected at times of swarming, might be dried, crushed, and stored in a dry place in skin bags for future use. Schapera also describes how the Nama, if faced with an occasional surfeit of meat, would cut it into thin strips and hang it on the branches of trees to dry

16　*Fragment of a grindstone, and a rubbing-stone. The latter is dimpled to help catch and turn the material being ground.*

naturally in the air. Meat dried in this way may be kept for years, and is excellent eating.

The archaeological evidence for such behaviour would be very difficult to identify. Grinding-hollows have been mentioned at De Hangen, and dished grindstones and pitted upper grindstones (fig. 16) are a fairly standard component of Holocene settlement sites. These, however, are used for the preparation of food for immediate consumption and are not in themselves proof of preparation for storage. More promising are undoubted storage pits found by Deacon at both Melkhoutboom and Boomplaas. About a dozen were found at Melkhoutboom and upwards of sixty at Boomplaas. They vary from 23 to 40 cm in diameter and 15 to 35 cm in depth. At Boomplaas about twenty such pits were found well down in the Wilton levels (at around 6 400 years ago), but most belong to the post-climax Wilton, about 2 000 years ago. The later pits are lined with grass, or with layers of leaves from a large, poisonous lily, and grass, and they are often capped or marked with one, two, or three flat slabs of stone. At Boomplaas four such stones had been painted, two with antelope, one with an ostrich, and one was indecipherable. The older pits at Boomplaas are unlined. Although a variety of plant remains survive, in some of the pits the commonest are fruits of three species said to be not very palatable, but with kernels rich in oil known to have been extracted and used by the Khoisan for anointing the skin. Whether these were the only things stored in the pits is unknown, and certainly fragments of edible-bulb leaves were found in at least one of the pits at Melkhoutboom. It is evidence which at least suggests the possibility that plant foods were stored to help cope with the lean season, and that such sites may have been used intermittently or continuously throughout the year.

There is, however, a piece of evidence which encourages continuation of the search for evidence of seasonal migration. An oral tradition surviving among the farmers of a remote valley in the

Longkloof mountains of the southern Cape describes the pattern of movement of a group of 'Bushmen' finally exterminated 200 years ago. This small group of seventeen men, women and children occupied a cave in the Baviaanskloof during the winter and moved to the Tzitzikamma coast for two months in the summer. The periods in between were spent based on caves in the Kouga River valley between the two. The tradition is important not only as an example of seasonal migration, but because it explicitly refers to a summer residence at the coast. It will be recalled that the proposed pattern for the south-west Cape was for a winter occupation of the coast, and the same is implied for any possible movement by the Melkhoutboom inhabitants. Recent study of the oxygen isotope content of seasonal growth layers in marine shells from Nelson Bay Cave also indicates that they were collected in winter.

But if we have an apparent conflict here it probably results from the temptation to look for simple solutions. The coast has many attractions to offer and these surely include plant foods as well as meat, and there may have been a variety of reasons for inland groups visiting the coast. If there was a risk of mussel poisoning in the summer months then shellfish may have been left alone, by visitors as much as by permanent residents. The stimulus to move might result either from a diminution of supply in the area temporarily abandoned, or from the appearance of some abundant or favoured food in the area of attraction. Shellfish are an obvious, abundant, and easily gathered food supply, but there are plenty of others. At Nelson Bay Cave well over a dozen species of fish were taken, some in great quantity. At Bonteberg on the Cape Peninsula crayfish were collected in substantial numbers. At least six species of whale inhabit the southern oceans and some at least are familiar visitors to the coastal waters. The Southern Right whale comes close inshore for calving in June and July (midwinter) and strandings are not uncommon. Early travellers from Europe often remarked on the avidity with which whales were hacked up and consumed, and whale and dolphin bones are not infrequent in coastal sites. There is a beautiful representation of a whale on a painted stone from the Knysna District (fig. 17), while one of the painted stones from Klasies River Mouth shows what appear to be four dolphins (fig. 18). Penguin eggs may be found at any season but are most common in summer, at which time the eggs or young of a variety of other sea birds also are available.

The Middle Stone Age inhabitants of Klasies River

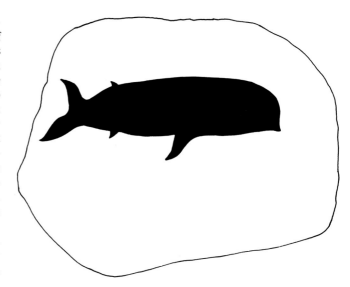

17 A splendid painting of a whale on a water-worn block of stone from a coastal cave near Knysna. The stone is approximately 30 cm long.

18 Painted stone from Klasies River Mouth. The animals appear to be dolphins.

Mouth were certainly securing part of their food supply from the coast. Seals, whales, dolphins, shellfish, and numerous penguins are all represented, although there are very few bones of flying seabirds or fish. But with the establishment of the Wilton culture within the coastal strip, exploitation of the marine resources appears to be on a completely different and altogether more professional footing. Fish and seabirds which eluded the earlier populations occur in deposits in great variety and greatly increased numbers, particularly in the case of fish. The enormous quantities of small fish found in some of the middens at Nelson Bay Cave suggest that they were being netted or trapped in tidal pools. Not infrequently in the summer months the upwel-

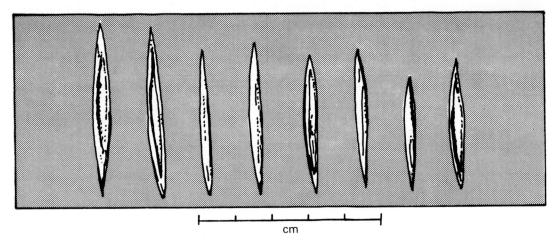

cm

19 Fish gorges

ling of cold water stuns huge quantities of fish, which can then simply be collected as they wash ashore. But other devices were in use. In a cave at the mouth of the Storms River and at Nelson Bay Cave, fish remains include those of red roman, a fish not affected by cold water upwell, and which does not come into shallow water. Such fish must almost certainly have been taken by line and hook or fish-gorge (fig. 19). Grooved sinkers (fig. 20) have been found in abundance at Nelson Bay Cave and two were found in an open midden site near the Storms River mouth. Identifiable fish-hooks have so far been reported only from sites in eastern Lesotho, but double-ended bone points that may have served as gorges have been reported from Elands Bay Cave and Nelson Bay Cave. In fact certain kinds of fish spine or even thorns might have made serviceable hooks which, even if they survived, might not be recognisable as such. Fishing as an activity was by no means restricted to the coast, for paintings of fishing scenes occur at several localities in the Drakensberg and at one in Rhodesia. Both lines and spears were used, and in the Drakensberg paintings of boats or rafts are depicted (fig. 21). Fish are represented in engravings even in the heart of the Karoo (fig. 22).

The combination of food remains, environment and artefacts reveals for us in a remarkable way the confidence and success with which the Holocene hunter and his womenfolk provided for the group. Plant fibres were spun into fine cordage which could be used as needed for traplines and bindings, or worked into fine, strong nets for catching or carrying. Wood was used with simple skill for pegs to keep things off the ground in cave or rockshelter, for arrowheads and bows, for digging-sticks and tool handles. Reeds were cut for arrow-shafts or woven into mats. Time, skill and taste were brought to the

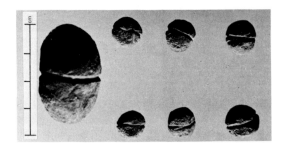

20 Grooved pellets of shale from Nelson Bay Cave, believed to have been used as sinkers for fishing-lines. Similar sinkers were reported by the Deacons from a site at the mouth of the Storms River, farther east on the south coast.

fashioning of beads and pendants and objects of bone, shell, and ivory at whose use we can only guess (fig. 24).

In all this we see evidence of masterly adaptation to the environment. But if most of the activities witnessed appear as individual efforts we are left with one that is surely communal, and which more than any other speaks of the group providing for all its members. For a thousand miles, from St. Helena Bay in the west to Kosi Bay in the east, in numerous places where the right conditions occur, tidal fish-traps have been built of large boulders. These may consist of a simple wall closing the outlet of a natural gulley or rock-pool, or of entirely artificial enclosures built out in great loops across the intertidal ledge (fig. 25). For the latter the conditions required are a gently sloping surface well strewn with boulders large enough to resist the scouring of the waves and small enough to be moved by human muscle power. Within such a situation boulders may be

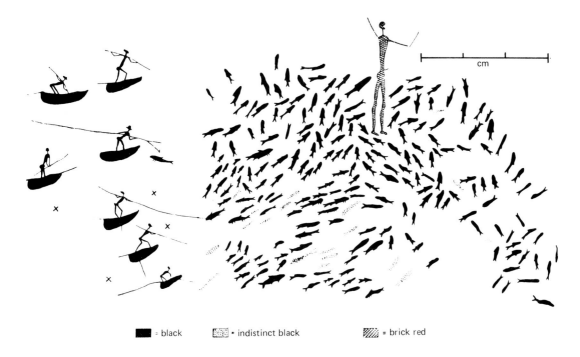

■ = black   ▦ = indistinct black   ▨ = brick red

21 A painting depicting fishing with spears from boats or rafts. From Mpongweni Mountain in south-western Lesotho.

cleared from a central area to create a large pool, and piled up to provide a broad, strong surrounding wall. The height is critical, for it must be such as to be covered by up to a metre of water at high tide. Fish enter the pools at high tide to feed and are trapped as the tide recedes. Traps may consist of a single enclosed pool, but commonly several occur together, and in at least one as many as nine sizeable enclosures occur in a single, joined complex.

So effective are the traps that some are still maintained and used by local inhabitants. They are said to be effective only for a few days during spring tides, and operate best when covered by high tide at night, preferably a dark night. The sea should be neither too calm nor too rough and there is evidence to suggest that the summer months are more productive than the winter.

But under ideal conditions the catches may be enormous. Few figures are available but in in one recorded sequence of catches over a three-month period, February to April, over 2 000 kg were taken, over 400 kg in a single catch.

The dating of the traps is based on information as

22 Engraving of a fish near De Aar, in the heart of the Karoo.

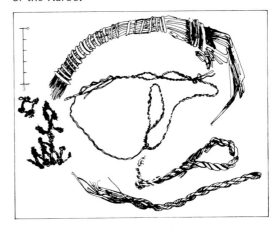

23 Netting from Melkhoutboom and various fibre articles from De Hangen.

113

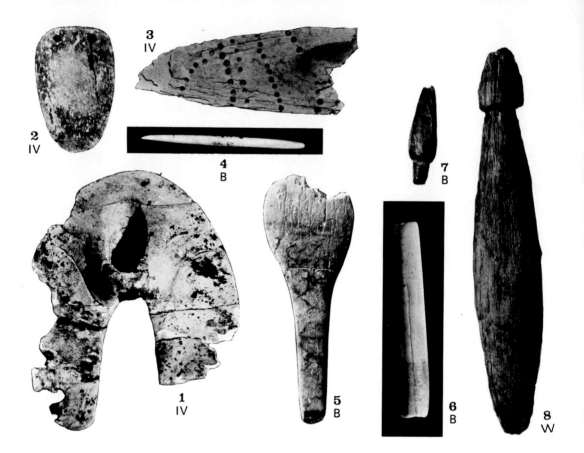

24 Bone, wood, and ivory were used for a wide range of tools, weapons and ornaments throughout the past 8 000 years. Nos. 1, 2, and 6, probably personal ornaments; 3, part of a knife; 4 and 7, arrow-heads; 8, missile head; 5, unknown. iv = ivory, b = bone, w = wood.

to when the sea stabilised at its present level, and this seems to have been between 5 000 and 3 000 years ago. Between 5 000 and 6 000 years ago the sea may have been only about one metre lower than at present, and many of the traps could have been operable from as much as 5 000 years ago, or more. Whether older traps exist under water and farther out is not at present known, but the traps appear to be a phenomenon of the Holocene. The amount of labour involved in maintaining the traps and their potential as a source of food might suggest that they were the property of groups that resorted regularly to them as part of a seasonal beat, or who may even have dwelled permanently at the coast. Whatever their position within the economy of the people who built them they are a truly remarkable achievement in the exploitation of natural re-

sources. They are the coastal counterpart of the pit-fall traps and fences used by hunters of the interior.

Signs of Change

Our knowledge of the interior during the Holocene is far less perfect and detailed than for the Cape mountains and adjacent coast. We have seen that for the earlier part of the Holocene the drier areas may have been very sparsely populated if indeed they were not quite empty. But we have no reason to believe that, apart from differing adaptations, man was any less successful in other areas than he was in the south; though undoubtedly nature was less generous in the more marginal environments. Within the time period 7 000 to 3 000 years ago we find evidence of sophisticated and successful populations employing with confidence a wide range of skills to support themselves in their chosen, or inherited territories. For some there may have been hard times when food was short, but rarely would it fail completely. For others life must have come close to ideal in terms of security. With a

25 *Part of an inter-tidal fish-trap complex at Still Bay, on the south coast.*

million and a half years of experience behind him man had reached the highest points of success in the evolution of the hunting–gathering way of life in Southern Africa. But changes were only a step away.

To illustrate this, we must turn once again to the southern Cape sites. By 2 270 years ago in the Wilton type site there were signs that the culture represented there had passed its climax and was changing. In her analysis of the uppermost levels (the death/birth phase) Janette Deacon remarks, 'The increased variance in the norms of scraper manufacture and the apparent disintegration of the cohesive factors governing artefact manufacture would seem to typify a cultural system in decline. . . . Inventories show a small variety of tool types with the complete absence of adzes and very few backed tools. . . . Pottery makes its first appearance.' Somewhere between 4 860 and 2 270 years ago the amount of sea shell reaching the site shows a marked decline, and the local freshwater mussel takes its place. Fifty kilometres away, at Melkhoutboom, the story is almost exactly the same, within virtually the same time-span. If anything, the

change to post-climax may be rather more closely dated to around 2 870 years ago. At Nelson Bay Cave, on the south coast, the Wilton levels are overlain by several feet of shell middens containing a very un-Wilton-like industry, which may represent the local expression of post-climax Wilton or something even farther along the path of change. The excavations at Nelson Bay Cave took place in two adjacent areas which have not yet been linked, and the precise details and dating of the transition from Wilton are not known. But dates from the post-climax levels indicate that classic Wilton had been superseded at least 3 000 years ago.

In discussing the evidence from the Wilton type site Janette Deacon hinted at a possible connection between the pottery in upper levels and paintings of fat-tailed sheep on the shelter walls. She posed the question whether the death/birth phase at the end of the sequence did not reflect the final disruption of the old hunter–gatherer society by the introduction of pastoralism into the area. She also suggested that

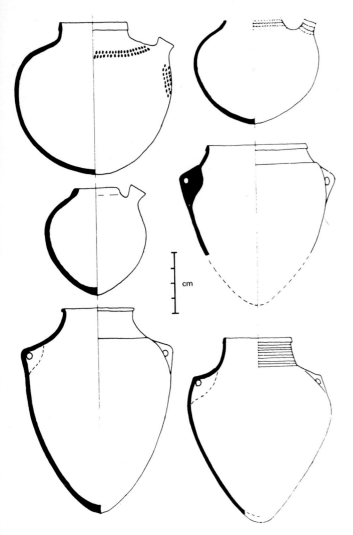

26 *Examples of pottery from L.S.A. midden sites on the south coast, at Jeffrey's Bay. The pointed bases, spouts and lugs are characteristic. It seems that pottery of this kind was made and used on the south coast more than 2 000 years ago, and may have been introduced together with sheep, and perhaps dogs.*

the shift from marine to freshwater shells in the post-climax phase at the site might reflect an interruption of coastal contact, with the implication that as yet unrecognised population movements might be responsible.

Until a few years ago pottery, which was well known from numerous coastal sites (approximately 150) and from a much smaller number of inland sites, was completely undated. The explanation for the existence of the pottery was, for many years, that Khoi pastoralists had migrated from East Africa, bringing, along with livestock, the characteristic pointed-based pottery, sometimes with lugs and spouts, similar to pottery known from parts of Kenya. But despite some similarities there are important differences in the details of the pottery from these widely separated areas, and nothing like either is known from the thousands of square miles

that separate them. With the advent of radiocarbon dating the supposed ancestral pottery in East Africa was shown to date to the sixteenth century A.D.; far too late to fit into the concept of a Khoi migration. In fact there are no good reasons for regarding the Khoi-speakers as other than part of the indigenous populations of Southern Africa in the Holocene. Both physical anthropological evidence and linguistic evidence favour a southern origin for the historical 'Hottentot' peoples, who would simply have formed part of the prehistoric substratum of hunter–gatherers. Not only are some hunter–gatherer groups of the Kalahari pure 'Hottentot'-speakers, but there is good evidence that groups of 'Bushmen' living along the Riet River at the beginning of the nineteenth century had been practising pastoralists for several centuries. It seems that by the time of the first European records, in the fifteenth and sixteenth centuries, some hunter–gatherers had adopted pastoralism as a way of life. Just when and how this happened is one of the most fascinating problems still to be resolved in South African prehistory.

One key to the problem lies in the dating of the earliest sheep (or cattle) remains, and the appearance of pottery may in some way be associated. Pottery, because of its weight and fragility, is something we do not expect hunter–gatherers to bother with, since they have to hump all their possessions around on their own backs. At the time of first European contact in the fifteenth century the pastoralists were accustomed to using their cattle not only for packing their household effects, including the poles and mat coverings of their houses, and pottery, but also for riding. It is not surprising then that pottery has generally been thought of as a hallmark of the pastoralists. It is not proven but it is conceivable that hunters, who had achieved a virtually sedentary existence in favourable situations such as the coast must often have offered, may have invented pottery or adopted it from others.

In fact both pottery and sheep turn out to be much older in Later Stone Age contexts on the south coast than anyone would have supposed a few years ago. At Bonteberg on the Cape Peninsula a radiocarbon date of 100 B.C. exists for a layer with pottery. To the

116

north, at Elands Bay Cave it is present early in the fifth century A.D. Eighty and a hundred kilometres to the east, at Hawston and Die Kelders, it belongs in the second half of the first century A.D. At Nelson Bay Cave it is probably present from the early part of the first century. Inland, where the pottery is of a completely different kind, the earliest dates seem to be much later; at present no earlier than the early thirteenth century A.D.

Sheep make their appearance at about the same time: early first century A.D. at Nelson Bay Cave, the second half of the first century at Hawston, and third to fourth century at Pearly Beach and Die Kelders. It certainly looks as if there is a real connection between the appearance of sheep and pottery. But cattle are notably absent. That paintings of sheep but not cattle occur in Namibia and the south-west Cape lends support to the conclusion that sheep were herded in the south before cattle. The art of painting remained vigorous and naturalistic well into the nineteenth century in the Drakensberg and the eastern Cape, and cattle are represented there. In the south-west Cape painting seems to have been a dying art in the seventeenth and eighteenth centuries, and it could be that the advent of cattle-herding in this area corresponded with, if it did not contribute to, the cessation of painting.

We do not know if the dates we have for pottery and sheep in the south and south-west Cape are the oldest that there are. The search has only been on for a few years, and excavation and analysis of material proceed slowly. But it is remarkable that almost every site examined in this area within the past few years has yielded pottery or sheep or both where its deposits span the period 3 000 to 1 000 years ago. It seems inescapable that pastoralism and new technologies had spread into the southern Cape region by the turn of the Christian Era. What is most intriguing is that these events seem to have nothing to do with the development of Iron Age farming communities far to the north in the interior of Africa. This is an argument which cannot be developed fully until the next chapter. For the time being, however, we may note that the introduction of domestic livestock into the traditional territory of the hunter, at least 2 000 years ago, marked the beginning of a relentless destruction, still continuing, of a way of life that had supported man in Southern Africa for upwards of a million years.

New Ways of Living

New Peoples and New Skills

'The dress of these Kaffirs is a mantle of ox-hide . . . They are shod with two or three soles of raw leather . . . secured to the feet with straps . . . In their hands they carry the tail of an ape or a fox . . . with which they clean themselves and shade their eyes when observing. This dress is used by almost all the negroes of Kaffraria, and their kings and chiefs wear, hanging to the left ear, a copper ornament made after their own fashion. These and all other Kaffirs are herdsmen and cultivators of the ground, by means of which they subsist . . . Of the same grain (millet) they make wine . . . which, when it has fermented in a vessel of clay . . . they drink with great enjoyment. Their cattle are very fat, tender, well-flavoured, and large . . . They use milk and the butter they make from it. They live in small villages, in huts made of reed mats . . . They obey chiefs whom they call Ancosses. The language is the same in nearly all Kaffraria, the difference being only like that between the different dialects of Italy and the ordinary dialects of Spain. . . . They value the most necessary metals, as iron and copper, and for very small pieces of either they will barter cattle.'

So wrote one of the survivors of the Portuguese ship *Santo Alberto*, which was wrecked in October 1622 somewhere not far from the Mbashe River on the south-east coast. His and other accounts by shipwreck survivors and early travellers focus attention on a number of important facts, all of which indicate peoples very different from the yellow-skinned hunters and herders met with elsewhere on the south and south-west coast (see chapter 4, fig. 2). The chief who, 'with about sixty negroes', greeted the survivors was 'of good stature, well made, of cheerful countenance, and not very black'. Such flattering remarks were never made of the 'Bosjesmans' or 'Hottentots', who were considered too ugly, almost, to be human, and were never well made or of cheerful countenance! These new people were 'negroes' and that was a term already well associated with dark-skinned Africans farther north in Africa, especially in West Africa. They not only kept cattle but also tilled the soil; a practice quite unknown among the 'Hottentots'. They used pottery and metals, and whilst the record quoted suggests that metals were rare and highly valued the same was not true farther north. South of Cape Cor-

rentes, Vasco da Gama described the use of tin for dagger hilts and sheaths, iron for spear blades, and an abundance of copper. The name given to the chiefs (Ancosses) is the same as the modern term 'Nkosi' used by the Nguni peoples. We are told of a wide-spread group of dialects apparently belonging to a single language-family, and others had noted that these were 'not so badly pronounced' as those of the 'Bushmen' and 'Hottentots'. Clearly we have to deal with peoples who were culturally and linguistically distinct from the yellow-skinned hunters and herders. Their way of life constitutes a complete contrast to that of the Holocene hunters with whom we were concerned in the last chapter, and it is our task now to enquire about these peoples and to try to ascertain when and how their new ways of living first began to alter the age-old habits of the hunter–gatherers.

Once linguistic studies were far enough advanced, in the later nineteenth century, it became apparent that the metal-using, mixed-farming Negroes of the south-east corner of the continent were part of a great complex of peoples occupying the major part of the continent from 34° south to 4° north of the equator, all speaking closely related

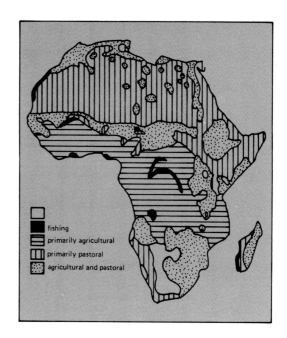

2 *The main types of subsistence economy in Africa.*

languages which linguists christened Bantu (fig. 1). Apart from speaking related languages it quickly became apparent that they had other things in common also. Despite some variation from place to place, all shared the more obvious Negro physical features of dark skin, woolly hair, thick lips, low bridge to the nose, and a tendency for the lower part of the face to project forwards somewhat (prognathism). There was, however, a widespread but ill-defined notion that the Bantu-speaking Negroes showed these features to a less extreme degree than the Negroes north of the 'Bantu line' and might, therefore, be a separate race. Everywhere there was a knowledge of the smelting and smithing of metals, though there was variability. Some were renowned iron-workers, others tended to be users rather than manufacturers, and there was much variability geographically in the working of such metals as tin, gold, copper, and brass. Some of this variability is certainly explicable in terms of the distribution of natural ores and the occurrence of alluvial or vein gold. In the case of farming, despite any cultural preferences, environmental factors such as rainfall, soils and temperature must have played an important part. But even in those areas where cattle were much prized some agriculture was always present (fig. 2). Pottery, which occurred as a rare commodity in the later part of the Later Stone Age, and among the historically observed Khoi, was abun-

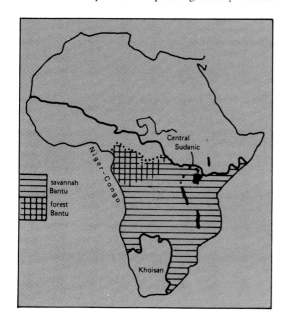

1 *The Bantu languages form a part of the Niger-Congo language family. The 'savannah Bantu' languages are thought to derive from proto-Bantu languages originally limited to the equatorial forest region. The surviving 'forest Bantu' languages form a group separable from 'savannah Bantu'.*

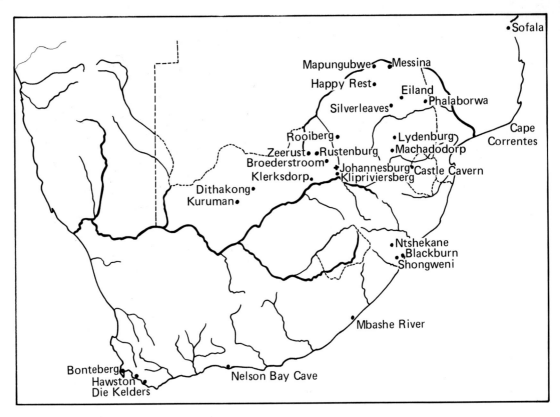

3 Sites and principal places mentioned in this chapter.

dant and in daily use among the Bantu-speakers. Huge pots were used for fetching water and for brewing beer, smaller pots for cooking or for containing milk, and a wide variety of open bowls for serving relishes.

It is small wonder that the term 'Bantu' quickly came to be applied to more than language. The three things, language, physical type and culture seemed inextricably associated and for many years nobody raised an eyebrow at such phrases as 'Bantu physical type' or 'Bantu culture'.

But in the 1930s the archaeological investigation of an ancient settlement on the top of Mapungubwe Hill, and in the valley below, at Bambandyanalo (fig. 3) produced evidence which started a wave of questioning. What puzzled the investigators was that they found what was clearly (to them) a 'Bantu culture' associated with skeletal remains which if not certainly Khoisan were at least considered to be non-Negro. Today the racial identity of the Bambandyanalo/Mapungubwe people is still not certain. But the discovery had the effect of sounding a warning about always expecting culture and human physical type to go hand in hand.

In the post-war years, as archaeological research in Zambia, Rhodesia and South Africa developed, much more became known of the metal-working mixed-farmers. To describe their culture in the archaeological record the term Iron Age was adopted. Although historians came gradually to accept the principle of the separateness of race, language and culture it none the less remained true that these three things seemed inextricably associated in the latest stages of the archaeologists' Iron Age; which was the equivalent of what explorers found in the areas east and north of the territory of the Khoi and the San. The San (Bushmen) certainly and the Khoi (Hottentots) less willingly were seen as living survivors of the South African Later Stone Age. Varieties of Later Stone Age culture were known throughout the area of Bantu distribution. Since there were no wild ancestors of sheep, goats or cattle in sub-Saharan Africa it seemed logical to link their presence in Southern Africa with the spread of other cultural traits (pottery, metal-working and agriculture) and of people. It was equally logical to see the Bantu-speaking Negroes as responsible, and so the search for the origins of the Bantu became a major historical or prehistorical issue.

The Question of Race

The physical characteristics of populations, as of individuals, depends on the transmission of genes. In the case of the individual this is a simple inheritance from the parents. What is inherited is a set of genes which equips the individual to react within certain limits with his environment. Environment and genes are complementary factors in shaping the individual, and environment is constantly exerting pressure for the retention of useful genes and the elimination of those that are not. But the unit of evolution is not the individual, it is the total population within which mates may be found. There is a constant mingling of genes within such a breeding population and it is the total gene pool in relation to the environment that is important in determining the characteristics of a population. As a result of constant gene mingling, mutation, and selection pressures, populations are continually changing, although in human populations the rate of change is generally very slow. Thus, if two populations initially similar remain isolated from each other for long enough they are likely to end up looking different from each other. The likelihood of such divergent evolution will be markedly increased if the two populations develop in differing environments. Apart from such gradual change resulting from genetic diversity (the constant mixing of gene combinations), mutation (the chance modification of genes by chemical processes), and natural selection (the role of the environment), changes may occur more rapidly if a population receives individuals from another population with very different combinations of genes. A few individuals would have little impact, but a large admixture might show itself very strongly.

Seen in these terms a continent as large as Africa, with such varied environments inhabited by 350 million people, could be expected to show greater variety than it does. Even at the height of enthusiasm for racial classification only half a dozen major groups were distinguished. Classification was based chiefly on measurable characters such as stature, head shape, face shape and the form of the nose. Skin colour and hair form were also included.

But such classificatory exercises treated races as static entities with sharply definable limits. Reality shows the falseness of this approach for there are always populations which occupy intermediate positions, explained as 'mixed races'. Modern anthropology has the advantage of a wider range of techniques than that of fifty or a hundred years ago, and with them have come new interests and new ways of viewing human populations. The study has moved from the external manifestations of genetic inheritance, so readily influenced by the environment (including diet), to the study of the underlying genetic compositon itself. The tendency is to give less prominence to those characters known to be controlled by a coplex of genes, and overly susceptible to environment, and more to those controlled by a single gene and less readily influenced by external factors. In this, most progress has been made in the study of blood-groups and the constituents of blood. The concern is no longer classification, but a better understanding of why the selection for particular genes and gene frequencies has taken place, and the usefulness or survival value of the particular genetic compositions encountered. The greatly improved knowledge of the genetic compositions of different populations resulting from these studies has brought with it an altogether more meaningful picture of the relationships of the inhabitants of the continent.

The contrast between the old somatic (body-form) approach to physical anthropology and the more recent genetic approach is rather like the difference between ordinary and X-ray photography. Despite the sharp line drawn by earlier anthropologists between Khoi and San on the one hand and Negroes on the other, genetic composition tells a very different tale. Recent studies show that the Khoi and San form part of a 'major gene constellation' with the other sub-Saharan Africans. Indeed the pattern of their blood groups is such that R. Singer and J.S. Weiner consider that they should be regarded simply as African Negroids with a long history of differentiation in the southern part of the continent. Not all anthropologists would put the matter in quite so positive a manner, but there appears to be general agreement that the contrasts between Khoisan and Negro are nothing like as significant as was formerly believed. As Professor Tobias has put it, 'the Khoisans have more in common genetically with Negroes than either group has with any non-African peoples'. Indeed, the Khoi and San are said to 'resemble or surpass' other African populations in precisely those genetic characters which distinguish African from non-African populations. They are ultra-African. At the same time it is clear that Khoi and San are much more like each other than either is like the Negro.

The same range of studies that have shown the Khoisan to belong to the same general African family as Negroes has shown even more clearly that the Southern African, Bantu-speaking Negroes cannot be separated in any sensible way, physically, from

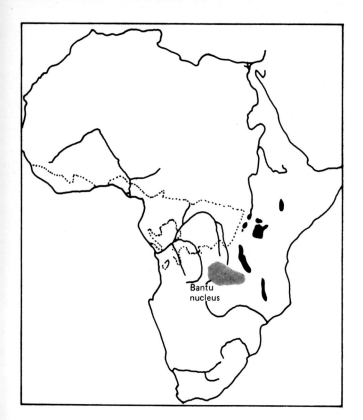

4 Linguist Malcom Guthrie saw the Bantu languages as having spread from a nuclear area south and west of Lake Tanganyika. This view is no longer supported.

the whole group of sub-Saharan Negroes. There is no such thing as the Bantu physical type, and the only basis for distinction from other African Negroes is culture, including language.

How might such a situation have arisen? Bushman-like skeletons have been found as far afield as the Nile Valley, and dating back to 12 000 or 14 000 years ago. By contrast the oldest Negro remains, also from the Nile Valley, are no older than about 6 000 years. Few Negro remains have been found at all, and of those known from Southern Africa none is older than about 1 500 years. Professor Tobias has suggested a proto-Negriform stock as being ancestral to both the African Negroes and the present-day Khoisan. Taking the Khoisan as ultra-African, and the Negro as representing a 'watered down' version of the genetic type, he considers that the ancestral stock probably bore a closer resemblance to the Khoisan of today than to modern Negroes. In other words the 'long period of differentiation in the southern part of the continent' proposed for the Khoisan was one in which they remained relatively unaltered in their isolation while populations to the north underwent change in the direction of the modern Negro. Such a proposal would require a mechanism for isolating two sections of the African population. It is tempting to see that isolation as represented by the period 9 000 to 4 500 years ago, when substantial parts of the inland plateau in South Africa appear to have been empty or only sparsely populated. To be sure of this will require much more research in the inland areas.

Wrestling with Words

Almost from the start the assumption was made that the Bantu-speaking farmers were immigrants to Central and Southern Africa. Whence they came, and when, were questions not easily answered. In simplest terms, since farming and stock-raising were ancient skills in North Africa and the Nile Valley, it seemed most reasonable to derive the Bantu from somewhere in the north. Accordingly in 1913 the great African historian Sir Harry Johnston saw them as hordes of warriors sweeping south through the continent, conquering with their superior weaponry and imposing their language on the conquered. The event was seen as rapid, and it was necessary that it should be so to account for the great similarities uniting the Bantu languages over such a large area. Sir Harry had little evidence with which to prop up his model and not much was forthcoming until the 1950s, when the African linguist Joseph Greenberg proposed an important revision of African language classification.

Prior to 1955 Bantu was considered to be an independent language-family of equal status with other language-families north of 'the Bantu line' (fig. 1). What Greenberg proposed, and what most linguists now accept, was that Bantu was simply a part of a larger language-family which included the former Western Sudanic family and several more easterly languages. For this newly defined family he proposed the name Niger-Congo (fig. 1). What was important for the debate on Bantu origins is that Greenberg argued that the greater degree of variability in the north-west corner of the Niger-Congo area, compared with the relative uniformity in the extensive former Bantu area, indicated that this was where the language had developed, and whence it had spread. Although he had not set out to explore the problem of Bantu origins his findings re-opened the debate and suggested a possible answer. If the 'proto-Bantu' had lived in the savannah region in the north-east of Nigeria and had embarked on a southward migration, those that were far enough east might have continued southwards, moving through the equatorial forest until they reached a familiar savannah environment south of it. If they came already armed with a knowledge of farming and metals, their subsequent expansion would neatly account for the widespread Bantu/Negro Iron Age. But there were problems with such a simple explanation, as we shall see.

A decade later another African linguist offered an alternative view. Malcolm Guthrie, working with common roots of words in a large number of Bantu languages, found high concentrations of these in a group of languages in the savannah country immediately south and west of Lake Tanganyika (fig. 4). This he regarded as the nuclear area in which proto-Bantu had developed and from which it had spread.

In order to explain the presumed ancient connection with Western Sudanic noted by Greenberg, he proposed a hypothetical group of 'pre-Bantu' who had lived in the region of Lake Chad. Some of these had moved south around the eastern margins of the equatorial forest and established themselves as 'proto-Bantu'-speakers in the nuclear area, whence they had expanded over the whole of the Bantu area. Others had spread westwards to Nigeria to give rise to other languages containing what Guthrie described as 'Bantuisms'.

This again was taken by some historians and archaeologists to provide a mechanism for explaining Bantu origins and the initiation of the 'Bantu Iron Age'. Attempts were made to unite the Greenberg and Guthrie evidence by suggesting that groups of pre- or proto-Bantu had moved through the forest from Nigeria to establish themselves in the nuclear area. This still required a remarkable population explosion, and presented difficulties relating to the origins of the cultural elements (farming, pottery and metallurgy) comprising the archaeologists' Early Iron Age. At the time when Greenberg and Guthrie first published their findings in the 1950s and early 1960s there was no sure evidence for an iron-using culture in West Africa that could have spawned iron-working proto-Bantu peoples. By the late 1960s iron-smelting was shown to be present in the Nok culture in Nigeria as early as the fourth century B.C. But for this to have been the parent of Guthrie's proto-Bantu would have required both a rapid and inexplicable movement of people through the forest followed by an even more remarkable and rapid population expansion.

Furthermore, important cultural elements present in the Nok culture are conspicuously absent in the Early Iron Age cultures of Central and Southern Africa.

Whilst Guthrie's notion of a proto-Bantu nuclear area has been questioned, his recognition of a group of languages in the forest areas of Gabon, Congo, and Zaire as forming a sub-group distinct from the Bantu languages to the south and east has been generally sustained. The group has been dubbed 'forest Bantu' in contrast to the savannah, or eastern Bantu, and more will be said of this presently.

From all this complicated linguistic evidence several important things emerge. First, the Bantu languages are part of a wider family including much of West Africa. Secondly the great diversification of languages, including those formerly known as semi-Bantu, in the Nigeria/Cameroons area suggest that this is the area from which proto-Bantu derived. Thirdly a distinction exists between forest Bantu and eastern Bantu. Fourthly, while there are important variations within the vast area of eastern Bantu the degree of similarity suggests that they have been spread relatively recently and rapidly throughout this area. Fifthly, while the historical implications of the relationships of the languages and the general pattern of their spreading are inescapable, there is no internal evidence for assigning an absolute dating to any part of the story. As we shall see, implications of population movement are present and it is even possible to make observations on matters of culture and economy at different stages of the reconstructed linguistic history. But the only basis for assigning a chronology lies in finding a match between proposed linguistic events and datable archaeological events.

The most recent and most remarkable linguistic contributions in this debate have come from the work of Christopher Ehret. In 1967 and 1968 Ehret concluded, on linguistic evidence, that cattle and sheep had been introduced to Central and Southern Africa by peoples speaking a Central Sudanic language at a time before Bantu-speakers (or Bantu language) had spread into these areas. The words are in fact not Bantu words, but have been borrowed by Bantu-speakers from other languages.

Following on the success of his earlier investigations Ehret extended his studies to a number of sets of loanwords of Central Sudanic origin recognisable in the word-lists of Bantu languages. Because of the relatively recent and rapid spread of the Bantu languages it has been possible to use the distribution of loanword sets to trace the pattern of their spreading and, within limits, to indicate the areas of contact in

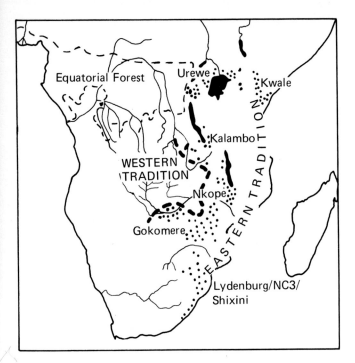

5 The eastern and western traditions of the
Early Iron Age as exemplified by pottery styles.
The main sub-groups within the eastern tradition
are indicated.

which particular borrowings took place.

The linguistic studies of Ehret and his co-workers draw in remarkable detail a story of linguistic history, cultural activities, and the movements of peoples. How, and to what extent this linguistic evidence can be wedded to the findings of the archaeologist we shall explore presently.

Patterns of Pottery

In the first section of this chapter we spoke of the combination of farming and metallurgy as representing the archaeologists' Iron Age. Although there is a good deal of variation in content from site to site the elements indicated by the term Iron Age are agriculture and/or stock-raising accompanied by the use of metals, and especially of iron. Pottery is invariably present and all these things are usually found in situations indicating at least semi-permanent settlement, in villages rather than in camp-sites. In the often acid soils of Africa, subjected to heavy rain and cracking dryness in alternating seasons, organic remains rarely survive. Bones, and especially teeth, tend to last better than plant material and, though our knowledge of domestic livestock is not good, it is infinitely

better than our knowledge of cultivated plants. Assumptions about agriculture derive in part from the linguistic evidence, and from the discovery of occasional hoes and grinding-stones, as well as the abundant pottery assumed to be related in part to the preparation and serving of cultivated vegetable foods. The substantial huts, for which there is evidence on many sites, including some of the earliest, are also taken to represent a permanence more likely to be associated with agriculture than with pastoralism.

But above all else the basis for the recognition of Iron Age occupation is domestic pottery. It has a number of advantages. The shapes and decoration of vessels tend to reflect the accepted norms for the particular society for which they were made. The pottery is usually abundant, and once fired it is very durable. Like language, pottery may evolve in divergent directions if a parent group splits to form new, separate groups. The derivative pottery traditions may be readily relatable to each other, and also to the parent tradition. It is on the basis of such ceramic (pottery) studies that archaeologists have generally divided up the Iron Age into chronological stages, and on which individual sites are linked into cultural groupings.

All the way from Lake Victoria to the Transkei coast the same general picture emerges of an Early Iron Age superseded roughly 1 000 years ago by a Later Iron Age. In general terms Early Iron Age pottery tends to be thick, pale (pink, buff, or reddish) in colour, and freely and boldly decorated. By contrast the Later Iron Age pottery is generally thinner and almost invariably grey (sometimes very dark), and whilst decoration may occasionally be extensive it has a more formal, less 'free' appearance than the earlier pottery. Red and black colouring are often applied and surfaces may be highly burnished. Radiocarbon dating has provided clear support for this typological division.

We cannot concern ourselves here with details of the cultural subdivisions within the Early and Later Iron Ages, but there are one or two broad generalisations which are central to our concern with the problems of Iron Age origins and the extent to which Bantu-speakers were involved. The first of these is that the ceramics of the Early Iron Age fall into two broad divisions, or traditions: western and eastern. The western tradition has been most clearly defined by D. Phillipson and J. Vogel and corresponds fairly closely to the territory of Zambia plus the south-east corner of Zaire. It is not certain what happens to the west of this, where research has been very limited. Knowledge of the eastern tradition has grown from the work of a number of archaeologists over the past decade, and despite the development of regional variations it seems fairly clear that the various identified groups belong to a tradition distinct from that of Zambia (fig. 5). The second observation of great importance made by Phillipson is that only in western Zambia and adjacent parts of Angola is there a continuity of tradition from Early to Later Iron Age clearly visible in the pottery. Elsewhere the change is abrupt and suggests anything but an evolution. Since the establishment of Later Iron Age pottery traditions about a thousand years ago there have been no major disturbances affecting the development of local expressions. According to Phillipson a general division of Later Iron Age pottery traditions can be made between areas north and south of a line joining Lakes Tanganyika and Malawi. We must now consider to what extent the linguistic evidence and the archaeological evidence can be welded.

Loanwords, Pots and People

The time has come to attempt an answer to that very important question, 'Who were the first farmers?' That they were physically Negroes seems almost certain, but at the distance of 1 500 to 3 000 years at which we may have to view them it is possible that they were not quite as familiar-looking as Negroes today. Two different language groups, Bantu and Central Sudanic, have been said to be involved, and it is our task now to see just what roles each may have played. If a clear answer could be given this chapter would not be so long. But there is no clear sure answer so we shall examine briefly in turn four models illustrating how things might have happened, given the linguistic and archaeological evidence which we have just reviewed. In each case it is assumed that Khoisan populations and the languages they spoke never extended north of the area indicated on the maps. The northern limit approximates to the boundary defined by the linguist E. Westphal.

Model 1 (fig. 6A). This is based almost entirely on Ehret's proposals arising from his study of loanwords in Bantu. Proto-Bantu-speakers living as hunter–gatherers in the equatorial forest spread southwards into the savannah to give rise to various savannah-Bantu groups (perhaps 600-400 B.C.). At the same time, or earlier, Central Sudanic groups had spread southwards and established themselves on the north-west side of Lake Tanganyika. Ultimately their spread carried them even to the south of the Zambezi, and whilst this may have occurred

later, it was none the less ahead of the Bantu-speakers. They were agriculturists, herders, probably iron-workers, and presumably made pottery. It was from these people that some Khoisan groups (perhaps Tshu Khwe) adopted sheep, and the word for them.

The eastern-most of the savannah-Bantu groups, moving eastwards, came up against the Central Sudanics at the north end of Lake Tanganyika and adopted their farming and iron-working practices, and the loanwords that went with them. Some continued around the north end of the lake and settled between it and Lake Victoria. Others spread to the south end of the lake where they acquired new Central Sudanic words. Here they split into two groups which have been named *Pela* and *Pembele*. The Pela spread eastwards to carry Bantu language into Tanzania, Kenya, and parts of Mozambique, while the Pembele spread south to bring the Bantu dialects to the south-eastern regions (Zambia, Malawi, southern Mozambique, Rhodesia and South Africa). Ehret sees Early Iron Age culture as being spread by the hands of the expanding Bantu-speakers, who completely absorbed the Central Sudanic groups.

There are several difficulties with this model. One is the archaeological invisibility of the Central Sudanic groups. There seems no reason why they should be invisible. Secondly the model says nothing of the *non*-Bantu Later Stone Age inhabitants who must be supposed to have inhabited the vast territories into which the Central Sudanics and the Bantu-speakers penetrated. If they had a genetic composition anything like the Khoisan it ought to show as it does in the south-east of South Africa. We must conclude that a vast reservoir of non-Bantu languages has left no recognised trace. The Bergdama of Namibia, the Kwadi of southern Angola, and the Hadza and Sandawe in East Africa could represent remnants of such replaced populations but one would expect more. If Bantu-speakers moving eastwards and southwards from the savannah west of Lake Tanganyika were the carriers of Early Iron Age culture, pottery traditions ought to follow the main lines of expansion indicated by the languages. Instead the boundary cuts across the projected migration routes. A way out of this last difficulty is suggested in model 2, which is based on suggestions made by D. Phillipson.

Model 2 (fig. 6B). In this model Later Stone Age proto-Bantu-speakers in contact with Central-Sudanic-speakers (from c. 1 000 B.C.) north of the equatorial forest acquired Early Iron Age culture traits and appropriate loanwords. They moved

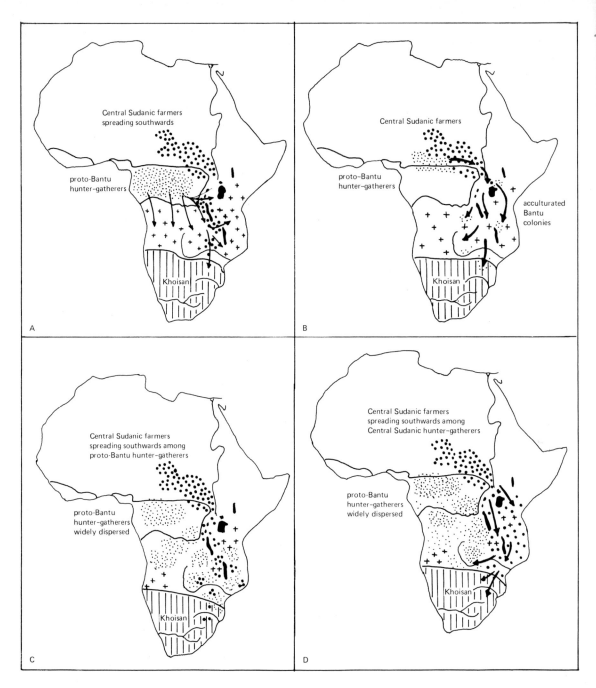

6 *Four ways in which farming, metal technology
and ceramics may have spread into Southern
Africa. Central-Sudanic-speakers are involved in
order to account for C. Sudanic loanwords in
modern Bantu languages. The four models represent working hypotheses to account for events
that probably occurred between about 750 B.C.
and 750 A.D. If any of these models is correct it*

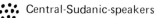 Central-Sudanic-speakers

proto-Bantu-speakers

+ hunter-gatherers speaking other
+ languages

*is likely to represent an over-simplification. No
allowance is made for the coast-wise spread of
ideas.*

through or past the Central-Sudanic-speakers and settled in the region of Lake Victoria giving rise to the Urewe tradition (c. 300 B.C.). Later (100-400 A.D.) an eastern stream spread southwards giving rise to the other Early Iron Age pottery groups of the eastern tradition. Only small numbers of people were involved. Sheep were present but not cattle. Later (400-500 A.D.) a western branch spread into Zambia taking cattle with them which they then passed on to the eastern-stream people and to some Khoisan groups in the south. Sheep may have reached Khoisan groups at an earlier date from the eastern stream. About 1 000 years ago, for reasons not yet apparent, a dramatic irruption of peoples took place, perhaps in south-east Zaire, which resulted in the rapid and far-reaching spread of Later Iron Age culture and of a newly emergent Bantu dialect (proto-eastern Bantu) to East and Southern Africa.

This model attempts to explain the presence of Central Sudanic loanwords in Bantu languages without invoking the presence of the people themselves in Southern Africa. The existence of variations of Central Sudanic words with the same meaning is accounted for by supposing long contact in the Central Sudanic homeland in which a number of dialects were involved. It explains the linguistic unity of modern Bantu languages in East and Southern Africa by suggesting that they derive from a rapid dialect-spread associated with the Later rather than the Early Iron Age.

The model has the same weakness as the previous one in not accounting for the Later Stone Age populations whose territories the Bantu infiltrated. We are told that small numbers of Bantu-speakers were involved yet they seem to have absorbed without trace a large indigenous population. It also ignores the point that the localities suggested by Ehret for his Central Sudanic groups were determined precisely, by a process of linguistic back-tracking, to account for the present distributions of loanword sets. It is not at all clear that such distributions could be accounted for in the manner suggested in the model.

An attractive feature is the idea that the present degree of similarity in eastern and southern Bantu languages might be accounted for by a rapid expansion of Later Iron Age peoples rather than in the Early Iron Age. In fact linguistically the model requires this because if we supposed that the present language situation arose from Early Iron Age events we would have to accept that the very dramatic Later Iron Age archaeological event had had no linguistic counterpart.

Models 3 and 4 are primarily alternative schemes for eliminating the problem of the missing Later Stone Age hunter–gatherers who must, in models 1 and 2, have occupied the huge area of Africa into which the Bantu-speakers intruded.

Model 3 (fig. 6C). The difficulty of the missing Later Stone Age populations and languages would be largely overcome if it were possible to see early or proto-Bantu speakers already widely dispersed as Later Stone Age hunter–gatherers. They might be viewed as sharing the central part of the continent with a number of other language groups (e.g. Sandawe, Hadza, Kwadi, Bergdama) much the way that the southern part of the continent was occupied by a variety of distinct Khoisan languages. Into this territory, in the manner proposed by Ehret, Central Sudanic farming groups moved, penetrating southwards mostly east of longitude 30° east. The process might, as Ehret suggests, have taken several centuries. The emphasis between agriculture and pastoralism could have varied a lot, and groups that were predominantly herders might move more rapidly than those that were not. In such a way sheep could have reached the southern part of the continent well in advance of either cattle or agriculture.

In such a model different Central Sudanic dialect groups may have been involved. Even after a long penetration of their territory first by sheep herders and then cattle herders, and after prolonged contact with agriculture on a long frontier, many Khoisan hunter–gatherer groups never adopted these practices. Thus there is no need to suppose that all who came into contact with the wandering Central Sudanics would have adopted their ways. Some Bantu-speakers may have done so, and perhaps some who were not Bantu-speakers. Others may have remained unaffected.

Phillipson's 'eastern stream' of Early Iron Age would be the archaeological reflection of this process. Individual sites, or clusters of sites represented by localised pottery variants of the eastern tradition, might have been created variously by Central-Sudanic-speakers, or by acculturated proto-eastern Bantu-speakers, or members of other language families.

Ehret has shown that the Malagasy obtained their livestock through contact with Central-Sudanic-speakers rather than through Bantu-speaking intermediaries. He supposes that the relevant stretch of coast was not yet occupied by Bantu-speaking peoples. This is an important reminder that Central Sudanic penetration was not limited to those areas where Ehret has pointed to linguistic borrowing. It also serves to remind us that ocean-going craft were involved in these early diffusions. This being so, it would be wise to make allowance for the role of coastwise trading in the transmission of ideas. Early coastal trading contacts are also reflected in the small numbers of Indian Ocean sea shells that turn up in a surprising number of the earliest of Iron Age sites in Rhodesia and Zambia and Malawi.

Phillipson's western stream would represent the acculturation of proto-eastern Bantu at the slightly later date he has suggested. The precise channels through which the contacts were made remain unknown in this model as in fact they do in model 2. Ehret suggested on linguistic grounds that cattle may have been few and relatively unimportant in areas that lie within the eastern stream, but this is not supported by the archaeological evidence. There is nothing in the archaeological evidence that requires cattle to have been introduced to the eastern stream from the west, as proposed by Phillipson.

Finally, the model would make use of the same mechanism as model 2 to account for the present Bantu language pattern: that is, the rapid development and spread of dialects associated with Later Iron Age events.

Model 4 (fig. 6D). This is really a variant model 3, in which proto-Bantu-speakers are limited initially to the more westerly savannah regions. To the east, instead of having populations of non-Bantu and non-Sudanic peoples we have an altogether greater extension of Sudanic-speakers, perhaps as hunter–gatherers. It is initially through these related language groups that agriculture, livestock and metallurgy are diffused, or spread by wandering groups from the north, as in models 1 and 3. The model does not add much compared with the others. It could be said to provide a greater ethnic unity for the eastern archaeological tradition in contrast to the western (Bantu) tradition. It might, however, be more difficult to lose a rather solid Sudanic or Central Sudanic language block in the face of Bantu expansion in the later Iron Age than to lose the mixture of languages visualised in model 3.

Well, we have indulged in a generous amount of speculation in an attempt to suggest possible ways of wedding the linguistic evidence to the archaeology. The exercise is in itself a fair indication that more research is needed before the range of possibilities can be narrowed. On the linguistic side, as Ehret has suggested, there is a need to search the Bantu languages for signs of possible non-Bantu and non-Central-Sudanic languages that might have been absorbed. On the archaeological side there is a great need to examine more closely the

phenomenon of the emergence of the Later Iron Age. As a generalisation it is attractive, but it will surely prove to be more complicated than has been suggested above.

We may not have progressed very far, but at least the reader should now be aware of the range of evidence and the possibilities arising from it, and that is a helpful start. What we can suggest is that the first metal-using farmers in South Africa were of negroid physical type, and may well have spoken an ancestral form of Bantu. But they might, just might, have been of Central Sudanic or some other stock.

South Africa's First Farmers

South Africa's first farmers are rather shadowy figures in the landscape. Little more than a decade ago the only real sign of them in South Africa was a handful of pottery sherds found at a site on the farm *Happy Rest* in the Soutpansberg mountains during the last World War. The site has not been dated, but pottery of similar type in Rhodesia (Gokomere tradition) is dated to the eighth or ninth century A.D. The impression given was that of a southward expansion across the Limpopo during a late stage of the Rhodesian Early Iron Age. Then, quite suddenly, from 1967 onwards have come a series of discoveries that have transformed our knowledge of the spread of farming and metal-working. The number of sites is not large and only one site, Broederstroom, has been extensively investigated. Nothing is known by more than scraps of information published in the form of preliminary notes.

In the mid-1960s the Anglo American Corporation began mining the immense iron-ore deposits of Bomvu Ridge (now called Ngwenya) in Swaziland. In the course of doing so a number of localities were found in which specularite, a soft and glistening form of haematite, had been dug out in antiquity. Rescue excavations were carried out at several sites including Castle Cavern, where radiocarbon dates indicate an early-fifth-century A.D. date for Iron Age occupation. Details of the excavation have not yet been published but scraps of rusted iron are mentioned in a preliminary note, as well as two stone ring fragments and a few stone tools including scrapers. Pottery from the site is described as thick and friable, representing vessels with well-defined necks, and decorated with single and multiple lines of broad, shallow grooving, parallel to and immediately below the rim. On its own the discovery is interesting and important, but it is only in its combination with later discoveries that the Early Iron

Age takes on some substance.

An important link in the chain of discoveries was provided by the sharp eyes of a Transvaal schoolboy, Ludwig von Bezing, now a medical doctor. At the age of 15, when his interests had widened to include such things as fossils and archaeological specimens, he recalled having seen, some years before, pieces of pottery lying on a hillslope a few miles from Lydenburg in the eastern Transvaal. He systematically collected what he had seen and a few years later, when studying medicine at Cape Town, brought his finds to the attention of the archaeology department there. And very remarkable finds they were. The fragments included parts of a large range of domestic pottery vessels, and the major part of seven most dramatic modelled heads. In addition there were a few beads of iron and copper, part of an ivory bracelet, fragments of two 'soapstone' bowls, which may relate to salt extraction, and a number of pieces of worked bone and ivory of unknown use.

The heads are, of course, exciting and beautiful objects, but they remain irritatingly silent as social documents. Two large heads appear to be helmet-masks intended to be worn by the user. The others are too small for this, but have holes on opposite sides of the base, as if for attachment to some other object. In view of their apparent age, the size and good preservation of the pieces suggests that they had recently eroded out from a pit or pits in which

7 Pottery fragments from an Early Iron Age site near Lydenburg in the eastern Transvaal. The thick buff-to-red pottery, with bold decoration, is characteristic of many Early Iron Age pottery traditions.

they had been buried or perhaps stored. The heads are the kind of object commonly associated with ritual occasions, such as initiation schools, and this is about as close as one can come to suggesting what their function might have been.

More useful archaeologically was the domestic pottery (fig. 7). The technique of decoration was that applied to the heads, but even more important both technique and decorative motifs were virtually identical to those found in the collections of pottery from the Natal coast many years before by John Schofield. Schofield's pottery, which he called NC3 (Natal Coast class 3) was associated in some cases with evidence of iron smelting but has never been dated. A single radiocarbon date of A.D. 490 was obtained for Lydenburg, though not under the most favourable circumstances. However, the general family resemblance between the Lion Cavern pottery (early fifth century A.D.) and Lydenburg suggests that the date may be correct. The distribution of this Lydenburg/NC3 pottery is carried far to the south by a series of finds on the Pondoland, Transkei and Ciskei coasts (fig. 8) of what their dis-

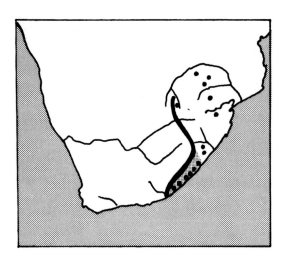

8 *General area over which apparently related Early Iron Age pottery is found south of the Limpopo. Localities of recently reported occurences are indicated by dots. The south-east coast sites are not known in detail.*

coverer, Robin Derricourt has called Shixini ware, but which clearly equates with NC3. In 1973 T. Maggs investigated a site with NC3 pottery at Ntshekane about 70 km north of Pietermaritzburg and located a number of pits about 2 m deep containing quantities of cultural material. Apart from pottery there are numerous grindstones, iron slag, bone tools, shell beads, and the bones of cattle, small stock, and antelope. This, however, is clearly a late development of the tradition, for the radiocarbon dates indicate a ninth century occupation. Pits with pottery of the Lydenburg type, and remains of sheep (or goats) and cattle were found by Evers at a site 2,5 km north of the 'heads site' at Lydenburg. The same investigator's survey of the 'heads site' shows that pottery, smelting sites, and the remains of hut floors occur over an area of about 10 hectares. But the best information on settlement details of the period comes from the site of Broederstroom in the Magaliesberg Valley about 60 km west-north-west of Johannesburg.

The Broederstroom site was discovered in 1973 and investigations were started later in the same year by Professor R.J. Mason of the University of the Witwatersrand. Although the site is badly eroded in places and is far from easy to work, Mason has already recovered much of relevance to our present story. The site is of a large village at least 2 hectares in extent. Twelve huts have been excavated and considerably more are known to exist. The huts were circular and about 2 m in diameter, though some

appear to be rather larger. In cases where huts were burned the mud plastering has been baked and preserved, showing that floors were plastered and the walls were built of poles and grass plastered inside and out with mud. Roofs were presumably conical and thatched. In some cases lines of vertically set slabs of shale remain standing in the floors of huts marking off a segment; in at least one case there are four lines dividing the whole floor evenly. It seems likely that the purpose of the slabs was to help support a platform of soil in order to raise the level of the floor, in part or entirely, above the general level of the ground. Most of the huts also have an internal setting of quartzite blocks apparently surrounding the hearth.

Two iron-smelting areas have been uncovered with fragments of the furnace blast-pipes. Nearby, a hut with associated nodules of unsmelted ore may represent the home of one of the artisans responsible for smelting. Iron has not survived well, and only a few scraps are known. A well-preserved copper chain, added to the evidence of the beads at Lydenburg, suggests that the Transvaal copper deposits were already being exploited. Two Indian Ocean sea-shells point tenuously to connections with the east coast. Perhaps one of the most curious things is the occurrence of hundreds of grooved sandstone fragments of a kind normally associated, in Later Stone Age contexts, with the grinding of shell beads. Fragmentary remains of sheep and cattle were found and upper and lower grindstones indicate that cereals were used and probably cultivated.

Human remains are represented by an adult maxilla and part of a juvenile mandible lying together in a pot. Fragments of leg-bones turned up in another part of the site. Although the teeth are said to fall within the size range of South African Negroids this hardly forms a very secure base for statements about the physical appearance of the Broederstroom inhabitants. It would, however, be no surprise if future discoveries showed them to have been Negroes.

The pottery from Broederstroom shares a number of features with the Lydenburg heads site and with NC3. But other features are more reminiscent of pottery from Eiland, in the north-east Transvaal, associated with salt-workings that seem to have remained in use intermittently from the Early Iron Age almost to the present. Some of the features of Broederstroom and Eiland are also found in what is currently the oldest Iron Age site in South Africa, on the farm Silverleaves, 16 km east of Tzaneen in the foothills of the Transvaal Drakensberg.

The Silverleaves site was discovered through road-cutting operations which exposed two pits from which the cultural remains were recovered by a local resident, Mr. M. Klapwijk. These included parts of 31 pottery vessels, pieces of charcoal, and some iron slag. The dating of the charcoals suggests that the site was occupied late in the third century A.D. or early in the fourth. The pottery is of great interest for two reasons. First, while it is clearly at home in the eastern tradition of the Early Iron Age and shares some features with pottery from Malawi (Nkope ware) and East Africa (Kwale and Urewe ware), it does not resemble *closely* the pottery from any of the other South African Early Iron Age sites. It may, therefore, be the first representative of a new, local tradition within the Early Iron Age. Its second claim to fame is that preserved within the fabric of the pottery were the impressions of seeds caught up in the wet clay when the pots were made. Some of these seed impressions have been identified as being made by the cultivated cereal *Pennisetum americanum,* thus Silverleaves provides us with the oldest direct evidence for cereal cultivation in the Transvaal.

In Natal, in the Shongweni South Cave, 25 km west of Durban, Dr. Oliver Davies recovered sherds of pottery similar to NC3 and dated to the end of the second century A.D. Well-preserved remains of the cereals *Pennisetum* (Bulrush millet) and *Eleusine* (African millet) as well as bottle gourd and melon were found at a slightly lower level and probably belong to the period of the pottery.

What is clear is that South Africa's first farming communities were established at least by the end of the third century. They were cultivating *Pennisetum* and in all probability a variety of other plants. By the fifth century populations were established in large villages of pole and thatch houses with plastered walls and floors. Their technology included the smelting and smithing of iron and copper, the manufacture of elaborate pottery, the carving of shallow bowls or dishes from soapstone, and the carving of bone and ivory. Salt was extracted from alkaline mineral springs by evaporation in soapstone dishes. The localised nature of such industry combined with the importance of the product almost certainly resulted in its being traded. Some form of trading contacts with the east coast are suggested by the occasional Indian Ocean sea-shells that turn up in so many sites (in Rhodesia, Malawi and Zambia as well as in South Africa). The occupants of Lion Cavern appear to have been involved in quarrying the glistening specularite in which the cavern was formed, and no doubt it too was traded. The only evidence of the use of such material at this time is on the Lydenburg heads, on which it was applied to the eyebrows and most of the incised areas of head and neck, but not to the face.

We have already remarked that over a large part of Southern Africa there are indications that this first phase of the Iron Age was terminated rather

A reconstruction exercise on fragments from Lydenburg. Initial work was done at the University of Cape Town, and pictures on the cover and p. 142 show heads after restoration by the British Museum. The 1 400-year-old heads are at present unique in the prehistory of Southern Africa.

abruptly about 1 000 years ago. The event is re-flected in the appearance of new pottery traditions and, in some areas, other new developments. This can also be seen to have happened in certain parts of South Africa. But our knowledge is too imperfect to be sure just what did happen in the 'middle ages' in South Africa. The Ntshekane site suggests that communities in Natal, represented by the NC3 pot-tery, had experienced no significant disturbance as late as the ninth century. Yet there is no trace of Early Iron Age traditions in the eleventh-century site at Blackburn, 20 kilometres north of Durban.

Nowhere in South Africa can we at present see an evolution from Early to Later Iron Age. In all the sites so far investigated we are in the presence of one or the other. The questions of precise time and pro-cess of transition are among the more fascinating challenges of South African archaeology. At the salt-working site of Eiland, Early Iron Age pottery is overlain by two successive levels representing two different Later Iron Age traditions. It could be a key locality for examining the problem. Another may be the important copper locality of Phalaborwa in the eastern Transvaal lowveld region. Preliminary investigations by R.J. Mason and N.J. van der Merwe indicate that copper and iron had been mined and smelted there for many centuries prior to the late nineteenth century. We shall refer to this again later, but in the present context we have to note that at least one of the ancient mine-shafts, 6 m deep and with a 9 m long gallery at the bottom, was dug in the eighth century A.D. and would therefore appear to have been the work of Early Iron Age metal workers. Unfortunately no identifiable cul-tural remains were associated.

Ancestral Societies

We have indicated in the previous chapter that at least some of the societies of the Later Stone Age must have been directly ancestral to the yellow-skinned hunters and herders of the seventeenth, eighteenth, and nineteenth centuries. Alas, al-though their genetic contribution to contemporary populations is often recognisable, their societies as such no longer survive except in attenuated form beyond the boundaries of South Africa. The same is not true of the Iron Age, for the Sotho and the Venda, the Tsonga and the Nguni are all surviving descen-dants of societies whose fossilised remains consti-tute the archaeological Later Iron Age.

We must assume that the inception of the Later Iron Age, at the very latest, marks the beginning of the history of the Bantu-speaking peoples of South Africa. There is no other event in the archaeological record that could mark their arrival or emergence at a more recent date. Indeed many scholars have ar-gued, and many probably still would, that the ances-tors of the present Bantu were emplaced at the time of the emergence in South Africa of the Early Iron Age. We prefer here to follow Phillipson's sugges-tion that the south-eastern Bantu dispersal, out-lined linguistically by Ehret, is to be correlated with the emergence of Later Iron Age cultures in or about the eleventh century A.D. Whether this new cul-tural phenomenon was superimposed on older Bantu-speaking groups or on non-Bantu-speaking groups may still be a matter for debate. The actual process by which it happened is still obscure, but it seems to have been rapid.

Fig. 9 sets out a range of probable effects on estab-lished pottery traditions of the arrival of new peoples. The important variables are whether men or women were traditionally the potters, both in the immigrant populations and in the host or indigen-ous groups. The other important factor is whether the immigrants are men alone, or men with at least some of their own women-folk. Out of the eight possible situations only one would be expected to result in a rather abrupt replacement of an estab-lished pottery tradition by a new one. It will be seen that this requires the intrusion of both men and women, among whom the women are the potters, into societies in which the menfolk were tradition-ally the potters. We must therefore suppose that the potters of the Early Iron Age were men, and that the Later Iron Age was initiated by the spreading of people, men and women, rather than simply of ideas. It is perhaps not without relevance that among the (non-Bantu) Bergdama of Namibia it was apparently the men who made the pottery.

The evidence leads us to these conclusions, but it is less helpful in suggesting why such a change, and such movements, should have occurred at all. It is in a sense the old problem of 'Bantu origins' updated from the early first millennium to around the eleventh century. To find potential mechanisms the most profitable source seems to be social an-thropology. We are reminded of historian Martin Legassick's remarks on the Sotho-Tswana oral his-tories. They are primarily concerned with the lineages from which the ruling chiefs were drawn. The chiefs themselves were powerful. They were generally wealthy and were at the centre of political, legal, economic and ritual life. Loyalty to the chief was paramount. But on those occasions when the succession was disputed conflict was often avoided

	Composition of Immigrant Groups (Potters in caps)	Potters in Recipient Groups	Possible Response in Pottery Traditions in Recipient Area
I	MEN only	MEN	new styles added to old temporarily or permanently
II	men only	MEN	no change
III	MEN & women	MEN	new styles added to old temporarily or permanently
IV	men & WOMEN	MEN	new styles may replace old if immigrant numbers are large enough
V	MEN only	WOMEN	old styles and new may exist side by side with little change
VI	men only	WOMEN	no change
VII	MEN & women	WOMEN	both styles may continue probably with no long-term change
VII	men & WOMEN	WOMEN	new styles may be added to old temporarily or permanently

by sons, or brothers, leaving the community with their followers to establish a new chiefdom elsewhere. This process produces what anthropologists call 'lineage-clusters', and the ideal conditions for its operation are said to have existed where relatively thinly populated territory was being colonised by an expanding population.

The linguistic picture created by Ehret seems to require the rapid dispersal, with accompanying dialect differentiation, of a dialect group which he calls proto-south-eastern Bantu. Social anthropologist Monica Wilson has explored the conditions required for such an expansion and concludes that a combination of polygyny and marriage with stock allows a wealthy lineage to increase much more rapidly than poorer lineages. She quotes the case of John Dunn, the Scottish trader who became a sub-chief in Zululand. Because he commanded wealth in cattle he was able to marry forty-eight Zulu wives and produce over a hundred children. 'Unto those that have shall be given': descent and inheritance in the male line ensures that wealth remains in the lineage, and the giving of daughters in marriage brings in more of the precious cattle, which may then be used to secure wives for the sons. The operation of such mechanisms in the past is recorded in the oral traditions of both Nguni and Sotho peoples

9 The table shows the probable effects on indigenous pottery traditions in response to various kinds of immigrant groups, depending on whether the potters in the groups involved are men or women. Whilst large-scale movements of men only, or men plus women, are allowed for, it is considered unlikely that there would be a large-scale movement of women only.

but the time-depth is uncertain. Professor Wilson believes that it was in such fashion that small groups of cattle-owners may have established themselves among hunters, or among cattle-owners with a different social organisation, and multiplied rapidly. An important aspect of such a process is that the children of women so absorbed tend to speak the language of the lineage rather than that of the mother's former group. Thus there might be a rapid growth in numbers of speakers of the language without the need to invoke a large migration.

Appreciation of such anthropological matters helps to bring an element of reality to otherwise rather abstract propositions. Yet they do not supply a simple and complete answer to the problem. The Bantu languages spoken south of the Limpopo – Venda, Sotho, Tsonga, Nguni (plus Chopi) – form a closely related group which is distinct from the

10 *Clay figurine of hump-backed ox. The horns are missing. Such figurines are common in the Later Iron Age. Together with the evidence of bones and ruined cattle pens they indicate an altogether more important role for cattle than in the Early Iron Age.*

Shona group of dialects of Rhodesia. But both ultimately derive from a common ancestral language said to have been located approximately in the extreme north of Zambia. The same dichotomy could also be argued from the archaeological evidence.

So far as we can see all of the material elements of the Later Iron Age were already present in the Early Iron Age. Cattle, sheep or goats, agriculture, pottery, iron and copper are all attested. What then might have provided the stimulus that set one small section expanding its influence and its language so rapidly?

Although cattle were present by the fifth century in many sites, they seem always to have been in small numbers. Faunal remains indicate that wild animals provided the bulk of the meat. But there is clear evidence in Rhodesia that cattle played an altogether greater role in the lives of the Later Iron Age communities, right from the beginning. Not only are cattle remains more abundant, but clay figurines of cattle appear in considerable numbers (fig. 10). In South Africa, too, evidence of a different kind points to a new importance for cattle. The archaeological evidence certainly suggests that the anthropological arguments about their role in expanding influence may have some substance.

Ehret seems quite sure from the linguistic evidence that the practice of milking cattle was introduced to the Bantu-speakers significantly later than the introduction of the cattle themselves. If we assume that Early Iron Age cattle were kept in small

numbers primarily as a source of meat, the introduction of milking may be seen as a powerful new factor in the economy. Milk and its by-products would constitute a new and highly nourishing element in the diet, and new attitudes to cattle could be expected to develop. Given favourable conditions herds in Africa can show an annual increase of from 4 to 10 per cent, an increase rate greater than that of their owners. Even at the lower rate of increase it has been said that the need for new land would grow alarmingly. Here we have the kind of mechanism needed to explain the rapid dispersals required by the linguistic evidence and suggested by that of archaeology.

Even so, it is not necessary, and perhaps not wise, to think in terms of this one factor only, important though it surely is. Other things might be involved. Could there have been an element of reaching out to secure, and perhaps exploit more fully, the monopoly of trade with foreigners on the east coast? In the middle of the tenth century a large sea-borne expedition from Indonesia sacked a number of towns and villages on the coast near Sofala; their attack on a fortified settlement, possibly in the Zambezi estuary, was not successful. They came to plunder for ivory, tortoise shell, leopard skins, ambergris, and Negro slaves, and it is curious that gold was not listed as one of the commodities sought. That they knew what they wanted, and returned a few years later, peacefully this time, suggests a history of such journeys reaching back well into the Early Iron Age. The east coast, perhaps as far south as Zanzibar, was the haunt of sea-traders from at least the first century A.D. Cosmas Indicopleustes, writing in the early sixth century, speaks of expeditions from Axum in Ethiopia to the land of Sasu for gold from its 'many goldmines'. The traders took oxen, lumps of salt, and iron, and the round trip occupied six months. We do not know where Sasu is, but it was 'near the ocean', and one is tempted to think of the prehistoric gold mines of Rhodesia. Al-Mas'udi was familiar with the gold trade through Sofala in the early tenth century. Could it have been the rich gold and copper deposits, already exploited before their arrival, that arrested the spread of the Shona between the Zambezi and the Limpopo, leaving the areas to the south for the south-eastern Bantu? Did the proto-Shona buy their way into the gold trade by way of marriages secured with cattle?

The pickings in gold south of the Limpopo were not so great, but half a dozen ancient gold mines are known (fig. 11). In all probability there are many more, and alluvial gold might have been panned in numerous places. Tin was mined in large quantities in the Rooiberg area. But the real wealth in minerals lay in the copper deposits. The evidence is clear also that iron was extensively mined and smelted, primarily in the Transvaal. If the foundations of the great Zimbabwe state lay in its wealth of gold, it is probable that in a more modest way iron and copper played an important role in the economy of the Sotho peoples. In particular Messina and Phalaborwa were important centres of copper production. It is through the ancient copper miners of Phalaborwa that we first come into contact with truly ancestral societies in the Iron Age.

Phalaborwa lies in the eastern Transvaal lowveld, 80 km east of the Drakensberg escarpment. It is scrubby bush-savannah country, hot, poorly watered, and (until this century) ridden with fevers and endemic diseases. None the less we have seen that the rich copper deposits attracted miners as early as the eighth century. We have no cultural associations for this one early-dated mine, but for other, later mines of the eleventh and eighteenth centuries we have better information. Apart from the mine-shafts and trenches, and the numerous smelting furnaces, many of the ancient volcanic hills (koppies) in the neighbourhood preserve evidence of settlements. These take the form of extensive stone-faced terraces designed to support flat areas on which one or more huts may be built. On the flat ground at the foot of the koppies larger groups of six or more huts occur as well as occasional large stone enclosures that must have been stockpens. Fifteen of these habitation sites have been investigated and give a useful picture of the lives of the inhabitants. The huts were circular, up to 3 m in diameter, with walls of posts and wattle, plastered inside and out with mud. Floors were plastered and roofs must have been thatched with grass. Grindstones, pottery, metal objects and bones comprise the common finds. Glass beads occurred on some sites but not others. The indications are that most of the hillside settlements belong to the eighteenth and nineteenth centuries, but one of the low-ground sites has yielded a series of dates ranging from A.D. 960 to A.D. 1130.

The most fascinating and important result of these investigations is the evidence they produced of continuity of tradition. Pottery from the eleventh-century site is virtually indistinguishable from that of nineteenth-century sites. Both are so similar to pottery made by modern Ba Phalaborwa in the area today that there can be no doubting that the Ba Phalaborwa are the direct lineal descendants of the ancient miners and metal workers. Similar

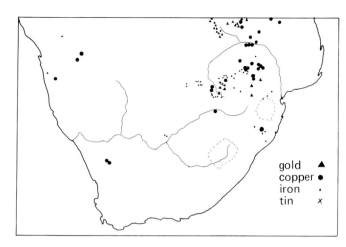

11 Main occurrences of pre-European mining. The number of sites is undoubtedly much greater, but it is unlikely that additional plottings would change the areas of occurrence significantly.

pottery is also made by the Lobedu 90 km to the north.

In the context of the peopling of Southern Africa this information is extremely interesting. There is at present no obvious ancestor in Southern Africa for the Phalaborwa pottery, nor is similar pottery known from elsewhere inside or outside South Africa. Yet stylistically it would be classed as Later Iron Age, and ought, therefore, to represent the arrival in the area of new influences, and probably new peoples. If this is indeed the truth then they must be among some of the earliest established Later Iron Age communities in Southern Africa. We must also note that while the Phalaborwa, the Lobedu and the Birwa form a local group of the north-eastern Sotho they lie over 400 km to the east of the area from which the Sotho, according to all their traditions, dispersed (fig. 12). In fact the Phalaborwa, Lobedu and Birwa are not linked to any of the important Sotho lineages. They are Sotho by language and custom only, and perhaps represent early settlers of different origin who have been subsequently absorbed into the expanding Sotho groups.

The greatest visible contrast between the Early and Later Iron Ages lies in the extensive use of stone for building after about the eleventh century. In Rhodesia the practice is closely associated with the rise of the Zimbabwe state and seems often to have been an expression of status. In South Africa stone buildings exist in vast numbers across the central and southern Transvaal and in the eastern half of the Orange Free State. Although some of the Transvaal sites undoubtedly spill over into mixed-savannah

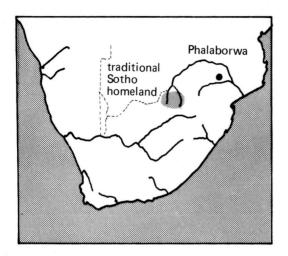

12 *The Ba Phalaborwa seem to have lived in their present locality for at least 900 years, and must therefore have been established early within the Later Iron Age period. This is hard to reconcile with their wide separation from the traditional Sotho homeland which, in the eleventh century, lay far to the southwest. Possibly the Phalaborwa have been absorbed into the Sotho milieu.*

country the great majority of the ruins lie within the highveld grasslands. In this case the reason for using stone was almost certainly because there was not enough timber. But this was not exclusively the case. In the Orange Free State, where the matter has received extensive and thorough study from Dr. Maggs, it is clear that the same basic architectural forms utilised whatever raw materials were readily available. Thus the walls of houses might be of stone or poles if the latter were available. Stockpens and linking walls might be of stone while house walls are of thick mud with a vertical reed core forming a kind of reinforcement. The rules were not rigid. Even in the highveld grasslands trees and shrubs occur, especially in stream valleys. What is certain is that the population densities represented by the ruins would rapidly exhaust timber supplies if they were used indiscriminately for building and for fuel. This is even allowing for the probability that not all the sites were occupied at the same time.

In the Transvaal Revil Mason made the first extensive study based on aerial photographs. He has given us not only a good idea of the areas over which the ruins are distributed (fig. 13) but also the first real indication of the incredible abundance of the ruins. His figures are somewhat difficult to use because he referred to each structure, or complex of walling which is not connected to another, as a 'set-tlement', whereas it is quite clear that in most cases these are merely components of settlements. In a broad zone across the south of the Transvaal, at the latitude of Johannesburg, from Zeerust in the west to Machadodorp in the east he has counted 6 237 structures. That his figures are probably very much on the low side is indicated by the work of Evers in the eastern section of Mason's survey area. From Lydenburg in the north to Machadodorp in the south, where Mason had estimated 702 of his units, Evers has identified 166 settlements, each containing an average of 32 of Mason's units. This would bring his figure up from 702 to over 5 000! But apart from these indications of locality and abundance, little in the way of detailed analysis has been published.

Evers has published two valuable plans from close to Lydenburg (fig. 14 shows one), showing two different types of layout using the same basic components. Cattle enclosures and huts cluster together in groups suggestive of family or extended-family units. These are contained in the one case within a rectilinear arrangement of walled tracks, while in the others the tracks radiate from a central area. The ground between clusters of enclosure units was presumably cultivated and the walled trackways were droves to contain the cattle on their way to and from their grazing lands. The age of the settlements is not known.

From Klipriviersberg, south of Johannesburg, Mason published the plan (fig. 15) of a site typical of the area. It seems to bear a close resemblance to Maggs's type N settlements in the adjacent area south of the Vaal (fig. 13). Magg's type N settlements are the oldest thus far known in the Orange Free State, and belong to at least as early as the first half of the fifteenth century. Eleven radiocarbon dates from four of Mason's sites span the period from 1640 A.D. to 1845 A.D., and all four sites were occupied in the seventeenth century.

Within the same area north of the Vaal, that is in the triangle from Rustenburg to Johannesburg and Klerksdorp, Mason has located nine village sites and a furnace linked by similar pottery and architectural features and spanning the time from 1060 A.D. to around 1610 A.D. None of these sites has buildings of stone. Floors were plastered, with raised, plastered platforms, and walls must have been of poles or reeds and plaster. Cattle and sheep (or goats) were kept and millet was cultivated. The villages, three of which have been fully excavated, were small, with ten to twenty huts arranged round a circular or oval area, and covering about 1 hectare. Until details are published we shall not know how

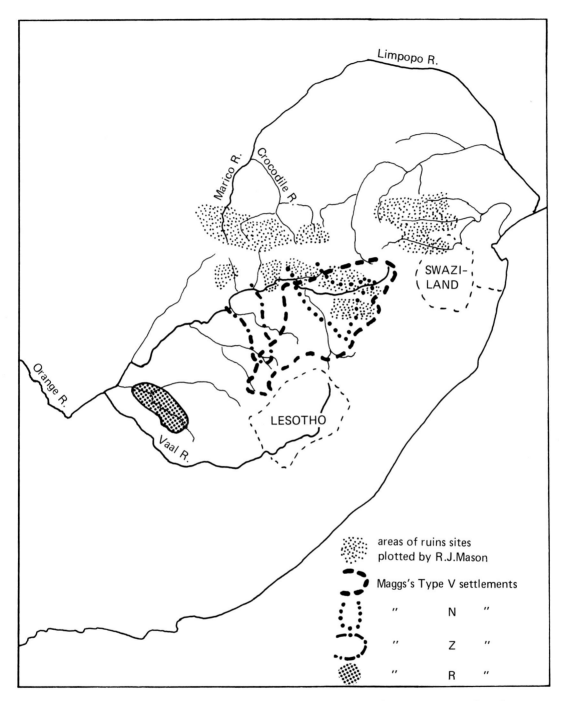

Limpopo R.

Marico R.

Crocodile R.

SWAZI-
LAND

Orange R.

Vaal R.

LESOTHO

⬚ areas of ruins sites
plotted by R.J.Mason

▬ Maggs's Type V settlements

＂   N   ＂

＂   Z   ＂

＂   R   ＂

13 Comparisons between the surveys carried out
by Mason and Maggs are not easy because of the
contrasting emphases used by the two workers.
It seems likely, however, that Maggs's type N
settlements (the oldest so far known in the
Orange Free State) extend through to the headwaters of the Crocodile and Marico Rivers, to the
traditional homeland of the Sotho peoples.

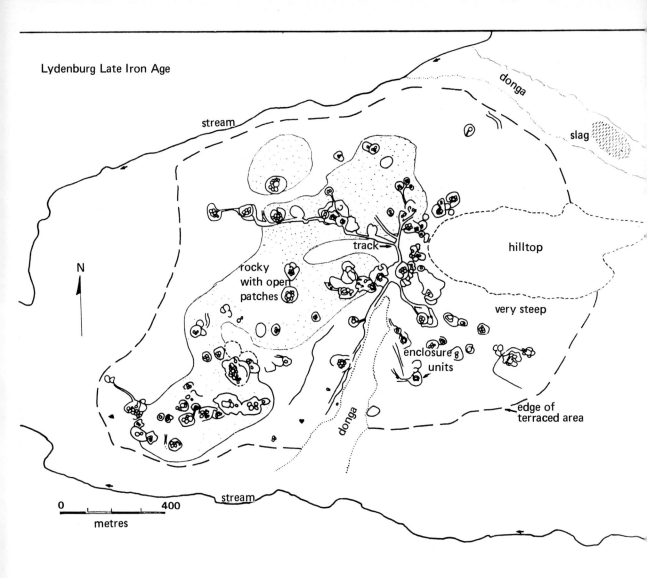

14   *Plan of a stone ruins complex near Lydenburg in the eastern Transvaal. A large number of units, each representing a small social unit, appear to be linked by drove-ways and terracing into larger 'village' units.*

closely the architectural arrangements and pottery might resemble those of the stone ruins, of the type N sites south of the Vaal. Nor is it safe to say at present just how much larger the area of distribution of these pre-ruins sites might have been.

The interest of the pre-ruins sites together with the type N and Klipriviersberg sites lies in their distribution as well as in their dating. They form a great swathe reaching from the headwaters of the Marico River, south-eastwards into the Orange Free State. The north-western part of this area of distribution reaches right into the heart of the territory from which the Sotho-Tswana peoples are traditionally said to have begun their dispersal at least 400 years ago. A correlation of these cultural remains with Sotho peoples seems therefore not to be out of place.

The radiocarbon chronology would carry their origins back at least to the eleventh century. The question which cannot yet be answered archaeologically is how the ancestral Sotho reached their homeland in the western Transvaal.

If the evidence north of the Vaal permits a provisional identification of archaeological remains with the Sotho-Tswana in a general way, the evidence from south of the Vaal is much more specific. In his remarkably detailed and clearly presented study of stone ruins in the Orange Free State, Maggs identified four main classes of settlement which he designated types N, V, Z, and R (fig. 13). Type N (fig. 16) we have already noted is the oldest of these groups and appears to be linked with an early stage of the expansion of Sotho-speaking peoples. Type V occupies the major part of the eastern Orange Free State between the Caledon River and the Vaal, spilling over into the Transvaal in the north-eastern area of its distribution. Type V is not a completely new departure, but utilises the same basic structures and settlement arrangements as Type N, except that the surrounding wall is generally not built, and stone-built, corbelled huts are added to the range of domestic architecture (figs. 16 and 17). What is clear is that its appearance in the late sixteenth or early seventeenth century marks a dramatic expansion of population. Areas between the older N settlements become built over, some N settlements are modified, and the whole area of occupation becomes enormously expanded. The limits in the east are set by the poorer grazing of the sourveld in the north and the high ground of Lesotho, where winters are bitterly cold and summers are very wet. In the west the limit was set by the 500 mm isohyet, beyond which rainfall was apparently too low for ideal grazing and agriculture. The V settlements in fact coincide closely with the best areas of grazing in the southern highveld.

But it is the type Z settlements to the west of the V settlements that pick up the links with contemporary peoples. Details of the architectural arrangements are shown in figs. 16, 18, 19. The basic unit is a circular hut with paved floor surrounded by a paved verandah. At the front of the house is a circular area enclosed by walls springing from opposite sides of the verandah. The cooking area is contained within this 'front yard'. At the rear of the hut is another circular area enclosed by an unbroken wall butted up to the walls of the front lobe. The 'back yard' was the working and storage area. It normally accommodated a large grain storage bin set on a circular stone base. Hut walls seem to have been of clay, and about 20 cm thick. It is not known if poles were employed, though this seems likely. The lobe walls are commonly of stone, but in some dwellings the front lobe walls were of mud with a single or double row of vertically-set stone slabs marking the base. These bilobial dwellings are grouped in a circular arrangement, sometimes closely packed so as al-

15   Plan, with suggested uses of structures, of the site at Klipriviersberg south of Johannesburg. This is one unit within a great complex of ruins, and bears a close resemblance to the type N sites of the Orange Free State.

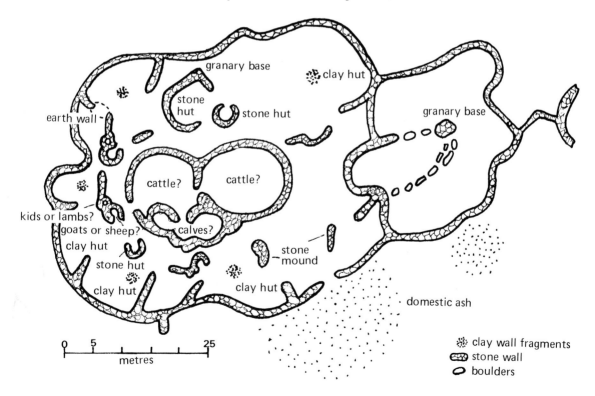

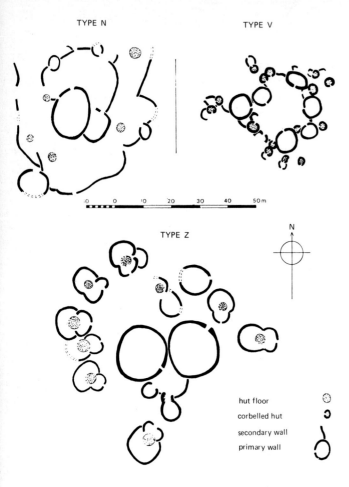

TYPE N

TYPE V

TYPE Z

N

hut floor

corbelled hut

secondary wall

primary wall

16   Plans of the three main types of settlement recognised by Maggs in the north-eastern part of the Orange Free State.

17   Part of the excavated 'V type' settlement on Makgwareng ridge, near Lindley in the Orange Free State. In the top right-hand corner is a fairly well-preserved corbelled hut, and two stone bases for grain-storage baskets show clearly in the central area. The channels mark the bases of reed- or grass-walled structures of an earlier settlement, or an earlier stage of the same settlement. The rough walling in the foreground is more recent and is not part of the settlement.

determinations, but at least one of the sites was occupied sometime between 1470 and 1650 A.D. The historical implications are important for they indicate that the Tswana had reached the southernmost limits of their expansion by the fifteenth century. The marked contrast between type Z settlements and ceramics and those of type V and N to the east show that important cultural distinctions had already emerged within the Sotho-Tswana group at least five centuries ago.

Nearly 12 million Nguni peoples (Xhosa, Zulu, Swazi and Ndebele) represent almost two-thirds of the Bantu-speaking peoples of South Africa. They live for the most part in the east, between the escarpment and the sea, in Swaziland, Natal, and the eastern Cape. For all their great numbers and great extent of territory we know precious little about their prehistory. Historical documents show Nguni-speakers to have been settled south of the Mthatha River well before the end of the sixteenth century, while oral traditions suggest that they were previously established in the foothills of the Drakensberg from as early as 1300 A.D. East of the escarpment rainfall is high and the landscape is generally well wooded. There was no need to build in stone and stone structures are rare, so archaeological traces of ancient settlements are not easily found.

18   A fine example of a bilobial hut, uncovered at a 'Z type' settlement just north of Ventersburg in the Orange Free State. In the centre is the hut, with its paved floor, and a paved verandah running about two-thirds of the way around it. In the foreground is the first lobe, which was the working-area and kitchen, with a screened-off hearth immediately inside and to the right of the entrance. A second fireplace is located on the verandah to the right of the hut. The second and larger lobe, behind, springs from the walls of the first lobe. It is larger, and served as the storage area for brushwood, grass, cattle dung, and probably grain-bins and other foodstuffs. If chickens were kept, they probably ran around here.

most to form an enclosing wall. Their doorways tend to face inwards towards the enclosed area, within which are generally three or four large circular cattle enclosures. The number of huts is rarely less than eight and often many more. Numbers of such groupings are commonly packed close together to form a major settlement complex, but always the clusters are separated from each other by a distinct gap.

The architectural details and grouping arrangements of these sites are so similar to those described from the early nineteenth-century Thlaping capitals of Dithakong and later (1820) Kuruman, and to the modern Tswana villages with their wards, that there can be no hesitation in identifying them as Tswana settlements. The chronology of the type Z settlements would benefit from more radiocarbon

A Later Iron Age burial from the Nagome 5 site at Phalaborwa. The skeleton is of an adult Negro male buried in a pit dug through the clay floor of a hut, and covered with stones. The burial is dated by radiocarbon at about 1750 A.D. The same burial custom is still followed by the Phalaborwa people.

Later Iron Age potsherds from Kgopolwe Hill, Phalaborwa, demonstrating remarkable continuity of ceramic style over 900 years. The site Kgopolwe 1 (SPK 1) dates from about 1900 A.D.; the same style was found in Kgopolwe 3 (SPK 111) radiocarbon dated to about 1000 A.D. Similar pottery is still made in the area.

A partial reconstruction of Lydenburg Head no. 2, an Early Iron Age ceramic sculpture dated to about 500 A.D. The head is about two-thirds life size, and a hole on each side of the neck provides for an attachment such as a supporting pole or hanging material.

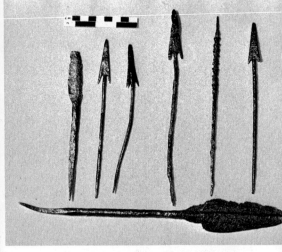

Six iron arrowheads and one spearhead from the Later Iron Age in Phalaborwa in the Transvaal. Note the bloodletting channels on arrows 2, 3, 4, and 6, the multiple barbs on arrow 5, and stepped midrib to strengthen the blade of the spear.

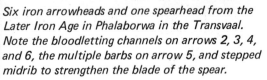

A drinking pot from the Later Iron Age at Phalaborwa.

A pot of unusual design (partly reconstructed) from the Later Iron Age at Phalaborwa. It was found in a rock shelter at Mapotweng Hill by Charles More, and contained a collection of items presumably belonging to a traditional healer, including some pieces of coral and seaweed.

An iron-smelting furnace of the Later Iron Age from the Transvaal Lowveld near Gravelotte. The side slits admit blasts of air from three sets of bellows; the central hole contains medicine to promote success in smelting. The diameter and height are both about 1 m.

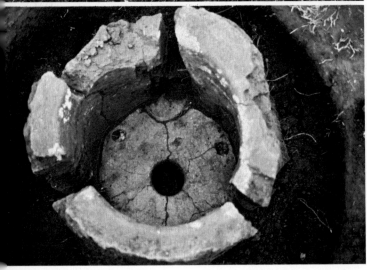

144

We have noted above that pottery of an Early Iron Age tradition (NC3 or Shixini ware) extends as far south as the Transkei and Ciskei coasts. But none of these sites is dated and it may be that they are relatively late representatives of the tradition. Certainly at Ntshekane near Greytown in Natal the tradition was still strong in the ninth century. But by the eleventh century something very different had been established at Umhlanga just north of Durban. Here Dr. Oliver Davies has excavated two houses of a village that may once have boasted a dozen or more. The houses were large (5,5 m diameter), circular bee-hive-shaped structures, apparently consisting of matting or thatch secured to a lightweight frame of osiers supported internally by one or more central posts. Food debris includes shellfish and a few fish-bones, bird-bones, zebra, hippo, bush-pig and antelope.

Iron is represented by a few scraps of slag. In searching for possible affinities one is thrown back on the pottery which, it must be confessed, is not very helpful. A few features such as notching of the upper edge of the rims of some vessels and applied studs of clay on another, combined with the simple forms, point to connections with undated pottery collections from Natal classified as NC2 by Schofield, and he suggested many years ago that his NC2 pottery bore some resemblance to Thembu (Nguni) pottery. The connections are highly tenuous but might be taken to suggest that ancestral Nguni were settled in Natal by the eleventh century. But it is not a happy connection, and it is complicated by the fact that some of these same pottery characteristics can be found sporadically through a large part of the ruins areas of the Orange Free State and the southern Transvaal. To try to pursue these would be likely to enmesh us in a web of speculation without contributing anything of real substance to the question of Nguni archaeological origins.

A Postscript on Pastoralists

At the end of the previous chapter we mentioned briefly evidence from within the final stages of the Later Stone Age for a shift in the economy from hunting and gathering to pastoralism. Maggs's Riet River settlements (fig. 13) in the eastern Orange Free State, spilling over into the northern Cape, provide interesting evidence for this for the inland area. The field evidence has been investigated by both Maggs and A.J.B. Humphreys of the Kimberley Museum, with similar results.

The sites are strung out along the line of the Riet River, usually in the hollows between groups of dolerite hills. The settlement units consist of a single large, circular, stone-walled enclosure, apparently for penning livestock, surrounded by several smaller enclosures which were presumably living quarters (fig. 20). Sometimes a unit of this kind occurs alone, but more often they are clustered in groups of from two to seven, with gaps of 5 km to 10 km between clusters. Some sites are very close to the river and others are up to 3 km distant, but most are from 0,5 to 1,0 km from the edge of the river. The arrangement is quite distinctive both in its plan-form and in its riverine distribution.

The associated pottery consists of simple bowls or wide-mouthed pots almost entirely lacking in decoration. In this, and in the mean thickness of the pot walls, it contrasts sharply with the Later Stone Age pottery from Sampson's Orange River dam scheme sites. Nor does it bear any resemblance to pottery from the type Z, N or V sites, or the coastal Later Stone Age pottery. It has all the hallmarks, like the settlements themselves, of being a purely local development. Stone tools of various kinds are characteristic and include grooved stones for grinding ostrich-eggshell beads, and the beads themselves. A few bone tools are present and a little iron and copper. Faunal remains include cattle and sheep (or goats) as well as a few species of antelope and a variety of small ground game. Burials were also of a distinctive kind in which the body was placed in a crouched position at the bottom of a circular shaft between 1 m and 2 m deep. Stones were placed in the shaft immediately above the burial, then soil, and finally a low mound of stones at the surface. Dates for the sites based on radiocarbon samples for two of the burials and one of the enclosures indicate that the sites may have been occupied in as early as the fifteenth century, but more likely in the seven-

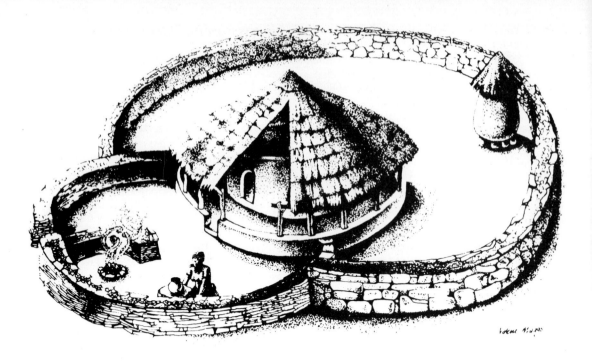

19　Reconstruction drawing of the kind of bi-lobial dwelling represented by type Z ruins in the Orange Free State. The arrangements closely resemble those of the nineteenth- and twentieth-century Tswana.

teenth and eighteenth centuries. Historical references indicate that the sites were abandoned by about the 1830s.

There are several points of interest about these Riet River settlements. The presence of typical Later Stone Age artefacts and the complete absence of any evidence for smelting or smithing immediately suggests that we are dealing not with Iron Age farmers, but with Stone Age peoples turned stockmen. The copper and iron must have been acquired by trade, presumably from the north and east. The settlements have none of the characteristics of the Khoi (Hottentots) encountered by European travellers from the sixteenth century onwards. The Khoi moved freely about the country carrying their houses (poles and mats) and their goods and chattels with them, on the backs of pack-oxen. The labour invested in the stonebuilt Riet River sites suggests a more sedentary existence. It seems likely that stock holdings could not have been very large, and perhaps not all the sites were occupied at the same time. There may have been a transhumant movement to and fro *along* the river. Perhaps the most interesting thing is the historical evidence of travel-lers such as Campbell and Burchell. Burchell speaks of the 'Bushmen' of Riet as being of mixed race, and speaking a variety of Bushman languages; and his companion visited one of their villages (of twenty-five huts) and spoke of their possessing sheep, goats and cattle. There seems little doubt that we are dealing with people traditionally regarded as hunter–gatherers who had intermarried to some extent with other groups and had settled to their own brand of pastoralism and with it a distinctive kind of social organisation reflected in their stone-built settlements. It is an interesting thought that they had themselves successfully made precisely the transition which governments today are trying hard to persuade the surviving Bushmen to make.

But the Riet sites reflect a relatively late process of acculturation and we must comment briefly on a much earlier example and one which has more important historical implications. The evidence is not yet extensive, but it is inescapable. It has been reviewed briefly but its import only becomes clear when considered against the background of the Southern African Iron Age. This is why this comment is reserved until last.

In short, we have evidence from the southernmost coast of South Africa for domestic sheep in the first century A.D. At Nelson Bay Cave an early first-century date is suggested, while at Hawston the second half of the century is indicated. The sites of Nelson Bay Cave, Die Kelders, and Bonteberg indicate clearly that fine pottery also was being made by the early years of the Christian Era, if not a century earlier. It is hard to escape the implication that sheep and pottery (and perhaps dogs) made their appearance as associated traits in the extreme south of South Africa at least 2 000 years ago.

Ordinarily it would be expected that such traits had been passed on by Iron Age farmers farther north. But we have seen that the earliest dates for Iron Age equivalents south of the Zambezi are 180 A.D. for Mabveni in Rhodesia, and 270 A.D. for Silverleaves in the northern Transvaal. These dates are too late to account for the south-coast sheep. It might seem easier to make use of Ehret's Central-Sudanic-speakers and say that they brought sheep to the southern part of the continent sufficiently in advance of the Early Iron Age to have enabled them to have spread to the south coast by 2 000 years ago. But even this is not an untrammelled solution. If sheep came so early with pre-Iron-Age herders why have they not been recognised in deposits of appropriate age in Rhodesia, the Transvaal, and the Orange Free State? If sheep and pottery were transmitted together, where is the ancestral pottery? Nothing like the coastal midden pottery is known from the Early Iron Age, and no pre-Early-Iron-Age pottery is known from the areas presumed to have been penetrated by the Central-Sudanic-speakers.

The situation is certainly enigmatic. Discussion

might proceed with a little more confidence if the territories of Mozambique and Angola had been more thoroughly explored archaeologically. If sheep and pottery came to the south via the south-west coast we still have to get them there, presumably from Rhodesia or Zambia, at an early date, and we are left with the absence of evidence in these central regions. It could be argued that they have filtered down the west coast from West Africa but the author is not aware of any evidence that would encourage such a view. If we turn to the east coast the same lack of occurrences of sheep and pottery confronts us. But the east coast does have the advantage of having attracted sea-going trade contacts from an early date. By the second century at least trade items, however indirectly, were reaching China. The ostrich made its first appearance in the Han court in the second century and a decorated tile of the early third century shows that it was the African, not the Asian, ostrich that was involved. The *Periplus of the Erythrian Sea*, a guide to the ports of Arabia, India and East Africa, and the connecting route to China, was written towards the end of the first century A.D. and gives the impression of knowledge that was not new. The east coast undoubtedly remains an attractive route for the diffusion of various culture traits, including the Persian fat-tailed sheep. The ancestor of the coastal pottery, if indeed it is not a local invention, remains unknown. Perhaps the answer lies beyond the shores of Africa. Whatever the answer, the origins of the south-coast pottery and pastoralism are an important and fascinating problem. They are a challenge to archaeologists over a wide area of Africa.

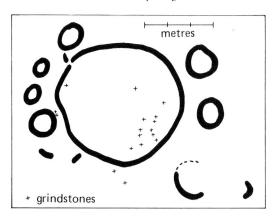

20   Khartoum 1. A type R (Riet River) site. Phosphate analysis at one site suggests that the central enclosure may have been a cattle pen. The surrounding enclosures may have been the foci of domestic activities. At Khartoum 1 the evidence was less conclusive and the concentration of artefacts of various kinds in the large central enclosure points to this as the centre of domestic activities.

6

The Peopling of Southern Africa

Fossils from East Africa and India indicate that the hominid line of evolution (the line leading to man) had separated from the pongid line (that of the apes) at least 14 million years ago, in the Miocene geological epoch. Because Southern Africa is lacking in relevant fossil localities of anything like this age, we have no way of knowing at present whether the southern part of the continent played any part in the very earliest stages of human evolution. But it seems unlikely, for the geological evidence suggests that large parts of the continent south of the Zambezi were very arid during this period (the later Tertiary). It was also an area of unstimulating stability unlikely to have provided fertile selective opportunities for any early primates that may have lived there. It is likely that the first representatives of the human line arrived in Southern Africa by migration from East Africa between 3 and 4 million years ago. These were the gracile australopithecines, *A. africanus*.

A. africanus was small-brained (about 494 cc) and although he habitually stood and moved in an upright position he was not an expert strider as modern man is. There are indications too that the wrist and hand were not as man-like as his overall appearance might suggest. He could not have been very fleet of foot, and in the absence of fangs or claws it seems quite certain that his survival was made possible by tool-using and perhaps useful forms of group behaviour in the face of threat. But the evidence would favour only the simplest kinds of tool-using: the wielding and throwing of sticks and stones, and perhaps the use of stones to crack bones and pulverise meat from carcases. *A. africanus* is probably best thought of as a scavenger rather than a hunter though he was undoubtedly capable of the limited degree of hunting observed in recent years among chimpanzees and baboons. For a million years or more he probably reigned supreme in the Transvaal and perhaps in Rhodesia too. There is no evidence to suggest that *A. africanus* spread as far as the Cape Folded Mountains or the southern coastal regions. His fate was probably sealed when a rather similar-looking creature moved onto the scene about 2 million years ago, and set up successfully in opposition to him. The competitor was an early form of man, and like *A. africanus* he had spread from East Africa.

These first true men to penetrate south of the

Limpopo could not have appeared very different from *A. africanus* even at a short distance. This is not surprising for it seems that they had separated from a common ancestor relatively recently in evolutionary terms (5 or 6 million years ago). They developed along very similar lines anatomically, in terms of their dietary habits, and perhaps in many aspects of behaviour. But the one took the lead over the other. The creature destined to become man developed more sophisticated behaviour with regard to the manipulation of stone and wood. Along with this went the expansion of the brain. By 2 million years ago his brain was half as big again as that of *A. africanus*. His brain capacity was far in excess of what was needed for the ordinary control of body functions and the surplus ensured his success in developing a material culture; in becoming man the tool-maker. With the manufacture and manipulation of tools undoubtedly came new, more complex, and apparently successful patterns of behaviour.

The view taken here that earliest man, like his australopithecine cousin, was a scavenger of meat is an extreme one that might not be shared by many anthropologists. It rests partly on the hypothesis that if both had been active hunters (predators) the abundance of game ought to have meant that competi-

Prehistoric camp sites among the dunes along the coast play an important part in helping us to reconstruct the past.

tion was not acute and *A. africanus* might have survived a good deal longer. The same might be true if *Homo* had hunted while *A. africanus* scavenged. But if both were scavenging, and employing basically the same techniques for doing so, there could have been an important clash of interests. The conflict would be settled when man had developed brain and culture far enough to deprive *A. africanus* utterly of the basis of his subsistence. We know that early in the Pleistocene there was a greater range of predators and scavengers than a million years later, and that the early part of the Pleistocene saw the extinction of a number of these. *A. africanus* was among them; man was not.

At the same time that the first men, or proto-men, spread into the Transvaal, about 2 million years ago, they were accompanied by *A. robustus,* a robust species of the genus *Australopithecus*. But being a vegetarian by preference, *A. robustus* was not in competition with man, and survived for a very long time alongside him. When he eventually died out, perhaps a million years ago or less, it may have been as a result of competition with creatures other than man. His history is even more marginal to the story of man than that of his more gracile, omnivorous relative *A. africanus*.

There seems no alternative to explain the presence of the first representatives of the human line in Southern Africa than to propose that they were immigrants. But having got man there, as a tool-maker, there is less need to invoke successive arrivals of new populations from the north. The Acheulian culture so well represented south of the Limpopo would be as natural an internal development from the Oldowan in South Africa as it was in East Africa. There are no sites in the south in which we can see the process occurring, as we can in Olduvai Gorge: nor is there much prospect of finding such a site south of the Zambezi.

In East Africa incipient tool-making may go back 3 million years. But the very simple tool-kit at Koobi Fora 1,8 million years ago suggests that an Oldowan level of technology may not have been attained until around 1,8 to 2 million years ago. By half a million years later the perfection of the handaxe and the cleaver had translated Oldowan into Acheulian in East Africa, and the timing of the process was probably not much different in the south. We are

Spending up to eight hours a day sifting through comminuted shell for small fish-bones is not a very pleasant task. It is the kind of drudgery that is necessary, however, to discover how prehistoric man made a living.

now in the early part of the Middle Pleistocene and we have few fossils to tell us about the biological evolution of man. But in widely separated parts of the world – Java, China, Tanzania, Morocco, and perhaps Germany – broadly within the time-range of the Middle Pleistocene the same species of man, *Homo erectus*, has been recognised. Some are estimated to be between 1,0 and 1,5 million years old. A thigh-bone from Java is quite indistinguishable from modern man; over-all stature is much greater than in Lower Pleistocene man, and the brain size greatly increased (around 1 000 cc). In East Africa and North-West Africa this kind of man is associated with Acheulian culture, and this was probably the case in South Africa.

Whether the technological step-up from Old-owan to Acheulian should be correlated with a period of relatively rapid expansion of the brain is not demonstrable, but it is not unlikely. What other features may have accompanied the transition we can only speculate about. We have seen that the number of Acheulian sites is much greater than for the Oldowan, and even allowing for some misreading of the evidence it seems likely that there was a significant increase in population. This would be a reasonable conclusion since it must be supposed that the development of the handaxe and the cleaver, which persisted for well over a million years, must have resulted in some advantage for their makers. There are indications in East Africa of the opportunistic hunting of large buffalo by driving them into a swamp, and the same may be true for elephant in Europe. There is no unequivocal evidence for the systematic hunting of individual animals at this time and more effective scavenging may have played as important a role as any advances in hunting. Clear evidence of hunting does not appear until the Upper Pleistocene about 100 000 years ago. There is some evidence in South Africa, as in East Africa, that patterns of behaviour in this time-range involved the repeated use of favoured localities resulting in the accumulation of vast numbers of artefacts.

By a quarter of a million years ago all the major regions of Southern Africa had been penetrated by man, with the apparent exception of Botswana, but the period from the Middle Pleistocene to well on into the Upper Pleistocene (perhaps 20 000 years ago) is in many respects obscure. We have outlined the technological changes that are visible in the archaeological record, but we have to admit that we still cannot see the processes and the progress of change. We see only the 'before' and 'after'. Within this very long period which we have dubbed a 'dark

age', particularly at the end of it, a number of changes are evident. We perceive that *Homo erectus* evolved into *Homo sapiens,* but we cannot say for certain just when or how rapidly this happened. The Florisbad skull is greater than 44 000 years old and Saldanha may be even older, so it looks as if the vital changes, especially the enlargement of the brain, had occurred fairly early in the Middle Stone Age. We badly need some well-dated early Upper Pleistocene cranial material to tell us just when the changes did occur.

We have already mentioned the interplay of factors sometimes referred to as 'feedback', and this is certainly the proper way to visualise what was happening. Once man had taken the road to culture, selective pressures must always have been operative, particularly for the enlargement and refinement of the brain. At times the process would be so slow as to be imperceptible, at others it was undoubtedly more rapid. It would not be far-fetched to suggest that the periods of rapid cultural change in the Lower, Middle, and Upper Pleistocene were each accompanied by an increased tempo of biological change.

If *Homo erectus* represents the maker of Acheulian artefacts it is tempting to correlate the emergence of

Professor R.A. Dart, discoverer of the australopithecines, among the remains of a prehistoric pastoralist settlement near the Riet River in the northern Cape.

types of *Homo sapiens* with the development of the Middle Stone Age. The evidence suggests another period of marked population increase. It might be going too far to imply that Acheulian man was not an active hunter, but whatever his prowess it seems likely that early Upper Pleistocene man was even more successful. We have suggested that his success may have stemmed from improvements in techniques of hafting resulting in more effective spears and perhaps knives too. The development of regional variants in technology as an accompaniment of population expansion in the Middle Stone Age points to possible far-reaching changes in social organisation compared with the Early Stone Age. We note too that some linguists feel that that may have been a crucial stage in the development of language, the evolution of which could have produced the first potential for sharply discrete ethnic groupings. By the late Upper Pleistocene most parts of Southern Africa were populated, though perhaps still sparsely, by essentially modern-looking people actively hunting and with an advanced technology. But although they exploited marine resources they did so less successfully than their Holocene successors.

Upper Pleistocene populations of the kind represented by the Tuinplaats and Border Cave skulls are seen as directly ancestral to the Khoisan (Bushmen and Hottentots), whose ancestors peopled the landscape during the past 10 000 years or more. They are also regarded as ancestral to the Negro, which raises interesting questions about the physical type of the Later Stone Age in areas to the north of the Khoisan, and the possibility that Negro populations were developing north of the Zambezi throughout the Holocene. If Negro and Khoisan derive from a common ancestor there ought to be a period when these two major populations were isolated from each other. Such a separation might develop on purely cultural grounds. Another possible mechanism exists in the apparent depopulation of some of the drier areas of the interior between 9 000 and 4 500 years ago. But rather more evidence is required from the plateau regions before we can speak with much confidence about this. What is important in the present context is that there is nothing in the evidence of either physical anthropology or archaeology that requires the introduction of new peoples. Indeed the population of Southern Africa may have been completely stable and developed within the sub-continent from early in the Pleistocene. Movement has surely taken place as the population has grown and expanded into previously unsettled plains and valleys. If the suggestion of a depopulation of the interior is correct this could have resulted in quite extensive population movements, more pronounced, perhaps, as conditions improved and attracted resettlement.

Even in the Holocene when population was at its densest it may never have exceeded half a million and resources could never have been severely taxed. The archaeological evidence all points to a mastery of the environment unparalleled in earlier times. Even allowing for the destruction of organic remains in sites older than 10 000 years it is clear that the range of artefacts, especially those of wood, bone and ivory, was far greater in the Holocene. Beads and pendants assume prominence, especially in the coastal sites where the living was good. If we have to look for a technological development that paved the way for better living it would be tempting to suggest the discovery of poison and the consequent development of the light-weight bow and composite arrow. In Zambia it was known at least 5 000 years ago and is represented in Southern Af-

rica by the bone components of composite arrowheads. Although the origins of art may lie in the Upper Pleistocene it is apparently in the Holocene that it assumes its finest expressions and its widest occurrence. The meaning of the art is obscure, but recent studies indicate that mythology and symbolism are involved and that the creation of much of the art was governed by strict rules of procedure. One has the feeling that the hunter–gatherers of the Holocene had in many cases attained a near-ideal existence and that leisure time was rarely in short supply. It is idle, but tempting, to speculate how such societies might have developed had not changes been forced on them from outside.

The first inkling of such changes is seen in the sheep and pottery on the south coast 2 000 years ago. Whether we view such innovations as being carried by coastal traders exploring the east coast, or by small groups of farmers filtering down from the north, makes little difference. The effect was the same: a two-million-year-old way of life drew to a close. We do not know the linguistic affinities of these early south-coast pastoralists, nor can we say much about physical affinities. The hunter–gatherers of the areas south of the Limpopo probably spoke San (Bushman) languages. Ancestral 'Hottentot' (Khoi) is believed to have developed from a Bush-related language Tshu-Khwe, spoken in western Rhodesia and northern Botswana. Whether sheep and cattle were dispersed at the hands of Tshu-Khwe-speakers, or by their Khoi-speaking descendants, or at the hands of San-speakers, we do not know, though indirect evidence might favour the Khoi. We should, however, remember that the Khoi themselves were at one time, perhaps 2 000 to 2 500 years ago, part of the hunter–gatherer population of Southern Africa. Whether they would be physically distinguishable in the archaeological record is questionable, for the greater stature and some other features which distinguished the historical Khoi from the San may have developed as a result of dietary factors linked to pastoralism. But be that as it may, the arrival of sheep (and perhaps goats) on the scene undoubtedly set peoples on the move and disturbed the ancient way of life.

There is no evidence, however, that any Khoi or San adopted agriculture as a way of life. But some peoples did, as the Transvaal sites have shown us. Between 1 500 and 1 700 years ago communities of cultivators and livestock-keepers, with a knowledge of smelting and smithing, established themselves south of the Limpopo. Just who they were and whence they came is still open to question. Tradition has seen them as the first, immigrant, Bantu-speakers, but recent archaeological evidence suggests they may have been otherwise. If we accept the presence in Southern Africa of wandering groups of Sudanic-speakers we could view them as belonging to these groups. Alternatively we could consider them as indigenous groups who adopted metallurgy and farming from other peoples just as some Khoisan adopted livestock. There will be debate on these matters for a long time to come. They were essentially subsistence farmers and there is no evidence at present to suggest any advanced form of political organisation. But there are faint traces of trading activities, in copper and in Indian Ocean sea-shells. If other goods were involved they have not been recognised, but it would be well to keep an eye on the possibility, for we know that men from outside Africa had an interest in its wealth from an early date.

The Mediterranean world and China had trading contacts, direct or indirect, with the East African coast as early as the first and second centuries A.D., if not earlier. Rhodesian gold may have been sought as early as the fifth or sixth centuries A.D., and the trade was well established by the tenth century. Indonesians were plying the east coast trade certainly by the ninth century and perhaps much earlier. As yet the consequences of such contacts for peoples south of the Limpopo are not evident but, whether they touched directly or not, they were the forerunner of more intensive contacts still to come.

If the identity of the first farmers is in doubt that of their successors is not. About a thousand years ago the ancestors of the present Bantu-speakers spread rapidly and effectively through Zambia, Rhodesia and Mozambique and into the Transvaal, the Orange Free State, Natal and the south-east Cape. There were not large numbers involved, but superior economic, social, and political systems led to the rapid absorption of indigenous peoples and a remarkable dispersal of lineages and language. By the fourteenth or fifteenth centuries the main outlines of Bantu distribution, as known historically, were established. Only the drier areas of the interior and the southernmost and south-western regions remained in possession of Khoisan hunters and herders. But the most dramatic event in the peopling of Southern Africa still lay in the future.

In a sense the earlier east-coast contacts lay at the root of what was to follow. For at the moment when the ancestral Sotho were achieving their greatest extension into the Orange Free State the Portuguese were fired with the desire to discover a sea-route to the Christian kingdom of Prester John, and to India.

Part of the Makapansgat Limeworks Cave, where fossil remains of numerous extinct animals, including Australopithecus, *have been recovered. In fact the great trench and the chamber to the left were cut by limeworkers quarrying into the 2½-million-year-old filling of the cave, in search of travertine for lime-burning.*

So it was that the first Portuguese ships, under the command of Bartholomeu Dias, rounded the Cape in 1488: the precursor of an increasing traffic in European vessels. By the late sixteenth century the Dutch, the English and the French were all sailing regularly to the East Indies and the spice-producing areas. The voyage was long and hazardous and scurvy was a constant scourge. The Cape of Good Hope was the ideal halfway stopping-point for water, meat, and a little 'scurvy grass'. In 1652 the Dutch formalised arrangements and established below Table Mountain a base in order to cultivate a garden whose produce would alleviate the sufferings of their sailors. The European presence in Southern Africa had begun, and the story of what was to follow belongs in the realm of the historian. But this does not mean that the story of the peopling of Southern Africa is complete. The introduction of slaves from East Africa and Malaya, for instance, contributed to the mixing of races initiated by European immigrants. The spectrum of physical types has been greatly widened and movements on a scale unparalleled in the previous two million years have taken place. This time the process is being documented, and it will be for historians, anthropologists and perhaps archaeologists of the future to sketch the ever-changing scene.

Glossary

ALBANY INDUSTRY: an industry in which there are few stone-tool types other than scrapers, most of which are large. There are no backed bladelets. At Nelson Bay Cave bone tools are relatively abundant, but have not been emphasised from other sites. Flourished between about 12 000 and 8 000 years ago.

AUSTRALOPITHECUS: a genus within the zoological Family that includes the genus *Homo*. Two species are known, *A.africanus* and *A.robustus*. Both became extinct early in the Pleistocene.

A.AFRICANUS: a species of the genus *Australopithecus*, lightly built (gracile), walking upright, and apparently adapted to an omnivorous diet. A tool-user, but not a tool-maker. Probably became extinct about 2 million years ago.

A.ROBUSTUS: a species of the genus *Australopithecus*, rather heavily built, upright-walking, and with massive teeth suggesting a specialised vegetarian diet. Not a tool-maker. Became extinct about 1,5 million years ago, or very soon after.

BANTU: a group of closely-related languages spoken over a large part of Africa. The name is commonly applied to the speakers themselves, but is incorrectly used if applied to physical type, or to material culture. The spread of the languages is generally associated with the spread of farming and metal-working in Central, East, and Southern Africa.

BRECCIA: a rock formed of broken fragments of other rocks, cemented firmly together. Pleistocene breccias in caves often contain fossil bones and stone artefacts as well as rock fragments.

CENOZOIC (or CAINOZOIC): a period of time (Era) in the geological history of the earth marked by the presence of essentially modern life-forms in the fossil record. It covers the past 70 million years, and is divided into two Periods, the Tertiary and the Quaternary.

DAGA: puddled clay used to plaster the walls and floors of huts in Africa. When burnt accidentally (or deliberately) it becomes reddened and hardened. In the Later Iron Age, in some areas substantial hut walls, benches, hearths, and pot-stands were made of solid daga and fired by burning grass and twigs to harden them.

GLACIATION: the accumulation and compaction of snow at high altitudes, leading to the formation of ice which flows under pressure of its own weight to lower ground. Valley glaciers are found in many mountain ranges today, but major ice-sheets are limited to Greenland and the Antarctic. At various times during the late Pliocene and the Pleistocene northern Europe and large parts of Canada and the United States were overwhelmed (glaciated) by massive ice-sheets.

GRACILE: an informal term (meaning slenderly built) often applied to *A.africanus* to emphasise its build in contrast to the heavier *A.robustus*.

HOLOCENE: the current geological Epoch arbitrarily agreed to begin some 10 000 years ago, at the end of the last glacial episode in the northern hemisphere.

HOMO: the genus to which man belongs. Three species are generally recognised: *H.habilis*, *H.erectus*, and *H.sapiens*. The first two are extinct.

H.ERECTUS: an extinct species of man widespread in the Middle Pleistocene. Associated in north-west Africa and East Africa with Acheulian artefacts. In China *H.erectus* was associated with a simple, non-Acheulian industry.

H.HABILIS: an extinct species of man that emerged late in the Pliocene and was replaced by *H.erectus* about 1 million years ago.

H.SAPIENS: the species of man to which all living populations of man belong. Early forms may have appeared by 300 000 years ago.

IRON AGE: a term applied by archaeologists in Africa to categorise the cultures of the iron-using, mixed-farming communities that began to replace the stone-using, hunter-gatherer communities in Southern Africa about 2 000 years ago, and somewhat earlier in West Africa and in the vicinity of Lake Victoria.

KHOI: a word used to refer to themselves by the yellow-skinned pastoralists encountered by Europeans at the Cape in the seventeenth century. Khoikhoi signified 'men of men'.

LEVALLOIS: a suburb of Paris whose name has been adopted to describe a particular method of stone-working first recognised there and subsequently at many sites in Europe and Africa. The method involves the shaping of a piece of stone (Levallois core) by flaking, to pre-determine the size and shape of a flake to be removed from it.

MIOCENE: the fourth Epoch within the Tertiary Period. It lies between about 25 million and 7 or 8 million years ago. During the Miocene the fauna begins to assume a generally modern appearance (compared with what had gone before), and among the Primates of the time *Ramapithecus* may have marked the beginning of the line leading to man.

OLDOWAN: the stone industry pre-dating the Acheulian in Africa, apparently associated with *H.habilis* in the Lower Pleistocene. Named from Olduvai Gorge in Tanzania.

PLIOCENE: the last Epoch of the Tertiary Period, between about 7 or 8 and 2,5 million years ago. The human and australopithecine lines differentiated during the Pliocene. Many parts of Africa were warm and dry during this interval, and fossil occurrences are rather rare.

POLYGYNY: the socially approved practice allowing a man to have more than one wife at a time

QUATERNARY: the most recent of the geological Periods, divided into two Epochs – the Pleistocene and the Holocene or Recent. The beginning of the period is rather loosely set at about 2,5 million years ago. The story of man's cultural evolution is contained almost entirely within the Quaternary.

ROBBERG INDUSTRY: an industry characterised by the presence of small bladelet cores and tiny blades derived from them. Small scrapers, backed bladelets and other tools are present in very small numbers. Very occasional bone artefacts occur. Flourished between about 19 000 and 12 000 years ago.

SAN: a variation of a word used by the Khoi (see above) to refer to the yellow-skinned hunter–

gatherers living in the south-western Cape in the seventeenth century, when the Europeans first made contact.

SMITHFIELD CULTURE: the name given to a group of stone industries first found near the town of Smithfield in the Orange Free State. The original concept has been much altered in recent years. Some of the problems are discussed in chapter 4.

STRATIGRAPHY: the study of the relationships between strata (layers of sediments), such as those formed by rivers or in lake-beds or by human activities, in archaeological sites.

TERTIARY: a Period of geological time from approximately 70 million years ago, to around 2,5 million years ago. Mammals achieved importance in the animal world, and among them the first Primates (the family of animals including man).

TYPE SITE: the site in which any given archaeological industry is first given proper definition, and which gives its name to the industry concerned.

WILTON CULTURE: an archaeological culture based largely on the production of microlithic (very small) stone tools (scrapers, segments, and backed blades) but using a variety of other materials (bone, ivory, wood, shell, skin, fibre), and named from a rockshelter on the farm Wilton in the Eastern Cape. It evolved about 8 000 or 9 000 years ago and disappeared about 4 000 to 3 000 years ago.

Further Reading

Chapter 1: Looking at the Landscape

Acocks, J.P.H. 1953. *Veld Types of South Africa*. Botanical Survey of South Africa. Memoir 28. Pretoria: Government Printer.

Bond, G. 1963. 'Environments of East and Southern Africa since the mid-Tertiary.' *S. Afr. Jour. Sci.* 59(7): 347–52.

Brothwell, D., and E. Higgs. 1969. *Science in Archaeology*. 2nd ed. London: Thames & Hudson.

Butzer, K.W. 1971. *Environment and Archaeology*. 2nd ed. Chicago: Aldine Atherton.

Clark, J.G.D. 1957. *Archaeology and Society*. 3rd ed. London: Methuen.

Clark, J.D. 1958. 'Some stone age woodworking tools in Southern Africa.' *S. Afr. Archaeol. Bull.* 13: 144–52.

Dingle, R.V., and J. Rogers. 1972. 'Pleistocene palaeogeography of the Agulhas Bank.' *Trans. Roy. Soc. S. Afr.* 40(3): 155–65.

Dorst, J., and P. Dandelot. 1970. *A Field Guide to the Larger Mammals of Africa*. London: Collins.

Gabel, C., and N.R. Bennett. 1967. *Reconstructing African Culture History*. Boston: Boston University Press.

Galton, F. 1891. *Narrative of an Explorer in Tropical South Africa*. 4th ed. London: Ward Lock.

Harris, W.C. 1963. *The Wild Sports of Southern Africa*. Facsimile reprint of 5th ed., 1851. Cape Town: C. Struik.

Hendey, Q.B. 1974. 'Faunal dating of the late Cenozoic of

Southern Africa, with special reference to the carnivora.' *Quaternary Research* 4: 149–61.

McCall, D.F. 1969. *Africa in Time Perspective: A Discussion of Historical Reconstruction from Unwritten Sources.* New York: Oxford University Press.

Semenov, S.A. 1964. *Prehistoric Technology.* Bath: Cory, Adams & Mackay.

Stevenson-Hamilton, J. 1929. *The Low-veld: Its Wild Life and Its People.* London: Cassell.

Story, R. 1958. *Some Plants Used by The Bushmen in Obtaining Food and Water.* Botanical Survey of South Africa. Memoir 30. Pretoria: Government Printer.

Thompson, B.W. 1975. *Africa: The Climatic Background.* Ibadan: Oxford University Press.

Trigger, B.G. 1968. *Beyond History: The Methods of Prehistory.* New York: Holt, Rinehart & Winston.

van Zinderen Bakker, E.M., and K.W. Butzer. 1973. 'Quaternary environmental changes in Southern Africa.' *Soil Science* 116(2): 236–48.

Watson, P.J.; S.A. le Blanc; and C.L. Redman. 1971. *Explanation in Archaeology: An Explicitly Scientific Approach.* New York & London: Columbia University Press.

Wellington, J.H. 1955. *Southern Africa: A Geographical Study.* Vol. I. Cambridge: Cambridge University Press.

Wells, L.H. 1969. 'Faunal subdivision of the Quaternary in Southern Africa.' *S. Afr. Archaeol. Bull.* 24: 93–5.

Chapter 2: The Earliest South Africans

Bates, M. 1961. *The Nature of Natural History.* (Revised ed.) New York: Scribner.

Bond, G. 1963. 'Environments of East and Southern Africa since the mid-Tertiary.' *S. Afr. Jour. Sci.* 59(7): 347–52.

Brain, C.K. 1958. *The Transvaal Ape-man-bearing Cave Deposits.* Memoir 11. Pretoria: The Transvaal Museum.

—1970. 'New finds at the Swartkrans australopithecine site.' *Nature* 225: 1112–19.

Campbell, B.G. 1966. *Human Evolution: An Introduction to Man's Adaptations.* Chicago: Aldine Publishing Company.

Clark, J.D. 1976. 'African origins of man the toolmaker.' In *Human Origins,* edited by G.Ll. Isaac and E.R. McCown. Menlo Park, California: W.A. Benjamin.

Clark, W.E. Le Gros. 1967. *Man-apes or Ape-men: The Story of Discoveries in Africa.* New York: Holt, Rinehart & Winston.

Dart, R.A. 1957. *The Osteodontokeratic Culture of Australopithecus prometheus.* Memoir 10. Pretoria: The Transvaal Museum.

Holloway, R.L. 1970. 'New endocranial volumes for the australopithecines.' *Nature* 227: 199–200.

Leakey, M.D. 1976. 'A summary and discussion of the archaeological evidence from Bed I and Bed II, Olduvai Gorge, Tanzania.' In *Human origins,* edited by G. Ll. Isaac and E.R. McCown. Menlo Park, California: W.A. Benjamin.

Tobias, P.V. 1965. 'Australopithecus, Homo habilis, tool-using and tool-making.' *S. Afr. Archaeol. Bull.* 20: 167–92.

— 1971. *The Brain in Hominid Evolution.* New York: Columbia University Press.

— 1976. 'African hominids: dating and phylogeny.' In *Human Origins,* edited by G. Ll. Isaac and E.R. McCown. Menlo Park, California: W.A. Benjamin.

Vrba, E.S. 1975. 'Some evidence of chronology and palaeoecology of Sterkfontein, Swartkrans and Kromdraai from the fossil bovidae.' *Nature* 254: 301–4.

Chapter 3: A Prehistoric Dark Age

Beaumont, P.B., and J.C. Vogel. 1972. 'On a new radiocarbon chronology for Africa south of the Sahara.' *African Studies* 31(2): 65–89; and 31(3): 155–82.

Butzer, K.W., and G. Ll. Isaac. *After the Australopithecines.* The Hague: Mouton Publishers. (See various chapters on early man, Africa, and Southern Africa.)

Carter, P.L. 1976. 'The effects of climatic change on settlement in eastern Lesotho during the middle and later stone age.' *World Archaeology.* 8(2): 197–206.

Carter, P.L., and J.C. Vogel. 1974. 'The dating of industrial assemblages from stratified sites in eastern Lesotho.' *Man* (N.S.) 9: 557–70.

Clark, J.D. 1959. *The Prehistory of Southern Africa.* Harmondsworth: Penguin Books.

— 1967. *Atlas of African Prehistory.* Chicago.

— 1970. *The Prehistory of Africa.* London: Thames and Hudson.

Deacon, H.J. 1976. *Where Hunters Gathered: A Study of Holocene Stone Age People in the Eastern Cape.* Claremont: South African Archaeological Society.

Deacon, H.J., and M. Brooker. 1976. 'The Holocene and upper Pleistocene sequence in the southern Cape.' *Ann. S. Afr. Mus.* 71: 203–14.

Howell, F.C. 1966. *Early Man.* Time-Life International.

Isaac, G. Ll. 1972. 'Chronology and the tempo of cultural change during the Pleistocene.' In *Calibration of Hominoid Evolution,* edited by W.W. Bishop and J.A. Miller. Edinburgh: Scottish Academic Press.

Klein, R.G. 1970. 'Problems in the study of the middle stone age of South Africa.' *S. Afr. Archaeol. Bull.* 25: 127–35.

—1974. 'Environment and subsistence of prehistoric man in the southern Cape Province, South Africa.' *World Archaeology* 5: 249–84.

— 1975. 'Ecology of stone age man at the southern tip of Africa.' *Archaeology* 28(4): 238–47.

— 1975. 'Middle stone age man–animal relationships in Southern Africa: evidence from Die Kelders and Klasies River Mouth.' *Science.* 190: 265–67.

Mason, R.J. 1962. *Prehistory of the Transvaal.* Johannesburg: Witwatersrand University Press.

Sampson, C.G. 1974. *The Stone Age Archaeology of Southern Africa.* New York: Academic Press.

Tobias, P.V. 1972. 'Recent human biological studies in Southern Africa, with special reference to Negroes and Khoisans.' *Trans. roy. Soc. S. Afr.* 40(2): 109–33.

Tobias, P.V. 1974. 'Homo erectus.' In *Encyclopaedia Britannica.*

Wells, L.H. 1972. 'Late stone age and middle stone age tool-makers.' *S. Afr. Archaeol. Bull.* 27: 5–9.

Chapter 4: A Way of Life Perfected

Avery, G. 1975. 'Discussion on the age and use of tidal fish-traps (visvywers).' *S. Afr. Archaeol. Bull.* 30: 105–13.

Axelson, E. 1954. *South African Explorers.* London: O.U.P.

Bicchieri, M.G. 1972. *Hunters and Gatherers Today.* New York: Holt, Rinehart & Winston. (Chapters 7 and 8 for the G/wi and !Kung Bushmen.)

Clark, J.D. 1959. *The Prehistory of Southern Africa.* Harmondsworth: Penguin Books. (Chapters 7–10.)

—1970. *The Prehistory of Africa.* London: Thames & Hudson.

Deacon, H.J. 1972. 'A review of the post-Pleistocene in South Africa.' In *The Interpretation of Archaeological Evidence.* Claremont: S. African Archaeological Society.

— 1976. *Where Hunters Gathered: A Study of Holocene Stone Age People in the Eastern Cape.* Claremont: S. African Archaeological Society.

Deacon, H.J., and M. Brooker. 1975. 'The Holocene and upper Pleistocene sequence in the southern Cape.' *Ann. S. Afr. Mus.* 71: 203–14.

Deacon, H.J., and J. Deacon. 1963. 'Scott's cave: a late stone age site in the Gamtoos valley.' *Ann Cape Prov. Mus.* 3: 96–121.

Deacon, J. 1972. 'Wilton: an assessment after fifty years.' *S. Afr. Archaeol. Bull.* 27: 10–48.

— 1974. 'Patterning in the radiocarbon dates for the Wilton/Smithfield complex in Southern Africa.' *S. Afr. Archaeol. Bull.* 29: 3–18.

Humphreys, A.J.B. 1973. 'A report on excavations carried out on a Type R settlement unit (Khartoum 1) in the Jacobsdal district, O.F.S.' *Ann. Cape Prov. Mus (Nat. Hist.).* 9(8): 123–57.

Inskeep, R.R. 1967. 'The late stone age in Southern Africa.' In *Background to Evolution in Africa,* edited by W.W. Bishop and J.D. Clark. Chicago: University Press.

Maggs, T.M.O'C. 1971. 'Some observations on the size of human groups during the late stone age.' *Supplement to the S. Afr. Jour. of Sci.* Special issue 2.

—1971. 'Pastoral settlements on the Riet river.' *S. Afr. Archaeol. Bull.* 26: 37–63.

Mason, R.J. 1962. *Prehistory of the Transvaal.* Johannesburg: Witwatersrand University Press. (Chapter 10.)

Parkington, J.E. 1972. 'Seasonal mobility in the later stone age.' *African Studies* 31: 223–43.

Parkington, J.E., and C. Poggenpoel. 1971. 'Excavations at De Hangen, 1968.' *S. Afr. Archaeol. Bull.* 26: 3–36.

Rudner, J. 1968. 'Strandloper pottery from South and South West Africa.' *Ann. S. Afr. Mus.* 49(2):441–663.

Sampson, C.G. 1972. 'The stone age industries of the Orange River scheme and South Africa.' *Memoir* 6. Bloemfontein: National Museum.

Schapera, I. 1930. *The Khoisan Peoples of South Africa: Bushmen and Hottentots.* London: Routledge.

Schweitzer, F.R. 1974. 'Archaeological evidence for sheep at the Cape.' *S. Afr. Archaeol. Bull.* 29: 75–82.

Vinnicombe, P. 1972. 'Motivation in African rock art.' *Antiquity* 46: 124–33.

— 1976. *People of the Eland.* Pietermaritzburg: Natal University Press.

Wendt, W.E. 1976. '"Art mobilier" from the Apollo II cave, South West Africa: Africa's oldest dated works of art.' *S. Afr. Archaeol. Bull.* 31: 5–11.

Westphal, E.O.J. 1963. 'The linguistic prehistory of Southern Africa: Bush, Kwadi, Hottentot and Bantu linguistic relationships.' *Africa* 33(3): 237–65.

Williams, J.D. Lewis. 1972. 'The syntax and function of the Giant's Castle rock-paintings.' *S. Afr. Archaeol. Bull.* 27: 49–65.

Chapter 5: New Ways of Living

Davies, O. 1971. 'Excavations at Blackburn.' *S. Afr. Archaeol. Bull.* 26: 165–78.

Davies, O. 1975. 'Excavations at Shongweni south cave: the oldest evidence to date for cultigens in Southern Africa.' *Ann. Natal. Mus.* 22(2): 627–62.

de Almeida, A. 1965. *Bushmen and Other Non-Bantu Peoples of Angola.* Johannesburg: Witwatersrand University Press (for the Institute for the Study of Man in Africa).

Ehret, C. 1974. 'Patterns of Bantu and Central Sudanic settlement in Central and Southern Africa (ca. 1000 B.C.–A.D. 500).' *Transafrican Journal of History* 3: 1–27.

Evers, T.M. 1975. 'Recent iron age research in the Transvaal.' *S. Afr. Archaeol. Bull.* 30: 71–83.

Hiernaux, J. *The People of Africa.* London: Weidenfeld & Nicolson.

Huffman, T.N. 1970. 'The early iron age and the spread of the Bantu.' *S. Afr. Archaeol. Bull.* 25: 3–21.

Humphreys, A.J.B. 1976. 'Note on the southern limits of iron age settlement in the northern Cape.' *S. Afr. Archaeol. Bull.* 31: 54–7.

Inskeep, R.R., and T.M.O'C. Maggs. 1975. 'Unique art objects in the iron age of the Transvaal, South Africa.' *S. Afr. Archaeol. Bull.* 30: 114–38.

Klapwijk, M. 1974. 'A preliminary report on pottery from the north-eastern Transvaal, South Africa.' *S. Afr. Archaeol. Bull.* 29: 19–23.

Maggs, T.M.O'C. 1976. 'Iron age patterns and Sotho history on the southern highveld: South Africa.' *World Archaeology* 7(3): 318–32.

— 1976. *Iron Age Communities of the Southern Highveld.* Occasional Publications of the Natal Museum, 2.

Mason, R.J. 1965. 'The origin of South African society.' *S. Afr. Jour. Sci.* 61(7): 225–67.

—1974. 'Background to the Transvaal iron age — new discoveries at Olifantspoort and Broederstroom.' *Jour. of the S. Afr. Inst. of Mining & Metallurgy* 74(6): 211–16. (This special issue contains a collection of interesting papers on iron age topics.)

Mason, R.J., *et al.* 1973. 'Early iron age settlement of Southern Africa.' *S. Afr. Jour. Sci.* 69: 324–26. (Several brief but important reports.)

Mauny, R. 1965. 'The Wakwak and the Indonesian invasion in East Africa in A.D. 945' *Studia* (revista semestral no. 15): 7–16.

Phillipson, D.W. 1976. 'Archaeology and Bantu linguistics.' *World Archaeology* 8(1): 65–82.

Potter, J.W. 1974. 'Chinese–East African trade before the 16th century.' *Ufahamu* 5(2): 113–34.

Thompson, L. (ed.). 1969. *African Societies in Southern Africa.* London: Heinemann. (Especially chapters 1–5.)

Tobias, P.V. 1972. 'Recent human biological studies in Southern Africa, with special reference to Negroes and Khoisans.' *Trans. roy. Soc. S. Afr.* 40(3): 109–33.

van der Merwe, N.J., and R.T.K. Scully. 1971. 'The Phalaborwa story: archaeological and ethnographic investigation of a South African iron age group.' *World Archaeology* 3(2): 178–96.

Wilson, M. 1970. *The Thousand Years Before Van Riebeeck.* Johannesburg: Witwatersrand University Press (for The Institute for the Study of Man in Africa).

Wilson, M. and L. Thompson (eds.). 1969. *The Oxford History of South Africa* vol. I. Oxford: Clarendon Press.

Index

Acknowledgements

Grateful acknowledgement is made to the following for photographs or illustrations supplied, or for permission to reproduce, in part or in whole, previously published illustrations (Fig. 1.5 signifies figure 5 in chapter 1):

Cover illustration British Museum (Mankind).

Fig. 1.5 R.V. Dingle & J. Rogers in *Trans. Roy. Soc. S. Afr.* 40(3); Page 13 below, A.A. Balkema (reprint 1969); Fig. 2.7 P.V. Tobias & Alun Hughes; Fig. 2.9 P.V. Tobias in *S.Afr. Archaeol. Bull.* 20(80); Fig. 2.12 W.E. Le Gros Clark and University of Chicago Press; Fig. 2.13 J.T. Robinson in *S. Afr. J. Sci.* 57(1); Fig. 2.16 M.D. Leakey and Cambridge University Press; Figs. 3.1, 3.3, 3.5, 3.6, 3.7, 3.8, 3.11, 3.12, 3.14, 3.15, 3.16, 3.17, 3.18, 4.16 P.V. Narracott & R. Murphy and Pitt Rivers Museum; Fig. 3.24 C.M. Keller in *Anthropological Records* v.28, copyright © 1973 by the Regents of the University of California, reprinted by permission of the University of California Press; Fig. 3.28 C.K. Brain in *Background to Evolution in Africa* by W.W. Bishop & J.D. Clark, copyright © 1967 by University of Chicago Press; Fig. 3.35 C.G. Sampson, *The Middle Stone Age Industries of the Orange River Scheme,* National Museum, Bloemfontein, 1968; Fig. 4.5 C.G. Sampson, *The Stone Age Archaeology of Southern Africa,* Academic Press, 1974; Fig. 4.6 C.G. Sampson in *Researches of the National Museum* 2(4), National Museum, Bloemfontein; J. Deacon in *S. Afr. Archaeol. Bull.* 29(1,2); Fig. 4.9 G. Silberbauer in *Bushman Survey* 1965, Govt. of Botswana; Figs. 4.11, 5.17, 5.18, 5.19 T.M. O'C. Maggs; Fig. 4.12 J. Walton & J.D. Clark in *P.P.S.* n.s. v.28; Fig. 4.18 J. Rudner in *S. Afr. J. of Sci.* special issue no. 2, May 1971; Fig. 4.21 P. Vinnicombe in *S. Afr. Archaeol. Bull.* 25(57); Fig. 4.23 J.E. Parkington & H.J. Deacon; Fig. 4.27 J. Rudner in *Ann. S. Afr. Mus.* 49(2); Fig. 5.2 G.P. Murdock, *Africa: Its People and Their Culture,* copyright © 1959 by McGraw-Hill, Inc., used with permission of McGraw-Hill Book Co.; Fig. 5.14 T.M. Evers in *S. Afr. Archaeol. Bull.* 30(3, 4); Fig. 5.15 R.J. Mason, *The Prehistory of the Transvaal,* University of the Witwatersrand Press, 1962; Fig. 5.16 T.M. O'C. Maggs in *World Archaeology* 7(3).

For unnumbered half-tone illustrations on the pages indicated as follows:

Pages 10, 69, 72 above, 83, Pitt Rivers Museum; pp. 36–7, Mrs. Sydney-Anne Wallace; p. 72 below, left and right, I. & J. Rudner, in J. Rudner, 'Strandloper Pottery from South and South West Africa', *Ann. S. Afr. Mus.* 49(2); p. 91 below, copyright 1956 A.R. Willcox, *Rock Paintings of the Drakensberg, Natal and Griqualand East,* Max Parrish, London; pp. 89, 90, 91 above, 92, R. Townley Johnson and the Rembrandt van Rijn Art Foundation; p. 142, photographed by Prof. N.J. van der Merwe from the University of Cape Town collection; pp. 143 above and below, 144 below, excavated and photographed by Prof. N.J. van der Merwe, University of Cape Town; p. 144 above and central, photographed by Prof. N.J. van der Merwe (artefacts from the Charles More Collection).

The following illustrations are based on or redrawn with permission from previously published material as follows:

Fig. 1.1 J.H. Wellington and Cambridge Univ. Press; Fig. 1.4 C.K. Brain in *Background to Evolution in Africa* by W.W. Bishop & J.D. Clark, copyright © 1967 by University of Chicago Press; Fig. 2.5 L.H. Wells in *S. Afr. J. Sci* 54(3); Fig. 3.9 R.J. Mason, *The Prehistory of the Transvaal,* University of the Witwatersrand Press, 1962; Fig. 3.20 A.J.B. Humphreys in *S.Afr. Archaeol. Bull.* 25; Fig. 3.22 A.W. Louw in *S. Afr. Archaeol. Bull.* 24 (part 2); Figs. 3.23, 3.31 P.L. Carter & J.C. Vogel in *Man* (n.s.) 9, 1974, Royal Anthropological Institute; Fig. 3.25 F.R. Schweitzer & A.J. Tankard, *Goodwin Series* no. 2, S. Afr. Archaeol. Soc.; Fig. 3.29 H.J. Deacon; Fig. 3.32 H.J. Deacon & M. Brooker in *Ann. S. Afr. Mus.* 71; Fig. 3.36 C.G. Sampson, *The Middle Stone Age Industries of the Orange River Scheme,* National Museum, Bloemfontein, 1968; Figs. 4.3, 4.4 E.O. Westphal in *Africa* 33(3), International African Institute; Fig. 4.10 J.E. Parkington & C. Poggenpoel in *S. Afr. Archaeol. Bull.* 26 (1,2); Fig. 4.14 J.E. Parkington (information); Fig. 5.9 J.W. Phillipson in *J. Afr. Hist.*; Fig. 5.20 A.J.B. Humphreys in *Ann. Cape Prov. Mus.* 9(8).

The author thanks Mr. L. Jacobson for compiling the index.